For Les, with all

Common Ground

Common Ground

The Story of Greenham

DAVID FAIRHALL

I.B. TAURIS
LONDON · NEW YORK

For Catherine, David and Jim

Published in 2006 by
I.B.Tauris & Co. Ltd
6 Salem Rd, London W2 4BU
175 Fifth Avenue, New York NY 10010
www.ibtauris.com

In the United States and Canada distributed by Palgrave Macmillan,
a division of St. Martin's Press, 175 Fifth Avenue, New York, NY 10010

Copyright © David Fairhall 2006

The right of David Fairhall to be identified as the author of this work
has been asserted by him in accordance with the Copyright, Designs
and Patents Act, 1988

All rights reserved. Except for brief quotations in a review, this book, or any
part thereof, may not be reproduced, stored in or introduced into a retrieval
system, or transmitted, in any form or by any means, electronic, mechanical,
photocopying, recording or otherwise, without the prior written permission of
the publisher.

ISBN 10   1 84511 286 5 (Hb)
ISBN 13   978 1 84511 286 8 (Hb)

A full CIP record for this book is available from the British Library
A full CIP record for this book is available from the Library of Congress
Library of Congress catalog card: available

Typeset in Monotype Baskerville by illuminati, Grosmont,
www.illuminatibooks.co.uk
Printed and bound in Great Britain by TJ International Ltd, Padstow, Cornwall

Contents

Foreword

JULIE CHRISTIE

Anyone who grew up, as I did, during or just after the Second World War must have wondered how they would have behaved if the country had ever been occupied. Would they have been part of the resistance or a collaborator or just kept their head down?

The women of Greenham Common, I always felt, were exactly the kind of people who would have formed part of a resistance against fascism and totalitarianism. They were committed, they were courageous, they were fearless and they were prepared to expose themselves to ridicule and worse for their beliefs. They were prepared to live outside in home-made shelters and taxing conditions through all weathers.

The name Greenham Common came to symbolise resistance against the odds, a feeling that if people were determined enough and persistent enough, even the most powerful military machine in the world could be halted or disrupted. To the tens of thousands of people who travelled to attend demonstrations there, and the millions who read with incredulity of what was happening, Greenham Common was both inspirational and educational. Greenham women inspired many others to risk imprisonment to support them because their strength and solidarity were so awesome. Had it not been an all-woman protest, it might never have gathered such support as so many women, myself included, felt drawn to be part of that magnificent demonstration of female strength. We went and were moved and inspired by the joy and determination we found there.

What difference did it all make?

The Greenham women were the most dramatic and visible part of an international movement against nuclear weapons that shaped the political context for agreements between the USA and USSR to drastically reduce the number of nuclear weapons. They showed people that however the odds were stacked, it was still possible to protest and survive. Democracy in action. It encouraged others, particularly women, to recognise that anything was possible.

Cindy Sheehan, the mother of an American soldier killed in Iraq, took her anti-war camp to the gates of President Bush's ranch in Texas. She was part of the tradition of the Greenham women, part of the tradition of the suffragettes and the Mothers of the Plaza de Mayo in Argentina and the Sandinistas in Nicaragua.

These are lessons that we constantly have to relearn and remember. We owe a debt of gratitude to the people prepared to back their beliefs with their actions – whatever the risks. If we let that go, we will turn into cowed and passive citizens and lose any pride in ourselves.

Preface

Anyone picking up this book might reasonably ask, 'Why is a man writing about the women of Greenham Common?' The answer is simple enough. This is not a memoir. It is the story of a place, an ancient stretch of common land that accidentally became an international political arena in which the final scenes of the Cold War's nuclear confrontation were acted out. As the drama reached its climax, tens of thousands of women mounted a protest comparable, in its passionate intensity and obstinate duration, to the suffragettes' battle for the vote. Many individual lives were permanently changed. And when the American cruise missiles left, some of that energy was transfused into a second battle, with its roots deep in English history – to recover Greenham Common for the people of Newbury.

As the *Guardian*'s defence specialist, I reported on the women's protest from both sides of the airfield's perimeter wire, as concerned to understand their fears as I was to explain or anticipate NATO's military strategy. I came to admire their courage, both physical and moral; their readiness to shed the protection of conventional respectability in pursuit of their anti-nuclear cause, and ultimately to risk repeated imprisonment. I was fascinated by the anarchic feminist communities that developed in the 'peace camps' scattered round the airfield's gates – named after the colours of the rainbow in deliberate contrast to the drab military camouflage inside the base, yet involved in acts of non-violent sabotage whose ingenuity any real military professional would admire.

Twenty-five years on, I have attempted to put their remarkable story in a wider perspective, to follow its strands through to the present day and assess its permanent legacy. Besides which, I was curious to discover what had happened to some of the individual women.

These were events that transcended their immediate context. Their influence spread worldwide. There are still plenty of 'Greenham women' around, active within the feminist movement. Moreover public concern about 'weapons of mass destruction' has been revived by continued nuclear proliferation, by the threat of terrorism, and by the immediate question of replacing Britain's deterrent force. As for our dwindling stock of common land, which at Greenham the protest indirectly helped to preserve, sadly the introduction of a 'right to roam' has not stopped its depletion.

The women who went to Greenham are fond of saying that none of them was typical. No one represented anybody else. I am grateful for that, being acutely aware that the personal, inevitably selective stories I have chosen to tell cannot remotely encompass a collective experience involving many thousands of people over more than a decade. But I make no apology for trying, because it is a story worth telling.

PART ONE
Trying to be Heard

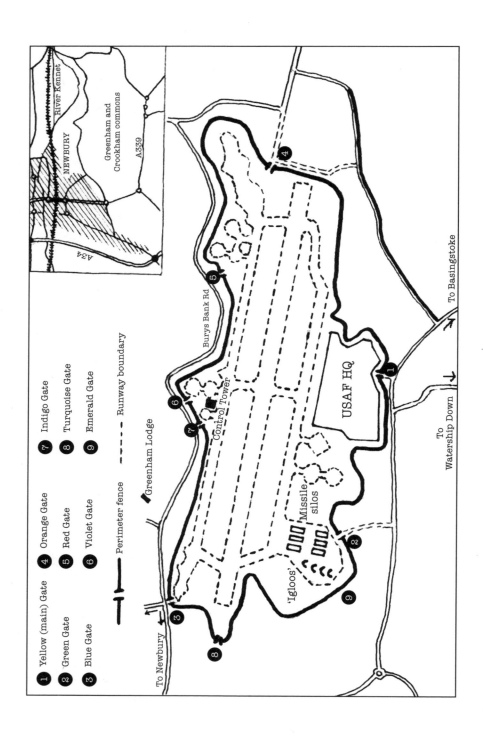

Legend:

1. Yellow (main) Gate
2. Green Gate
3. Blue Gate
4. Orange Gate
5. Red Gate
6. Violet Gate
7. Indigo Gate
8. Turquoise Gate
9. Emerald Gate

— Perimeter fence

- - - Runway boundary

▲ Greenham Lodge

Map labels:

River Kennet

NEWBURY

Greenham and Crookham commons

A339

A34

To Basingstoke

To Watership Down

USAF HQ

Burys Bank Rd

Control Tower

Missile silos

'Igloos'

To Newbury

A call to action

Llanwrtyd Wells is a long way from London's corridors of power. It is still more remote from the NATO command bunkers where during the summer of 1981 the climactic moves in the East–West nuclear arms race were being plotted. A voice protesting against the basing of American cruise missiles in Britain was unlikely to be heard, especially if it belonged to a middle-aged woman, tied to house, family and job in this small Welsh town.

Helen John realised that many people thought she was paranoid about the nuclear danger. And perhaps she was unduly suspicious of the vast military excavations she came across in the hills above Sennybridge, thinking they might be connected with the missiles. Yet she remained convinced that these 'awful weapons' threatened the survival of future generations. She had five children of her own to think about and, as a midwife, had brought many more into the world. For her, the intellectual jargon of nuclear deterrence was simply a euphemism for collective suicide.

So she decided to call a public protest meeting, in a hall opposite the railway station. She had never organised such an event before, let alone chaired the discussion. She didn't expect many people to turn up, but on the night the place was packed out. And crucially, the speaker she invited to address them – an anti-nuclear campaigner from Carmarthen, Ann Pettitt – brought news of a group of like-minded women who were planning a march to Greenham Common, where the American cruise missiles would be based. Calling themselves 'Women for Life on Earth', they intended to deliver their protest personally by walking the hundred or so miles from Cardiff City Hall to the Berkshire airfield – and demanding a televised debate with Margaret Thatcher's Defence Secretary, John Nott.

Even then, Helen nearly missed the event that was to transform the rest of her life. Confirmation of a start date for the march was late in reaching Llanwrtyd Wells. With less than a week to go, and her mother-in-law expected at any moment, there was barely time to make arrangements for her family while she was away.

About forty women set out for Greenham on Thursday, 27 August – just before the end of the school summer holidays. Some brought their kids along. And there were four male 'supporters', whose presence in what was essentially a women's protest was already contentious. Ann Pettitt, the original instigator, had no intention of excluding men. But Helen recalls returning from a supply trip in their van with another woman – who vehemently opposed any male involvement – to find two of the men right at the front carrying the 'Women for Life on Earth' banner: 'And she just screeched to a halt and said: "Stop. Give that banner to the women. Get to the back, and don't ever let me see you at the front again."' It was the first stage in a process that would eventually establish the unique, women-only nature of the Greenham protest. 'But the banner is heavy', the men explained. 'And the women are strong', came the authentic feminist reply.

The walk was expected to take about ten days, with informal meetings along the way to discuss their concerns. There was a certain amount of press interest, but not at all the sort Helen had anticipated:

> All they asked about was how our husbands were coping back home, and weren't we irresponsible exposing our children to all that carbon monoxide. We just could not get them to engage in serious conversation. So some of us decided to try a different approach – to take a leaf out of the suffragettes' book and engage in civil disobedience.

Helen's own resolve to take some sort of direct action even if it meant facing arrest – like chaining herself to the airfield gates – crystallised on the last night before they reached the US base. In nearby Hungerford, she was offered lodging by a man who turned out to be caring for a three-year-old daughter on his own. And he evidently shared the women's fear that nuclear confrontation might lead to nuclear war, because he was beside himself, worrying that his little girl would not survive to become an adult.

The father's anxiety strengthened Helen's determination to make her personal protest, whatever the consequences. 'I spent that night awake', she recalls, 'working out that for the first time in my married life I wasn't going to ring my husband and ask his permission, or even involve him. I was 44. And I knew it might cost him his job, but that was not enough to stop me.' This was something I was doing for myself, as an adult human being.'

The crucial decision came two days later, outside the entrance of what was officially known as 'RAF Greenham Common', though in reality it was of course a forward base for the US Air Force. Four of the women

How it all began. The first 'Greenham women' (Helen John on the right) chain themselves to the airfield fence, 5 September 1981, in imitation of the suffragettes.

– Helen, Eunice Stallard, Lynnie Seward and Lynne Whittemore – had indeed chained themselves to the wire-mesh fence by the main gate as soon as they arrived, in suffragette fashion, using flimsy baggage padlocks bought in Newbury. They had expected immediate arrest – or something equally dramatic. But it didn't happen, and they weren't quite sure what to do next. The rest of the marchers turned up. Somebody took photographs of the women looking 'determined'. Local people from the Newbury Campaign against Cruise Missiles offered cheerful support. Yet, almost inevitably, after all that effort, there was also a touch of anticlimax – a feeling more of picnic than protest. In fact 25 years on, one dedicated supporter still regards that very first demonstration as 'barmy'.

Karmen Cutler did manage to read out their demands – basically that they wanted a public debate about the cruise missiles – to a solitary MoD policeman, who at first mistook them for the cleaners, arriving a bit early. Then, after a while, another policeman came over to tell Helen it was best to move on because, it being Saturday night, 'the Jack Daniels would be flowing' and they might be raped by drunken Americans. When she rejected this kindly advice, he went off looking thoroughly baffled.

Next to appear was none less than the US base commander, the very man to whom they wanted to deliver their protest:

> And he stood there – and I've never forgotten his knuckles, they were white with fury – and said he would like to machine-gun the lot of us. And he added the words that really did change the course of my life: 'As far as I'm concerned, you can stay there as long as you like.' And at that moment – I think it was about half past six – we decided that was exactly what we would do.

This was the moment, in other words, that turned a one-off demonstration into an open-ended campaign. 'I've always felt we owed that American commander a huge debt of gratitude', Helen says now. 'Without his contemptuous dismissal, we wouldn't have stayed – I had five kids to get back to.'

In fact they did much, much more than just stay. Within months, Helen herself had abandoned her family – though I don't imagine she would describe it like that – fallen in love with a woman, asked for a divorce, and exchanged domestic respectability for the uncomfortable life of a political activist.

Many other women's lives also were transformed by that small drama on 5 September 1981. It was the start of a decade-long protest the like of which Britain had not seen since the suffragettes fought for the vote in the early years of the century. There were eventually tens of thousands of Greenham women – and not only from Britain. They also came from the United States, Western Europe, Australia. On one occasion 35,000 linked hands around the 9-mile perimeter fence. And Greenham Common, this obscure piece of communal land, occupied for NATO by foreign military forces, the local arena in which the last stage of the Cold War would be fought out, became familiar across half the world.

On the march

Greenham women reminiscing about the protest are fond of saying there is no such thing as a 'Greenham woman'. By which they mean there is no single stereotype that represents the thousands of women who came through the camp, or supported it as best they could from a distance. Each individual brought different skills to the communal effort, and took different experiences away. The stereotypes existed only in the minds of tabloid newspaper editors.

Indeed right from the start, the four women who chained themselves to the airfield fence were deliberately chosen to represent the different ages of women. Eunice Stallard, already in her sixties, was the grandmother; Helen John had teenage children; Lynnie Seward had young children; Lynne Whittemore was a student. Yet they did have important things in common besides their gender, both that first group and the network of camps and support groups that developed from it.

It was not mere accident that the original marchers came from South Wales, where the mining valleys are steeped in the politics of Old Labour. Tiny white-haired Eunice, full of subversive vitality even now she is in her eighties, has a montage on her kitchen wall celebrating, among others, the National Union of Mineworkers, Welsh CND and the National Union of Women's Suffrage Societies. Her proudest moment, she says almost seriously, was having a railway breakfast with Nye Bevan, ministerial founder of the National Health Service, on his way to an important Coal Board meeting in London.

Others on the march, I would guess, were disillusioned by party politics – as many Greenham women were – but they could hardly grow up in that part of the world without acquiring some sort of political background. Typically, they had tried the Campaign for Nuclear Disarmament (CND) and become impatient with talking and walking that seemed to get nowhere. They were looking for a bit of direct action.

Ann Pettitt's inspiration for the Greenham protest came from a chance reading of *Peace News*, which carried a report of a women-led march from Copenhagen to Paris. 'For some reason it just grabbed me.' Cardiff to Newbury didn't have quite the same transcontinental ring to it, but planning a 120-mile, ten-day trek, with at least a few kids trailing along, nevertheless required considerable determination and organising ability – qualities she and her early collaborator Karmen Cutler (now Thomas) evidently possessed in large measure.

In 1981, Ann and her partner Barry were getting their boots muddy nurturing plants and animals on a hillside smallholding above Carmarthen, bringing up two children, and campaigning against, among other things, the dumping of nuclear waste in Wales. She and Karmen had met briefly years before – without at first remembering this – at a squat in London's East End. By now Karmen also had a small child.

Work on planning the march was divided out among a small band of volunteers. Lots of telephoning (no emails in those days) to solicit financial support, arrange overnight stays with local Labour Party or church groups, seek advertisement in newspapers and women's magazines (including *Cosmopolitan* as well as the *Guardian*, so that they weren't all woolly liberals), and alert the various police forces whose escort was required. They quickly learnt a basic lesson: unless your organisation has a proper name, no one will take you seriously. So they called themselves 'Women for Life on Earth'.

If you think that sounds rather grand for a bunch of Welsh housewives, you would be wrong. The most striking common characteristic I found among Greenham women – or at any rate the ones I came to know personally – is that they believed in their cause seriously, simply and directly. Preserving life on earth was exactly what they were about. They did not see nuclear cruise missiles through the filters of military routine, academic war games, political expediency or journalistic cynicism. For them, these weapons were vividly present – far more powerful than the bombs dropped on Japan and, given the way the Cold War seemed to be intensifying, only too likely to invite the devastation of our own towns and countryside.

Helen John's determination to do something about it had reached critical pitch one day as she was driving to fetch her eldest child from school, dropping down to Builth Wells among the headwaters of the River Wye: 'It was a beautiful sunny afternoon – and suddenly I had this overwhelming vision that all the trees would be destroyed – I had to pull over – it reminded me of a Pathé newsreel I'd seen as a kid, of the devastation of Hiroshima.'

Helen's account reminded *me* of visiting Chernobyl, in the Ukraine, where a line of trees opposite the exploded nuclear power station was indeed shrivelled dead and brown by radiation. By 1986, when the Soviet accident occurred, the Greenham protest had been running for five years. Chernobyl came as a terrible reminder that civil nuclear power and nuclear weapons are intimately connected, scientifically, industrially and politically. To understand just how intimately, take a quick look at the nuclear raw material uranium.

In this dangerous business, uranium metal is subject to a process called 'enrichment', which makes it more radioactive. And the process is used in both civil and military programmes. *Slightly* enriched uranium makes fuel for a type of power reactor which can either drive naval submarines or generate electricity for civilian use; *highly* enriched uranium provides a bomb (like the 'Little Boy' dropped on Hiroshima). It is this particular technical ambiguity that makes the current international argument over Iran's nuclear programme so difficult to resolve.

Uranium irradiated in a reactor also creates plutonium, another bomb-making material (used for 'Fat Man', which annihilated Nagasaki). In fact the Chernobyl power station design, like the British Magnox stations, was derived from plants originally built to produce plutonium for weapons. When the Ukrainian reactor exploded, it was as potent as a bomb in terms of the radioactivity spread across Europe.

Another personal memory of 1986 is of going over to the *Guardian* news desk to report that the radioactive cloud from Chernobyl had just crossed the English coast at Dungeness. Our news editor at that time was Melanie Phillips (nowadays a columnist elsewhere) and in her momentary alarm she forgot the story, concerned only with what she should do about her children. The radioactive dust drifted on westwards, to be rain-washed down on to the Welsh sheep pastures.

Back in the late 1970s, after a decade during which CND's membership had slumped to a few thousand, and the women's libbers were concentrating on other things, increasing public awareness of this close connection between the civil and military aspects of nuclear power was one of the factors that revived the peace movement. Concern about the health effects of nuclear power stations or waste dumps read across to weapons, and that led, in one momentous instance, to the march on Greenham.

Occupation

The train of circumstance that led the women to Greenham Common reaches back at least to the beginning of the Second World War, when it was requisitioned, along with the adjacent Crookham Common, as an emergency airfield. To understand fully why it was chosen by the RAF, and why the local townspeople were so determined to recover it after half a century of military occupation, one needs to go back much further.

Berkshire's River Kennet is the gentlest of waterways, so readily manageable that eighteenth-century engineers turned it into a canal linking London with Bristol and Bath. Yet not so long ago in geological time, the whole valley now sheltering the market town of Newbury was filled with an icy postglacial torrent, scouring the chalk bedrock to hurl great banks of flint and shingle along its margins. One of those gravelly ridges forms what is now Greenham Common.

So this quiet heath began in violence. And in different ways throughout its history, it seems always to have been a battleground. Invading armies came and went. The Gauls were here, and the Romans. But it was not just armies that were fighting for control. Heathland is itself the result of an ecological struggle, between incompatible plants, trees and animals. And while we tend to think of it as a 'natural' landscape – simply because it has been there for so long – the contest is often crucially mediated by human intervention.

Once farmers settling the Kennet valley began to move their cattle up on to the ridge to graze the tall grass and birch scrub, other plants, especially heather and gorse (which round here they call furze), seized their chance to take over. As the high ground was cleared, rainwater ran more freely, carving deep gullies into its southern slopes, where the surviving birch trees were soon crowded by thick clumps of alder. Grazing cattle were joined by wild creatures – larks, butterflies, adders – which also thrived on open heathland.

This particular heath is common land, or, to be precise, two adjacent commons: Greenham to the west, larger and of course far better known, but also Crookham, equally important to the local community. So as well as being an ecological battleground, it was also a setting for the centuries-long fight to protect commoners' rights of access from the encroachment of farming enclosures. These two commons survived enclosure as long as they did because they were poor, stony ground – the 'wasteland of the manor' – on which neighbouring commoners had historic rights to graze animals, collect firewood or dig for peat and gravel. In the modern world, one of the few activities the land suited was playing golf (the former Crookham golf course, later rivalled by Greenham, lays claim to be the first inland course in England). But as the town of Newbury expanded, spreading its arms to east and south, its residents came increasingly to value access to such open countryside, however rough, and whether or not they had any formal rights.

By the 1930s, the commons formed part of two large family estates, both of which were sold at auction in the run-up to the Second World War. And crucially, in the light of subsequent legal battles, Newbury Borough Council stepped in to purchase the manorial rights of Greenham Common – for £225 – and then established a legal right of public access (which had already been granted at Crookham, because this enabled the landowners to control what public activity took place).

In 1941, an RAF surveyor searching for a suitable wartime airfield site would have looked down from his biplane on a long broad swathe of flat, open heathland between the valleys of the Kennet and its tributary the Enborne, aligned roughly east–west (the best alignment for a runway, because of the prevailing westerly winds), with the old Basingstoke road running straight down the middle of it. This place not only had potential as an airfield; from a distance it must have looked as if it already *was* an airfield.

By May 1941 the RAF was in possession, having used its emergency powers to requisition both commons, and the first runway was indeed laid out approximately along the line of the old road, but just north of it so it could still be used. Greenham was originally intended as a satellite airfield for nearby Aldermaston, which would later accommodate Britain's atomic weapons establishment. But construction was barely complete when it was decided the base should be loaned to an American unit – the first of many that were to occupy it, with brief intervals, for the next 50 years.

In September 1943, the US Army's 101st Airborne Division descended on Newbury, followed early the next year by the great fleet of Dakota aircraft and wooden gliders that was to carry them into Normandy. With typical organisational flare, the American ground crews used the enormous crates in which the glider fuselages and wings arrived as instant building blocks for their own accommodation.

This first US visitation produced none of the arguments that surrounded later, post-war deployments. The Yanks had answered a desperate call for help. In the crowded Newbury pubs there may have been the odd jibe about their being 'overpaid, oversexed and over here', but it was blindingly obvious that without them there could be no hope of driving the Germans back through France.

Final preparations for D-Day were kept as secret as possible. Even so, townspeople must have realised what was happening on 5 June 1944 as Newbury's streets, like many others, were suddenly deserted by the American troops, and the evening quiet was broken by the drone of 80 Dakotas taking off at 11-second intervals.[1] The allied supreme commander General Eisenhower was there at the airfield to tell his young soldiers, so heavily encumbered by equipment they could barely clamber aboard the aircraft, that 'the eyes of the world' were upon them. Three hours later they were dropping across the marshes north of Carentan, behind the Americans' 'Utah' invasion beach.

As the war ended, Greenham was handed back to the RAF, to be closed in June 1946 and de-requisitioned a year later. It was one of dozens of surplus, more or less derelict airfields across the southeast of England. Newbury assumed it would soon be getting its commons back. The borough council even formed a committee to organise their restoration. Of course the concrete runways would take some digging up, but the makeshift wartime base had not even been fenced in. The old Basingstoke road could easily be cleared and patched up.

Such parochial plans reckoned without the onset of the Cold War – the Berlin crisis of 1948 and the rush to form a defensive transatlantic alliance against the Soviet Union. NATO was created in 1949, as one of its British commanders saw it, 'to keep the Russians out, the Americans in, and the Germans down'. Keeping the Americans in meant, among other things, providing them with forward bases for their nuclear bombers, and not asking too many awkward questions about how they might be used in the event of another war.

GREENHAM
the first protests

When it was announced that Greenham Common was to become a permanent US Air Force base there was massive local opposition

GREENHAM COMMON PROPOSED AIRFIELD

TO THE

INHABITANTS OF NEWBURY
AND THE
SURROUNDING VILLAGES.

At the Town's Meeting held at the instigation of the NEWBURY AND DISTRICT CHAMBER OF COMMERCE in the Plaza, Newbury, on Thursday, 22nd March, 1951, to discuss the proposed new Airfield on Greenham Common, the following resolution was passed unanimously:

1. This Meeting, whilst fully conscious of the urgency of the Defence Programme, cannot contemplate without dismay and distress the grave injury which would be done to the Town and District by the construction of a permanent aerodrome on Greenham Common, on the very borders of the Borough of Newbury.

2. This loss, now and for ever, of ancient Common Lands and Liberties would be a disaster; these are for us essential parts of that peaceful way of life for the protection of which the Defence Programme has been undertaken.

3. We declare that we are far from being convinced that the admitted military requirements can only be met at the cost of so drastic a sacrifice by so many people; or that no adequate alternative site can be found.

4. We therefore most urgently pray that the project be not proceeded with.

PETITION FORMS WITHIN.
COME IN AND
SIGN TODAY!

The land referred to commands a gorgeous view of the Berkshire and Hampshire downs. In the spring it is a blaze of yellow broom and in the autumn a carpet of blue heather. It has always been regarded as common land, but the people appear to have permitted the landlord certain rights over it because he presented himself as the guardian of its immunity . . .

Nye Bevan on Greenham Common, in a letter to Clough Williams-Ellis at the Council for the Preservation of Rural England, 30th August 1938.

Where Greenham was concerned, Air Ministry officials were pleased to realise that the emergency powers they needed to re-acquire the airfield were still in force. The Americans took a not-so-discreet look in February 1951 and a month later it was announced that they would soon be back, with their nuclear bombers. That meant noisy six-engined B-47 Stratojets, not friendly little propeller-driven Dakotas, plus a much longer, 12,000-foot runway, a security fence and permanent diversion of the Basingstoke road.

This time the people of Newbury were appalled, angry and vociferous. A 'Town's Meeting' was called at the Plaza Theatre – not by troublesome political activists, but by stolid members of the Chamber of Commerce with Greenham commoner Lord Teviot in the chair – to register 'dismay and distress' at the 'grave injury' a permanent aerodrome would cause. A resolution was passed unanimously, declaring that 'the loss, now and for ever, of ancient common lands and liberties would be a disaster; these are for us essential parts of that peaceful way of life for the protection of which the defence programme has been undertaken.'

Emboldened by such vigorous public support, borough councillors made clear they would not voluntarily relinquish Greenham Common. Local MP Anthony Hurd delivered a petition to Parliament with 10,000 signatures on it. In the political circumstances of the day, however, he was wasting his time.

Prime Minister Clement Attlee's government was struggling – unsuccessfully – to reconcile three strategic policy objectives: an overriding requirement to entangle the United States in the defence of a devastated Western Europe against the perceived threat of a nuclear-armed USSR, an appeal for reluctant American assistance in the UK's own nuclear bomb programme, and some degree of control over US weapons based in the UK. Whether or not the burghers of Newbury were 'dismayed and distressed' at the prospect of turning their ancient commons into a launch pad for NATO's nuclear strike force was definitely not a major concern. Within days, the Cabinet had formally overruled their objections and given USAF engineers the go-ahead for a two-and-a-half-year construction programme at Greenham.

The scale of the work made it clear that the Americans were there to stay. The vast runway – the longest in Europe at that time – was surrounded by a great sprawl of taxiways, hard standing, hangars and bomb storage 'igloos'. There was no room for the old commons road, which had to be rebuilt around the southern perimeter. The Ark Tea Room and the Volunteer Inn were demolished. And when the first B-47 bomber wing took possession of the airfield in October 1956, local people's worst fears about noise were realised. These heavy six-engined jets not only produced a penetrating roar on take-off; they landed with relatively high power against a drag parachute. Even when they weren't flying, their engines often had to be tested.

The B-47s belonged to the US Strategic Air Command – motto 'Peace is our Profession'. For the six years 1958–64 they operated the Reflex Alert scheme, standing by at a few minutes' notice to take off on bombing missions against the Soviet Union.

These were the early, dangerous, frenetic days of the Cold War, and Newbury was involved in more than one way. It had become a dormitory town for the Atomic Weapons Research Establishment at Aldermaston, six miles away, where British boffins were struggling to catch up with their American counterparts, having been cut off for more than a decade from the benefits of their wartime cooperation by the 1946 McMahon Act – a US congressional measure to prevent the sharing of nuclear information. The British nuclear industry was immature and in a hurry. Corners were inevitably cut.

Given the inherently secretive nature of the British governmental process, overlaid in this case by additional military security, the public at large knew little of what was happening. But every now and then they caught a glimpse of what a dangerous game this was. Events like the USAF B-47 accident at Lakenheath, Suffolk, in 1956, when a nuclear bomb store was set alight, or the disastrous fire in an atomic pile at Windscale in 1957, could not be totally hidden. And in February 1958, Newbury was jolted by a fatal accident at its own neighbourhood base – a fire which totally destroyed a parked B-47. Was there a nuclear bomb on board at the time?

A full account of this alarming incident belongs much later in the Greenham story, because none of the details, or the unexpected, secretive way it became linked with Aldermaston, was disclosed at the time. By the time they were revealed, in 1996, along with rumours of an earlier accident, local people were much more sensitised to nuclear safety issues, not least by a suspiciously high rate of childhood leukaemia in their town.

If accidents like this alarmed Newbury, they also raised uneasy questions in Whitehall and Westminster – questions that were to resurface in a different form during the cruise missile deployment of the 1980s.

In normal circumstances the British authorities would not have allowed foreign, nuclear-armed aircraft to operate from RAF bases without complying positively with British regulations and procedures. But such was the pace of events, and the deferential nature, then as now, of the 'special relationship', the Americans were given a virtually free hand.

Two months after the Greenham accident, in an almost obsequious letter dated 6 May 1958, Prime Minister Harold Macmillan wrote to the US President General Eisenhower asking for some sort of advance warning and information about US aircraft flying from or over the UK carrying nuclear bombs. His 'Dear Friend' Eisenhower would be aware of the agitation such flights were causing, Macmillan wrote, and unless at least a few people in London knew what was going on, it was difficult to resist political pressure on the issue:

> When, last year, you agreed that we could fly components for our Christmas Island trials over your country we were, in my view quite properly, required to comply with certain conditions that were imposed for the safety of the United States. Broadly speaking we have to satisfy your authorities as to our safety procedures in transit and to provide advance notification of the flight plans of each individual flight, with a statement of the general nature of the cargo, and to make arrangements so that immediate information about the detailed nature of the cargo could be furnished to your airbases in the event of an accident.
>
> This is just the kind of information and assurance about your flights over this country which I now lack. The reason is easy enough to understand and springs from the way in which arrangements for your aircraft to be here were first made in the days of the Berlin Airlift. But the domestic interest in these matters has grown since then and I feel I ought to ask you to provide the British authorities with the same sort of information about future flights of your aircraft into, out of and over this country when they are carrying nuclear weapons or their components.
>
> Of course, I do not want to embarrass you, by asking for details of weapon design which are barred by your present law, but our own experience shows that it is possible to avoid this and yet comply with your own safety conditions. Such information would naturally be restricted here to the few officials who would need to know.

As the letter makes clear, that particular stable door should have been shut ten years earlier, when the first 'temporary' deployment of US bombers to the UK had been agreed as a show of strength during the Berlin crisis. During that same critical period, Clement Attlee's government had failed to obtain any written understanding on a much more vital issue – a British veto over the use of American nuclear weapons based in this country. It was not until January 1952 that any public statement was made – and then only a communique, issued after the new prime minister, Winston Churchill, met US President Harry Truman. The British ambassador in Washington had prepared the ground just before the election, but by this stage the best even Winston could squeeze out of a reluctant US administration fell far short of a veto.[2]

The communique merely reaffirmed that use of the bases in an emergency would be 'a matter for joint decision' by the two governments 'in the light of the circumstances prevailing at the time'. From then on, whenever British governments were challenged to say whether they retained ultimate control of the US weapons, they fell back on this limp formula. And so it was with Prime Minister Margaret Thatcher and her Defence Secretary, Michael Heseltine, when ground-launched nuclear cruise missiles were deployed to Greenham in the 1980s. American officials confronted with the same question could, and did, point out that these missiles were based in the UK as part of a collective NATO strategy, and subject by then to an integrated command structure in which Britain played an important part. But that did not stop MPs from both sides of the House of Commons calling for what came to be called a 'dual-key' control – meaning that the weapons could not be fired unless both governments agreed.

In truth, Britain had by this time settled into its role as the United States' 'Unsinkable Aircraft Carrier' – the title chosen by the iconoclastic journalist Duncan Campbell in 1984 for his compelling analysis of the US military presence.[3] The 'Iron Lady' was never likely to give those obstinate, protesting women encouragement by questioning established American command and control arrangements. However the Social Democratic Party (SDP) leader David Owen – who led the debate on this issue – did find a new line of attack, arguing that missiles based on British territory were essentially different from aircraft simply using our airfields, and should therefore come under our direct control.

The citizens of Newbury reckoned they already knew the difference. Aircraft could be hideously noisy, while missiles – at least until they were launched – would be completely silent. The departure of the SAC B-47s in 1964 brought a long period of relative quiet. Indeed one might have expected the military to pull out altogether, since the emergency powers under which the airfield was requisitioned expired in 1958. In fact, the RAF had no intention of leaving. The Air Ministry had already purchased

Crookham Common from its private owners, and before the Americans left it persuaded Newbury Borough Council to sell 600 acres of Greenham Common inside the base (importantly, though, not the 200 acres outside the perimeter) by 'voluntary' conveyance. Much of it, after all, was by now covered with thick concrete.

The ministry is believed to have paid only £7,500, because the land was subject to various ancient rights of common. The men in bowler hats must have been rubbing their hands with satisfaction at the deal, since their next move – planned years previously – was to extinguish those awkward commoners' rights. At a stroke of a lawyer's pen, this would both eliminate any right of access and restore the land value in case the airfield was eventually sold for redevelopment.

In the event, whether through an oversight or just bureaucratic complacency, the second part of the plan was never followed through. The commoners retained their ancient privileges, even though their legitimate access to the base was physically barred by a tall wire fence. By that time, with the base so well established, MoD officials probably thought they were dealing with no more than a technicality, an insignificant legal anomaly. If so, they got it badly wrong. This omission was to have far-reaching consequences – for those inside the wire as well as outside. Right through to the 1980s, it lay there like a time bomb.

Nor was the borough council completely supine where the commons were concerned. It extracted a half-promise from Whitehall that if ever the airfield was no longer needed for military purposes, Newbury would have a chance to buy it back – or at least be consulted about its future.

Over the next few years this tug-of-war between Whitehall and Newbury continued. In 1965 the Commons Registration Act, badly flawed though it was, gave rural communities all over the country the chance to halt the erosion of their common land. Greenham and Crookham commoners were among those who took advantage of it to register both the commons and, much to the irritation of the Ministry of Defence, their continued rights of access to the base. It took years of negotiation, but was finally agreed on condition that individual rights – to graze cattle, collect firewood and so on – would be 'in abeyance' as long as the airfield was needed by the military.

It was while this argument was under way at local level that NATO lost the use of French airfields (because President de Gaulle withdrew his forces from the integrated command structure) and Greenham was offered back to the Americans as a standby base. During the next decade it was used intermittently by the USAF, and for a few months in 1972–73 to house Ugandan refugees.

The next test of strength came in 1978, when the MoD announced that Greenham had been chosen by the Americans to base a force of KC-135 in-flight refuelling tankers (the military plane from which the Boeing 707 airliner was derived). Fearful of the noise they would cause, Newbury residents waged the same essentially 'NIMBY' campaign they had organised 20 years earlier against the SAC bombers – protest meetings, marches, a petition. And this time, to their delight, they won. The MoD backed off, and told the Americans they would have to take their noisy aircraft to Fairford, in Gloucestershire (where there is still a major US airbase).

In December of the following year, however, at a special NATO ministerial meeting in Brussels, it was decided to deploy a new force of American ground-launched nuclear cruise missiles throughout Western Europe, and the search for bases was on again in the UK – this time to take 160 of the new weapons. At first it was thought they might go to Lakenheath in Suffolk, or Upper Heyford, Oxfordshire, where nuclear bomb storage already existed to service USAF F-III bombers (the aircraft later used to bomb Libya). Then in June 1980 word went round Whitehall that two unoccupied bases had been chosen, but that an announcement was being delayed while Margaret Thatcher's government prepared for what was bound to be a controversial, politically sensitive deployment.

As the *Guardian*'s defence correspondent, I therefore set myself the job of prising this secret out of the military authorities. It took several days of telephoning. I called everyone I knew whose post would require their knowing which the bases were – although, of course, nobody was allowed to tell me. Finally, by collecting hints and snippets of information, I was able to put together two profiles to compare with a list of all the USAF facilities in the UK. Greenham was a pretty obvious choice. But the second base, a 'Defence Property Disposal Office' at Molesworth off the A1 – a sort of military scrapyard, without even a small runway – was a total surprise. Still, the profile fitted exactly. My editor, Peter Preston, decided to back the story, and I waited anxiously for confirmation – which came the next day, 17 June, in a Commons statement from the then Defence Secretary, Francis Pym.

It also became clear just how politically sensitive these cruise missiles were. The MoD had taken the unprecedented step (this was way before the days of 'spin doctors') of preparing thousands of leaflets justifying NATO's strategy, reassuring local residents that the noise disturbance would be 'minimal', the risk of an accidental release of radioactive material 'negligible', and so on. The pamphlet also contained the statement – simply incorrect, and later to be publicly challenged – that none of the nuclear weapons stored in this country for many years had been involved in an accident.

From Whitehall's point of view, the reaction in Newbury was reassuringly muted. Next day in the *Guardian* I quoted Mrs Caroline Holbrook, a leading light in the earlier campaign against the noisy KC-135 tankers, to the effect that the 'Greenham watchdog committee' had no objection in principle: 'We are pro-NATO, pro-defence, and we fought against the KC-135s because they were noisy and dirty, whereas cruise missiles are supposed to be nice and quiet', she said.

However, another local resident, Joan Ruddock, later to lead CND and go to Westminster as a Labour MP, was already 'phoning round urgently to set up the Newbury Campaign Against Cruise Missiles. The women's march from Wales was of course still far over the horizon, but the stage was now set for an extraordinary protest that would make Greenham Common a familiar name far beyond the boundaries of the county of Berkshire.

Women's Peace Camp

The camp acquired its name by an extremely roundabout route. News of the protest, barely noticed throughout the rest of Britain, was instantly picked up – for obvious propaganda reasons – by an East German radio station. From there it was somehow relayed around the world, so that a few days later a letter arrived from Australia addressed to 'The Greenham Common Women's Peace Camp'. A sign was duly painted – in the suffragette colours of purple, white and green – to announce this identity.

At first, the encampment developed slowly and hesitantly. None of the marchers, after all, had originally intended to stay, and those few who were able and willing to do so somehow had to acquire tents, bedding, cooking equipment and so on – lent in the first instance by local Newbury people. Ann Pettitt and the others made intense efforts to get publicity and build support through CND (for example, by speaking at the Campaign's rally in Hyde Park that October) and various feminist networks. But, inevitably, during those first months, the campers were thin on the ground.

Eunice Stallard, with no immediate family responsibilities, stayed for a few weeks until she broke her wrist. Several times, she recalls, the camp dwindled to just three women. Helen John remembers actually being there on her own.

Gradually, the elements of a permanent camp were assembled: a donated caravan, a standpipe for water, a makeshift postal service (all of them facilities that would come under attack as opposition to the women's activities built up in later years). Tents began to be augmented by igloo-shaped structures, which soon became a Greenham symbol – 'benders'. In their classic form, these were framed by pliant branches, covered with transparent plastic sheeting, and made comfortable inside with whatever materials came to hand (benders later became only too vulnerable to the council's bailiffs). In these early, innocent days there was also a splendid sort of plastic marquee, built round a poplar tree.

Tents and 'benders', the plastic-covered shelters that became a Greenham symbol.

At the community's heart was its campfire – increasingly valued as winter approached. A place for endless talking, a gathering point to welcome visitors (who often brought firewood as a gift, since cutting live wood was forbidden). Add somebody who could play a guitar, and it also provided a natural setting in which the women would sing – something they did a great deal as the protest swelled.

Their compositions were eventually compiled in a Greenham songbook containing more than 50 numbers. Some were a female take on familiar 'men's' tunes ('Lily of the Arc Lights' to the tune of 'Lili Marlene'); others were blatantly political ('I Am a Witness to Your War Crimes'). They could be ironic ('We Work for the Russians'), explanatory ('We Are Gentle Angry Women'), based on Greenham slogans ('Take the Toys from the Boys'), or intended to draw historical comparisons ('Our Diggers' Song' or 'We Are the Witches'). Perhaps the most familiar, belted out to raise morale during a sit-down blockade, or to puncture the ritual of a magistrates court, was 'You can't kill the spirit/ She is like a mountain, old and strong.'

The first crucial turning point in the camp's story – without which it may never have developed further – came early in February 1982, when

YOU CAN'T KILL THE SPIRIT

it was decided that from then on the protest should involve women only. The decision was prompted in part by an official warning from Newbury District Council that the women would be evicted from common land outside the main gate in a fortnight's time. There was a feeling that if a physical confrontation was in prospect, the fewer testosterone-fuelled males around the better. Besides which, a number of women felt that the men who stayed were simply not pulling their weight. Too much late-night talking, not enough washing up.

More positively, the women were determined to experiment with their own form of non-violent protest. They wanted to assert their identity, to take their own decisions in a way their pre-Greenham lives had not always permitted, to represent themselves in dealing with the authorities. In short, they preferred to run their own show. And a press release announcing the new policy went further: the peace camp intended, or at any rate hoped, to deal only with female representatives of the authorities and the 'media'. This second, distinctly feminist aspiration could never be completely fulfilled, though I do recall a group of women (at what later became Blue Gate) refusing to talk to me because I was a man.

There were several meetings, small and large, before the women-only consensus was confirmed over a period of two or three weeks. Nancy Orrell remembers an unseasonably sunny day and 'a huge circle in front of main gate' within which everyone – in authentic Greenham fashion – was invited to have their say. Young men impatient to interject were told to wait their turn.

For Nancy, the issue was a difficult one, because her husband Bob was both a prominent campaigner in his own right (as a veteran of the D-Day landings, he was chairman of Ex-Services CND) and an active supporter of the Greenham protest. Bob's 'black bags', containing a mixture of firewood, kindling and firelighters, were part of the camp's essential supplies.

Nevertheless, she found the women-only arguments persuasive. As a mother, she understood the anxiety of another woman at the meeting who said she would not let her 16-year-old daughter stay in a mixed camp. And when it was her turn to speak, she was conscious of her own responsibility for a 16-year-old boy – the youngest member of her CND group in Christchurch, Hampshire – who had joined the Orrells that weekend. She had noticed during other demonstrations, she told the meeting, how 'the police immediately pick on young men and throw them out'.

Greenham's long-winded, egalitarian, consensual approach to decision-taking, which probably owed something to the Quakers as well as to the women's liberation movement, was one of its strengths. Here was the antithesis of the political meeting where a strong chairman forces through a vote on a prepared resolution. It did not mean, however, that everyone immediately agreed. Helen John had only gradually come round to the idea of women-only, on pragmatic grounds, though in retrospect she regards the decision as 'pivotal'. Karmen Cutler, among the organisers of the original march, was never reconciled to it. She recalls collecting generous contributions from the Welsh miners only to be told, when she delivered the money to Greenham, that the miners themselves would not be welcome there – 'just because they were male'.

As for the men who were actually asked to leave, some were outraged. They didn't buy the line that a women-only policy was not anti-men, merely pro-women. As they saw it, the peace camp's purpose was preventing the deployment of nuclear cruise missiles – an aim they all shared, regardless of gender – not conducting a feminist experiment. Helen remembers one of them (a 'non-violence trainer' apparently) getting so carried away that he flung coins at her because they had the Queen's head on them and then tipped a cauldron of water into her lap.

The women-only decision also posed problems for CND as an organisation. As it happened, the Campaign had just appointed a woman 'chair', Joan Ruddock, who was thoroughly sympathetic towards the peace camp. Not only did she live nearby, at Burghfield Common; she and a colleague from Newbury Labour Party had started the town's campaign against the cruise missiles within hours of reading that the nuclear weapons were on their way to Greenham. It was also her initiative, through CND, which provided the camp with its first portacabin. But she had to face the fact that many within the organisation – at that time predominantly male – regarded the women-only policy as divisive and unfair. Whereas she and the CND

COMMON WOMENS DAY

Women come to GREENHAM Common on the first Saturday in every month and become VISIBLE. (Starting from May) Please come and make your own contribution, from simply being here, Planting, Picnicing, Singing, Sharing Experiences, ect to non-violent direct actions.

There will be no Leaders, and every Women is asked to take responsibility for making each big gathering possible and non-violent. You may want to offer a work-shop or share skills and information - or this may be your first visit and you just want to see the base for yourself.

If you cannot make it on the Saturday, Come on the Sunday - Stay the weekend if you want to.

PLEASE TREAT THE COMMON AS YOUR HOME

The Situation will be different from the usual - as we may not be allowed toilets, so come prepared and informed on how to deal with WASTE, The Nature of the Common and everything that lives on it is very finely balanced. You may need to bring shovels or trowels to make laterines — - Water Containers will be useful. Pick up and burn, or take away with you every scrap of TOILET PAPER, and everything that is not compostable/biodegradable. Also DO NOT take/cut Live wood only gather dead wood that has fallen of the trees, if you have fires. IF we all follow these LAWS OF NATURE - we should leave everything as good as we found it.

There are Safe Spaces around the Common that can be used as Play Areas for children. If you can offer Theatre, Energy, Music, Toys ect. Please go ahead - nothing will be specifically laid on from the Camp. THANKS -

YOU ARE THE ENERGY FOR MAKING THIS DAY HAPPEN. PLEASE DUPLICATE AND PASS IT ROUND

* WOMEN PLEASE CONTINUE TO COME AT OTHER TIMES AS WELL *

WOMEN ONLY PLEASE

Men can support by helping financially, taking care of children at home ect.
Basically we are asking men to STAY AWAY the first weekend of every month.

(margin, clockwise: MAY · JUNE · JULY · AUGUST · SEPTEMBER · OCTOBER · NOVEMBER · DECEMBER · JANUARY · FEBRUARY · MARCH · APRIL)

general secretary Bruce Kent took the view that the Greenham women were exceptional, and should be treated as such, it took 'a huge amount of negotiation and discussion' to carry the movement with them: 'We were asking people who were raring to go, wanting to be there – because there was a huge sense of wrong, that the Americans were going to site their missiles at Greenham – to stand back and give the women space.'

It was therefore essential, in Ruddock's view, that the CND national council should take a formal position on the issue, 'because otherwise our membership, or some of the members certainly, would have been on a collision path with the women – and that would have been hugely damaging to the peace movement'. After much debate the council did eventually agree that Greenham should be regarded, in her words, as 'a special place for a special group of people', and that the organisation would suppress its reservations (about tactics, as well as the question of gender) so as to offer continuing support.

As a journalist looking back at all this, I have to say that whatever the reasoning behind it, making the camp women-only was a stroke of public relations genius. Every news editor in the country was instantly provided with a clear-cut storyline. And this one was not about just another anti-nuclear demonstration, to be 'spiked' along with many others. Here was a courageous band of 'peace women' taking on a military superpower – a story that would run and run.

For the moment, however, this was still a low-key affair. Whilst the women may have arrived at Greenham with strong anti-nuclear convictions – why else would they have stayed – their tactics were cautious. The early 'actions', as they always called them, took the form of passive blockades. It was almost a year before they actually entered the base – for just a few yards, to barricade themselves inside the sentry box at the main gate. In retrospect, comparing this with later actions in which women armed with bolt cutters hurled themselves at the fence, it seems almost like a schoolgirl prank. And it was still relatively good-humoured, on both sides.

The first mass incursion, just before dawn on New Year's Day 1983, produced one of the enduring visual images of Greenham: dozens of women dancing in a circle on top of one of the half-completed missile silos. The press had been widely alerted, and their pictures of these small defiant figures silhouetted against the construction site's floodlights went around the world. Yet even at this stage the women had deliberately decided not to cut the fence.

The idea for the silos action came from an observant Glaswegian called Elena, who noticed that although multiple fences were being erected to protect this most sensitive area, where the nuclear weapons would be stored, there were still gaps to let construction traffic through. So for the time being only one layer of fencing barred the women's access. The women surmounted this with ladders, plus carpets to cover its barbed wire, then made a rush for the top of the nearest silo, somehow managing to outpace the pursuing constabulary through the cloying mud. (Coming from Maldon in Essex, where the annual mud race is typically won by lightly built runners who skip across the surface, rather than by powerfully built men who sink through it, I can understand this.) The many women arrested on that occasion were charged with 'breaching the peace'.

In retrospect, there were several reasons why the protest escalated so gradually and cautiously. One has to remember that when the original marchers arrived, the Americans were not much in evidence. The cruise missiles were not scheduled to arrive for another two years. The airfield's main perimeter fence, later to become such a significant barrier, physically, legally and symbolically, still had gaps in it. The huge, hump-backed silos in which the missile launchers would be hidden had not been built – 16 months later, as we have just seen, they were still at the mud and concrete stage.

Another reason (though women who lived through the whole protest tend to make light of it) was uncertainty as to how the military authorities would react. It takes courage and determination to lie down in front of a bulldozer, all the more so when the outcome may be arrest and possible prosecution. A respectable family woman, with kids and a job to think about, does not lightly acquire a prison record. Nor, for that matter, does an ambitious young woman about to embark on a professional career.

Ideologically, the women took an inordinately long time to work out for themselves what 'non-violent direct action' should mean in this situation. At one level, they were confronting immediate practical questions such as whether to climb over a 10-feet-high fence using a ladder and a carpet, or cut straight through it (inviting a charge of criminal damage). Much more broadly, they wanted to embrace the principle of non-violence – to challenge those who would resort to military action as a means of settling international disputes, and learn how to be politically effective without violence.

Di McDonald, who saw the peace camp from many angles and later became a prime mover in the Cruisewatch campaign to stop the missile convoys exercising outside the base (her daughters still think of themselves as 'Greenham women', although they were small children at the time), recalls the solemn way in which these issues were debated. 'Non-violence' was one of the camp's two golden rules (the other being 'no men overnight'). It was obvious that people should not if possible be injured in the course of a protest, but what about damaging property?

It sounds unlikely, given the turmoil that occurred later, but Di remembers 'about two years of anxious discussions, meetings, dialogue and philosophising' before they actually decided to cut the fence. The argument which tipped the balance was that, while it might technically be a violent act to destroy the fence, it was justified 'to prevent the greater crime' being planned within the base. This satisfied consciences and seemed to offer the basis of a legal defence – 'It wasn't accepted, but that didn't invalidate it in our view.'

In debating the limits of non-violence, and the comparative merits of direct action, as opposed to a conventional political campaign, Greenham women were of course recapitulating arguments that divided CND during the late 1950s and early 1960s, at the time of the Aldermaston marches. More intriguingly, they were walking the same intellectual ground as their feminist sisters the suffragettes, fighting for the vote many years before in the run-up to the First World War.

Of all the earlier movements that inspired the Greenham protest,[4] it was the militant suffragettes who had the most immediately obvious influence. The four women who chained themselves to the wire outside the main gate in September 1981 were consciously imitating their Edwardian predecessors. When the arrests started at Greenham, many women followed the suffragettes' example by choosing imprisonment rather than paying a fine. The camp notice board was painted in suffragette colours and many of the ribbons fluttering from the perimeter wire were chosen with the same historical reference in mind.

Sitting recently in Di McDonald's kitchen, listening to her stories of Greenham and discussing this very point, she surprised me by fetching a long swathe of purple, white and green ribbons she still keeps by her. Unsure why those particular colours were originally chosen, I later sought help from the curator of the Women's Library in Whitechapel. It seems the colour scheme was devised by Emmeline Pethick Lawrence, treasurer of the grandly styled Women's Social and Political Union (WSPU). Writing in the suffragettes' journal *Votes for Women* in 1908 she explained the symbolism:

'Purple ... is the royal colour. It stands for the royal blood that flows in the veins of every suffragette, the instinct of freedom and dignity ... white stands for purity in private and public life ... green is the colour of hope and the emblem of spring.'

Living up to such high-flown inspiration would clearly take some doing. Looking beyond that, the historical comparison is complicated and contradictory. The suffragettes of the WSPU – led by Mrs Emmeline Pankhurst and her daughters Christabel and Sylvia – were a militant faction within a much larger women's movement fighting for the vote. Many of those involved were simultaneously campaigning to prevent the war which engulfed Europe in 1914 – and would instantly have understood what was happening at Greenham – while others focused exclusively on winning the vote. So when war did come, the movement became deeply split between those adopting an internationalist, even pacifist approach, and those who loudly supported the war effort.

Moreover both the 'suffragettes' (according to Roy Hattersley, this was originally a scornful journalistic term coined, just as it might be today, by the *Daily Mail*[5]) and the less aggressive 'suffragists' were in the first instance seeking justice for their own sex. That their influence as voters might benefit the nation as a whole, or their success help the cause of those men who still did not have the vote, was a secondary matter.

Of course the Greenham women, too, were more or less united in their feminism. Hence their decision to exclude men. But that was a matter of tactics (at least for the originators of the protest), of personal preference and mutual understanding. Their declared cause – the removal of the cruise missiles and, by extension, an end to nuclear confrontation – transcended any question of gender. As they saw it, this was a matter of human survival.

Where Greenham women closely matched the suffragettes' approach was in their belief that well-publicised direct action was the best way to make men in authority take notice. The original marchers arrived at the Berkshire airfield with what they thought was a reasonable demand: a televised debate with Defence Secretary John Nott. To this extent it was still a conventional political campaign. It was when this polite request was comprehensively snubbed, as it was always likely to be, that their mood changed to one of obstinate protest. And even then, as we have seen, they moved only slowly across the direct-action spectrum from passive sit-downs to massed assaults on military property.

The suffragettes, for all their long skirts, were less ladylike. Like other Edwardian women fighting for the vote, Mrs Pankhurst and her followers did initially pin their hopes on a parliamentary campaign. But repeated frustration with MPs and ministers, who often expressed sympathy yet never translated that sympathy into political action, eventually turned them into outright militants. And once convinced of the need for direct action, they really waded in. For some, it was a case of the more violence the better – often symbolic, certainly, but sometimes personalised, or just plain destructive.

Chaining themselves to Whitehall railings was the least of it. They swept down Oxford Street smashing windows (surely a magnificent sight as they clutched precarious hats in one gloved hand, hammers in the other). They set fire to pillar boxes, slashed paintings, posted letter bombs, hurled stones at No. 10 Downing Street. A substantial bomb was planted in Lloyd George's house (though they probably knew it was empty at the time). Winston Churchill, an avowed sympathiser who would not deliver the political goods, was horsewhipped on Bristol Temple Meads station (much more satisfying, one imagines, than merely jostling Michael Heseltine when he visited Newbury).

The question hotly debated at the time – and which reads across to the Greenham protest – was whether militant action actually furthered the women's cause. A much larger body of suffragists, led by women like Mrs Millicent Fawcett, president of the National Union of Women's Suffrage Societies (NUWSS) – whose banner is on Eunice Stallard's kitchen wall in memory of her mother – never accepted Mrs Pankhurst's dictum that the most effective political argument is a broken pane of glass. For them, politics meant reasoned persuasion, though they certainly shared much of the suffragettes' anger when their allies in the House of Commons (probably a majority of MPs) repeatedly shied away from the necessary legislation.

As the suffragettes became increasingly violent some of their staunchest supporters, such as the *Manchester Guardian*'s legendary editor C.P. Scott, began to see their tactics as counterproductive. Even the Labour Party leader Keir Hardie, always the women's champion and extremely close to Sylvia Pankhurst, had his private doubts. Lloyd George was notoriously susceptible to women, and was prepared to give them the vote on certain terms, but, after being injured by a flying missile, he said plaintively that they would do far better to exchange such intimidation for some old-fashioned feminine blandishments.[6]

On the streets, suffragettes sometimes faced the Edwardian equivalent of the yobs jeering at the Greenham peace camp from passing cars. However, the brutality they suffered at the hands of the prison service – solitary confinement, force-feeding through tubes – won them widespread sympathy. Churchill, on becoming Home Secretary, did rule that suffragettes should be treated as 'political prisoners' (which is certainly how the Greenham women saw themselves). And some well-placed suffragettes already enjoyed special treatment, such as meals sent in from expensive hotels by well-wishers. In the main, however, the punishment they endured was far more rigorous than the conditions their modern counterparts faced in Holloway, deeply unpleasant though these were. Such courage was bound to be an inspiration to future feminist generations.

The outbreak of the First World War in 1914, and the resistance to it that later developed, divided the suffrage movement in dramatically new ways. It even split the Pankhurst family, with Emmeline loudly demanding conscription for men and munitions work for women, while Sylvia stuck to her pacifist, socialist principles. The moderate NUWSS was divided between internationalists and conventional national patriots, its president Mrs Millicent Fawcett – a non-militant in the suffrage context – declaring that it was almost treasonable to talk about peace until the Germans were defeated.

Two wartime movements which anticipated Greenham, in the sense of harnessing feminist solidarity in the cause of peace, were the Women's International League (nowadays the Women's International League for Peace and Freedom, to which Di McDonald belongs) and the Women's Peace Crusade. The League was formed with the explicit aim of linking the women's and pacifist movements. The Crusade, following the introduction of conscription in 1916, brought thousands of working women on to the streets to protest at the way their men were marched off to feed cannon in the trenches of the Somme. But of course none of these women had the vote. Many of their hopes for a more peaceful world were still pinned on the advent of universal suffrage, when women's voices would be heard in Parliament for the first time.

Military victory in 1918 was accompanied by partial victory in the suffrage campaign – women of 30 and over got the vote. While historians have argued ever since as to how credit for this success should be shared out, the simple version of the story most of us inherited gives it mainly to the militant suffragettes. Hence those padlocks at the Greenham main gate in

September 1981. For me, certainly, the slogan 'Votes for Women' prompts a familiar newspaper image of the vociferous Mrs Pankhurst being arrested outside Buckingham Palace, ladylike feet swung high off the ground, waist clasped in the arms of an enormous uniformed constable. (Helen John suffered a similar indignity during the sentry box action.)

So far as I can discover, the only public memorial to the sensible Mrs Fawcett at Westminster is an inscription added to her husband's monument in the Abbey, recording that she 'won citizenship for women'.[7] The outrageous Emmeline Pankhurst, by contrast, has her own bronze statue, prominent among the plane trees alongside the Houses of Parliament. It was erected in 1930 by public subscription (from both men and women) 'as a tribute to her courageous leadership of the movement for the enfranchisement of women'. The statue is flanked by two bronze plaques. One depicts the medal awarded to more than 1,000 women imprisoned for the suffragette cause – the convict's broad arrow on a Westminster portcullis (Mary Richardson, whose medal was recently auctioned, had a record eight bars added to her award; her exploits included taking an axe to Velázquez's 'Rokeby Venus' in the National Gallery and dumping a petition against force-feeding into George V's lap). The other plaque shows Christabel – even bossier than her mother and by all accounts an insufferable snob – who 'jointly inspired and led the Militant Suffrage Campaign'.

The intended moral, presumably, is that one broken pane of glass is worth a hundred letters. Some of their modern sisters would endorse that, but note those references to 'leadership' – not at all part of the predominant, non-hierarchical ethos of the anti-cruise-missile campaign. Bossy women surfaced at Greenham, too, as they were bound to do. But any statue would quickly have suffered the same fate as Saddam Hussein's.

Embracing the base

The first attempt to get rid of the Greenham women by physical eviction came four months after the first warning letter from Newbury District Council, on 27 May 1982. Bailiffs turned up at the main gate with bull-dozers, backed by a heavy police presence, and simply wrecked the peace camp. Distraught women watched their carefully constructed benders swept aside, along with the improvised facilities they had developed for cooking, protecting children, welcoming visitors and so on. Their poplar tree, supporting its marquee, was among the casualties.

The odd thing was that part of the camp was nevertheless left unscathed. The eviction turned out to be a selective affair, only covering common land owned by the Council outside the base. Caravans on immediately adjacent land owned by the Department of Transport (DoT) were not disturbed. So as soon as the bailiffs left, the women simply moved across and re-established themselves as best they could – though a number still ended up in court charged with a 'breach of the peace'.

This was the beginning of a sort of giant game of hopscotch played by the women over the next year, as they responded to successive evictions by jumping back and forth between different tracts of land. In September it was the turn of the DoT to obtain an eviction order for its land, associated with the nearby roads. It reinforced this assault by dumping tonnes of rocks to make re-establishing a camp much more difficult. Eventually, the district council and the DoT were joined by Berkshire County Council (urged on, no doubt, by the MoD and its American guests) in a coordinated campaign to eliminate the protest. It never succeeded. On the contrary, the publicity provided by the evictions (women against bulldozers – wonderful pictures) attracted still more women to Greenham. It also made them increasingly aware that the law, though certainly not on their side, could often be used to their advantage – especially where common land was concerned. Even an unsuccessful legal challenge could buy valuable time. And by now women were working the system in more positive ways, such as adding their names to the electoral register using the main gate of RAF Greenham Common as their address.

That autumn turned out to be one of the wettest on record. Rebecca Johnson remembers it raining on a biblical scale, for 40 days and 40 nights. It was not good camping weather, even without the bailiffs:

> We were living in a sea of mud under these sagging bits of plastic we called the washing line, facing what for me was the absolutely frightening prospect of my first trial and possible imprisonment. Yet at the same time we were building this crazy idea of getting 25,000 women down to Greenham to encircle the base — because that is how many we thought it would take.

Rebecca — a 27-year-old postgraduate student at the time — had first visited Greenham in the previous March, just for the day with a couple of friends, bearing a 7 lb pot of honey that nobody seemed to want. She was recently back from two years living in Japan, and busy with a Master's degree at the School of Oriental and African Studies (SOAS) in London. Her thesis dealt with US–Soviet relations during the reconstruction of Japan, embodying her conviction that the nuclear destruction of Hiroshima and Nagasaki was not so much the last act of the Second World War as the first act of the Cold War. Rebecca returned to Berkshire on 9 August (the date of the Nagasaki bomb). Having seen an appeal for Greenham reinforcements in *Time Out*, she put a tent on the back of her Honda 175 motorbike and rode down for what she expected to be more or less a week's holiday. As she arrived, Helen John was having 'a blazing row' about drugs — that is, about the danger of drugs discrediting the women's protest if they were allowed in the camp.

Three days later Rebecca's holiday turned into a permanent commitment: 'I suddenly decided I would have to live there.' She made another motorbike trip to London for the portable typewriter and books she needed to continue work on the thesis, returning to Greenham in time to join the sentry box action that would lead to her first experience of Her Majesty's Prison Holloway. The week's visit lasted five years.

The trial Rebecca had been dreading was delayed until 15 November. Much to the defendants' surprise (and quite out of keeping with later practice), Newbury magistrates agreed to adjourn the case to give them time to call expert witnesses. The women were delighted to grasp this opportunity to take on the system, and to demonstrate that, so far as they

Photo: Ed Barber

Things start getting rough. A limply non-violent Rebecca Johnson is arrested 'for standing on top of a pile of stones and singing', 5 October 1982.

were concerned, bringing nuclear cruise missiles to Greenham was a far more important breach of the peace than a few minutes occupying a sentry box.

They worked from the premise, Rebecca wrote later, that people should take personal responsibility for their actions, not hide behind uniforms or professional protestations that they were just doing their job:

> We decided to approach the legal system as we do the military establishment and break it down into its component human beings. Police officers, judges, lawyers, clerks, magistrates and juries could all be challenged to question the part they play in maintaining an oppressive system. We defied the traditions and protocol and made it clear that our respect could only be won by their individual actions, not by their robes and rituals.[8]

To make the most of the case, and the political platform it offered, they wanted not just good lawyers, but lawyers who shared their fundamental views. And the important precedent they set, after much discussion, was to have only women lawyers, such as the solicitor Jane Hickman. Their expert witnesses included the campaigning historian E.P. Thompson (author of the pamphlet *Protest and Survive*), the Bishop of Salisbury and Dr Barbara Cowie, who spoke about the medical effects of nuclear weapons. The Labour politician Tony Benn, no doubt recognising the women as heirs to a tradition of protest going right back to the seventeenth-century Diggers, also turned up to show solidarity. As for the women themselves, they took the witness stand one after the other to expound their concerns about cruise missiles and their duty (for example, under the Nuremberg Charter) to speak out against them. A pregnant woman proclaimed her unborn child's right to a healthy future.

The centrepiece of Rebecca's evidence (at least it sounded like the centrepiece to me, on hearing about it much later) was the recurrent nightmare she developed after returning from Japan the previous autumn, where she had visited the museum at Hiroshima. Her nightmare was not so much prompted by what she heard from the Japanese, although they were of course the only people actually to have suffered a nuclear attack. She was shocked to find that her friends in England, who had never been particularly political, were talking openly of their fear, 'and within a few months it had seeped into me'.

Rebecca was living at that time high up in a block of flats on Old Street, London, just north of the City. In her dream she would wake up, open the window, and look out towards the River Thames across a scene of complete devastation:

> The weird thing was, my room would be there, intact, and then I'd go to the window and it would be London that wasn't there. It was a familiar view, but completely distorted, broken, crushed. I seemed to have extraordinary vision – I could distinctly see the broken dome of St Paul's cathedral (which was of course echoing the broken A-bomb dome at Hiroshima). So somehow my subconscious had put together the views I'd seen at the Hiroshima museum and this discussion that seemed to be all over the place in England – that there was going to be a third world war and we were going to get caught in the middle of it.

Such visions of a devastated future were not exactly the routine fare of Newbury magistrates' court proceedings. Nor indeed was the Genocide Act 1969, discovered by the women's legal team, forbidding the destruction of any national, racial or ethnic group. The magistrates were courteously dismissive, ordering all eleven women to be bound over, under archaic legislation dating from 1361, to keep the peace for a year.

That was supposed to be the end of the matter. But the women, in true suffragette fashion, refused to be bound over (in their view they were already trying to keep the peace), which, to the magistrates' apparent dismay, meant automatic imprisonment. This obstinate tactic also seems to have surprised the police authorities, because Rebecca recalls five hellish hours locked in the cubicle of a 'meat wagon', being transported first to Reading, then Slough, and finally Holloway in North London, as the police tried to find prison places for them all.

They emerged two weeks later to a joyous welcome from their supporters, and a lot of press and television cameras – just the publicity they needed for the big demonstration they were planning in a couple of weeks' time. 'If we can go to prison for 14 days', Rebecca told them, 'you can come to Greenham for one day.'

The date chosen for the demonstration that came to be known as 'Embrace the Base' was the anniversary of the NATO decision to base US cruise missiles in Europe: Sunday, 12 December. The women had the idea that they should demonstrate their collective will to stop the military preparations going on inside by linking hands around the entire 9-mile perimeter. It was a simple idea, but the arithmetic was daunting. The smallest number anyone reckoned would close the circle was 16,000, and more cautious calculations put it at around 25,000. So that was what they secretly aimed for – quite unprecedented so far as Greenham was concerned – and, just in case, those attending were asked to bring scarves to stretch between them. Rebecca remembers drafting an appeal – three pages where she knew it should have been one – which spread outwards as a chain letter. Each recipient was asked to make 10 copies and pass them on.

Helen John was working on the appeal in London, by now separated from her long-suffering husband Douglas, who, after pleading with her to return to Wales to care for her children so that he could resume work, had reluctantly decided that divorce was the only option. The speed with which their two lives diverged seems to have shocked them both. For Helen, it was as if by marching to Greenham she had entered some parallel but quite different, fast-expanding universe, peopled almost entirely by highly motivated, emotionally charged women. Within months she was off to publicise the protest at a conference in Amsterdam – the first she had ever attended – where 25 different nationalities were represented. After the domestic routines of Llanwrtyd Wells it must have been intoxicating, but perhaps also bewildering. She says, in retrospect, that the one thing she really regrets is not being able to find the words to explain to Douglas what was happening to their relationship.

Preparing to 'Embrace the Base', 12 December 1982. Greenham's first mass demonstration against the US nuclear cruise missiles.

Douglas evidently worked it out from what he heard and saw, though at first barely able to believe either. He did his best to seem supportive, driving down to the camp with fresh supplies. But he was eventually forced to accept that his wife genuinely believed campaigning against nuclear weapons was more important to her children's future than caring for them back in Wales.

Helen now found herself stuffing envelopes in a borrowed basement in Islington, deeply impressed by the efficient way regional networks spread word of the 'Embrace the Base' demonstration through the Midlands, Wales and Scotland, using contacts such as CND and WILPF. Their posters used the symbol of a spider's web, already adopted at Greenham because it combined a feminine delicacy with unexpected strength.

Even so, no one anticipated the overwhelming response. At dawn on the 12th, Rebecca crawled out from beneath the black plastic of her 'washing line' shelter to find 300 women who had driven down overnight already gathered by the airfield gate – 'a surreal group standing there, with candles, in the sleet, totally silent, and I knew it was just going to be the most incredible day of my life'.

Throughout the morning, roads leading to Newbury were jammed with coaches and cars. Ann Pettitt, up from Carmarthen for the occasion, cried when she realised they were full of women. Thirty-five thousand turned up that day, plus a few male supporters – not that big a crowd for a crucial football match at Wembley, maybe, but as a signal that Greenham women meant business it could hardly have been more emphatic. And they really did 'embrace the base'. After a lot of chaotic manoeuvring to close the gaps, they decorated the wire, as requested, with an array of personal items representing their lives – family photographs, children's toys, ribbons, balloons, paintings, tampons, flowers. Darkness came early on a mid-December day, giving the television newsreels one strong, final image as thousands of candles and torches illuminated the encircling wire.

Press reaction was predictably varied. The *New Statesman* gave the event its solid endorsement. Greenham Common, its editorial suggested, had developed a political importance that reached far beyond the issue of cruise missiles. The way the women had entered a national political debate in their own right and on their own terms was 'a direct and disturbing challenge to established political conventions.'[9] The *Sunday Telegraph's* hard-hitting columnist Peregrine Worsthorne said his reaction to Greenham women was exactly the same as to women who try to tear to pieces men accused of child murder as they arrive for trial: 'sympathy for the strength of their emotions and contempt for the weakness of their logic'.[10] The *Guardian* sent down its resident champagne revolutionary, Richard Gott, who began by feeling snubbed as a male (when told men were supposed to stay at one particular gate, he 'felt for a moment like a woman who has entered the Men's Bar at the Gymkhana Club') but left feeling privileged to have attended a 'genuinely historic occasion'. It was, he wrote, 'a triumph for the women's movement' and 'a powerful advertisement for anarchy'.[11] The *Daily Express* had an angle: 'Russian TV cameras roll as 30,000 women ring missile base in anti-nuclear protest.'[12]

About 6,000 of the women stayed overnight at the base, and many of them took part next day in the second half of the demonstration – a blockade to 'Close the Base'. And the police suddenly got a lot rougher. Women were grabbed, dragged and thrown aside in an effort to keep the gates clear. Rebecca, afterwards nursing a badly torn ear, put the changed tactics down to the fact that whereas the Sunday event was a symbolic demonstration, Monday's blockade was a serious effort to disrupt the operation of the base.

Looking back at it all many years later, Helen felt that for her that cold December weekend 'was when Greenham really started'. Thousands of women made their first visit – but not their last – and in doing so took their first political action. The peace camp no longer consisted of a small, obstinate group. It had become the centre of a mass protest, continuously monitored by press and television, sustained by a countrywide web of women's support groups.

A Greenham rainbow

Among those who became intoxicated by Greenham that winter was Lorna Richardson, a dark-haired schoolgirl from Kingston-upon-Thames. Her story is not typical, because nothing about Greenham was typical, but it is illustrative of the way in which so many lives were suddenly and permanently changed.

Lorna had visited the camp once before, aged 16, after seeing some photographs of it outside the Quaker meeting house in Kingston. Four friends hitchhiked down at the weekend. There was lots of excitement. They came back 'absolutely knackered' and bunked off school the next day to recover. At the time she was studying science, and dreamed – as many girls do – of maybe working with animals. But politics were never far away: 'it was part of the family culture to go on marches and stuff envelopes'. Her aunt was the stalwart feminist Labour MP Jo Richardson, member for Barking in London's docklands, friend of Clare Short and 'an enormous influence' on her young niece. It was Jo who first explained some of the issues surrounding nuclear power after taking her to see the film *The China Syndrome*.

After returning to Greenham for the 'Embrace the Base' demonstration in December 1982, Lorna became a regular visitor and was soon in the thick of the wire-cutting action. That led to arrest, and eventually, in 1984, along with other women, to the Crown Court in Reading, The trial date coincided with her A-level examinations, so rather than pay fees for exams she would be unable to take, she cancelled them: 'I didn't have any money, and I'd left home, so I thought "Let's just do things properly, shall we" and moved down to Greenham full time.'

Lorna remained there, in the sense that it was her main home, and the address where she was registered to vote, for the next four years. All youngsters see the world in vivid colours, but Greenham was something else again. She witnessed the mass evictions that preceded the cruise missiles' emergence from their fortress, learnt to deal on equal terms with all kinds of women, from aggressive young lesbians to elderly grans. She took part in lots of actions, and therefore had to come to terms with imprisonment (genuinely can't remember whether it was seven or eight times). Eventually, she did resume her education (Ruskin College, Oxford, then SOAS, London), but thinking back she says: 'If you like, Greenham was my university.'

If Lorna were recounting all this to another Greenham woman, she would not need to describe it in such detail. A strange sort of shorthand – which they all use – would suffice. Rather like the chairman of a military conference introducing a retired general – as they all do – by listing the regiments in which he served and the battles he fought, one woman can instantly comprehend another's experience by hearing which actions she took part in and, above all, which of the several gates she lived at, each with its different sociological mix. To decipher the code, you have to know something of the local geography.

Newbury is an ancient town (though, as its name indicates, in Norman times it was literally a 'new town') established on the historically important junction of the London-to-Bath road and the north–south route from Oxford to the ports around Southampton. RAF Greenham Common occupied the south-east quadrant of the cross formed by their modern equivalents, the A4 and A34, so that aircraft taking off to the west climbed noisily across the town's southern suburbs, and some houses on the eastern side of the town looked out across the airfield's perimeter road – and were therefore cheek by jowl with several of the women's encampments. This juxtaposition became a sore point as, almost inevitably, friction between local residents and the peace women increased.

Publicity following the vast demonstrations of December 1982, coupled with the knowledge that the actual nuclear missiles would soon be arriving, meant that the small group of women who had sat it out at the main gate were joined by dozens more during 1983, and weekend visitors were counted in hundreds, or even thousands. As the numbers grew, the original camp gradually became too much like a goldfish bowl for many women. It was cramped by earlier evictions, the buses stopped there, and it was the first point of call for most visitors. So during that busy year a series of breakaway satellite camps, or 'gates', was established, mostly corresponding to the eight real gates used by military traffic.

To make as big a contrast as possible with the drab olive green of the American military equipment, the gates were named after the seven colours of the rainbow – beginning with Yellow (the new name for Main Gate, at the airfield's south-eastern corner), then Green, Blue, Indigo, Violet, Red and Orange, plus Turquoise to cover the eighth military entrance, Emerald (between Green and Turquoise, with no real gate, but a good view of military activity around the silos) and Woad, where a new entrance was created in 1985. Once acquired, these names stuck. They became so much part of Greenham's language, even the MoD police habitually used them, and the women still do so. The names also acquired distinct reputations, which in turn rubbed off on those who chose to live there.

The first additional camp was Green Gate, established in January 1983, deep in the woods from which the silos' action was launched. From the start it was women-only. It was a place where seriously lesbian women congregated. A word often used to describe its atmosphere is 'cosmic', a reference among other things to the fact that the symbolic Greenham practice of weaving webs seems to have originated there.

Blue Gate was set up in the summer of 1983 on Rebecca Johnson's initiative, partly because she was finding Yellow Gate 'claustrophobic', partly because it suited the tactics of protest. This was the nearest of all the gates to the centre of Newbury, on Burys Bank Road at the far north-western corner of the airfield (For some reason the actual gate, daubed in blue paint, has been left untouched, still barring the path of people walking their dogs on the reopened common). The women wanted a visible presence there, so that official visitors coming straight from Newbury could not slip into the base without being aware of their protest. The cost of that presence, however, was high. Some nearby residents objected strongly. Local yobs gave vent to their feelings as they passed. And this gate was the first, early-morning call for council bailiffs intent on eviction. It developed a hard-earned reputation as a community of tough, occasionally rowdy youngsters, some of whom were overtly lesbian.

The fact that Greenham contained a lesbian community was one of its strengths. At a time when homosexuality was less acceptable than it is today, this was an extraordinary place where lesbian women could not only admit to unorthodoxy, but actively celebrate it. They had a second, positive reason for putting up with discomfort and harassment, and since they tended to be young, with fewer family commitments, they were more prepared to live there permanently.

Lorna Richardson spent much of her time in the seclusion of Emerald Gate, near the silos, keeping an eye on British 'squaddies' guarding the perimeter (the young soldiers' behaviour varied wildly, from throwing stones at the women to exchanging coal for kindling through a hole in the wire in a mutual effort to keep out the winter cold). However, the period she then spent at Blue Gate left her with enormous respect for the women who made it their home: 'You'd wake up to the sight of a bailiff's knife slashing the plastic above your head.'

> There didn't seem to be any restraints on what the bailiffs were able to do at Blue Gate – possibly because the women were younger, possibly because they were more likely to be working class. Or maybe because it was the first eviction of the day and they were getting something out of their system – who knows. Anyway I thought the women there had a rough deal, and I thought they did a fabulous job, which is why I moved there.

Orange Gate was established around the same time as Blue, during the week-long massed blockades of July 1983, shortly after Mrs Thatcher was re-elected. But it developed a quite different character. Its position, well back from the road at the eastern end of the airfield, meant it was relatively secure for children. Older women who wanted some privacy, and whose background was more likely CND or the Quakers than women's liberation, also preferred to stay there.

The remaining gates were set up at the end of that year, to cope with a vast influx of women around the time of the second December 'gathering' – even bigger than the first. By this time the nuclear missiles had actually arrived, prompting a renewed intensity of protest, and perhaps a little private despair.

Three of the new camps – Red, Violet and Indigo – were along the northern perimeter road, with Turquoise Gate tucked away at the western end of the runway. The Turquoise cuisine was austerely vegan, in contrast to the carnivorous high-living at Violet Gate – sometimes known as the 'frocks gate' because its residents adopted a more conventional feminine style, including chatting up soldiers through the wire. 'God, they looked like models', recalls a woman who saw them through a distinctly Orange filter. 'They'd say, "I can't come, I haven't finished combing my hair."'

The other distinction Greenham women drew among themselves turned on how long they spent there. There were the 'campers', some of whom made the airfield's perimeter their only home for years at a time; there were 'stayers', who came for shorter periods; and there were 'visitors', who were naturally much more numerous.

For some, these categories formed an obvious hierarchy: campers at the top, confronting the military day-in, day-out, in all weathers, while others swanned off on speaking tours or whatever, and at the bottom, casual visitors who only turned up when the sun was shining. For others, any hierarchy was – and still is – politically incorrect in a feminist community. And those who take this view often go further, arguing positively that every woman who joined the protest was a 'Greenham woman', whether she spent one day at the camp or ten years. She might be contributing vital support from elsewhere, or simply encumbered by other responsibilities. Besides which, if the cumulative time spent by regular stayers were added up, it might come to more than that contributed by some of the campers.

The argument was never settled. It became one of many small, cumulative issues contributing to a bitter division within the Greenham community in later years.

Nuclear politics

Michael Heseltine was on holiday in Tobago when he received a call from Prime Minister Margaret Thatcher on the morning of 6 January 1983, offering him the post of Defence Secretary. He accepted without hesitation.

With a general election already in prospect, the job confronted Heseltine with two challenges: one departmental; the other of wider political importance to the Conservative government. First, he had to sort out the financial wreckage of the Falklands campaign, during which the Royal Navy's vital contribution had put paid to his predecessor John Nott's plans to scrap large parts of the fleet. Then he had somehow to win the public debate about nuclear weapons and nuclear deterrence which a Labour Opposition under the leadership of Michael Foot – veteran of the Aldermaston marches – was bound to initiate: 'It was an immediate imperative; there was no alternative.'

At Greenham, far more was at stake than the outcome of a domestic election. The US military had chosen to plant their nuclear banner there to challenge what they perceived as a threatening deployment of mobile Soviet SS-20 missiles throughout eastern Europe. The British base was part of a collective NATO programme, which it was hoped would also involve Germany, Italy, the Netherlands and Belgium in the counter-deployment of Tomahawk cruise and Pershing II missiles.

As Defence Secretary, Heseltine also became *ex officio* Britain's representative in NATO committees, such as the Nuclear Planning Group, which developed this controversial strategy. Of the 572 weapons planned by the Alliance, 464 would be cruise missiles, of which 160 were coming to the UK. Moreover Greenham Common had been chosen to become the first operational cruise missile base, so as to set a resolute example to political waverers in the Netherlands and Belgium. The NATO plan therefore put a heavy responsibility on Heseltine to deliver British cooperation with the minimum of embarrassing protest, and to ensure that operational deadlines were met. Had the Greenham women been able to halt the deployment – unlikely though this may have seemed, even at the dramatic height of their protest – there is little doubt that the allied strategy would have begun to unravel. In Heseltine's own words: 'the continuing effectiveness of the strategy of the whole Western Alliance was at risk'.[13]

One of Heseltine's first moves on arriving in Horseguards Avenue was to set up a new section within the defence secretariat, DS19, to support his own propaganda campaign. It was headed by a vigorous young assistant secretary, John Ledlie, evidently chosen because he had useful experience of dealing with the press as well as the appropriate administrative skills. Whatever the reasoning, it was a shrewd choice. Ledlie also worked well with Heseltine's private secretary, Richard Mottram, another civil servant with the intellectual self-confidence to deal straightforwardly with journalists or politicians (later, when he was much more senior in the MoD, I watched him silence members of the Commons Defence Committee simply by telling them the plain truth – a rare tactic in a department so deeply imbued with secrecy).

So far as Ledlie was concerned, DS19 was just another bunch of officials charged with the normal work of supporting ministers – in this case a varying group always chaired by the Defence Secretary. Their joint brief, according to Heseltine, was 'to coordinate government policy in the widest sense on this issue – to win the intellectual case and the political case for the government'. Outside Whitehall, however, and certainly within the senior ranks of CND, DS19 soon acquired a sinister reputation as a 'dirty tricks' department being fed information by the security service MI5. Suspicions later erupted into public scandal when Cathy Massiter, an MI5 intelligence officer who claimed she was asked to report to DS19 on the 'subversive political affiliations' of certain CND officials,[14] blew the whistle on the whole operation in a Channel 4 television programme.[15]

During the election campaign, the Defence Secretary made no bones about his intention to discredit the peace movement as a whole, and CND in particular, by publicising the fact that its membership included Communists and Marxists. He saw himself as fighting a legitimate propaganda war in which he spoke for 'the real peace-keepers' – members of the armed forces.[16] He chose, for example, to counter CND's Easter demonstration, in which 70,000 people linked arms to form a human chain from Greenham Common to the Burghfield atomic bomb factory by way of Aldermaston, by ostentatiously visiting troops guarding the Berlin Wall.

For Cathy Massiter, MI5's relationship with DS19 raised a question of principle for which she was prepared to risk years of imprisonment under the Official Secrets Act. Was the security service entitled – under its own guidelines – to supply information derived from tapping a senior CND official's telephone for 'political' purposes? The official concerned was Dr John Cox, an honorary vice-president and a member of the Communist Party, who (conveniently for those listening in) often called Joan Ruddock or the general secretary, Bruce Kent, from his home in Pontypool. According to the guidelines, such eavesdropping should only have been allowed if MI5 suspected the person concerned of engaging in 'major subversive or espionage activity' – which as far as she knew it did not.[17]

Cathy's boss at that time was Stella Rimington, who later became the first female director general of MI5. In her circumspect autobiography *Open Secret*,[18] Mrs Rimington admits that her colleague's whistle-blowing came as 'a massive shock' to a service whose personnel were brought up not even to tell friends they worked for MI5. Her line on the episode is that Soviet officials *did* encourage fellow travellers to infiltrate the Western peace movement, an activity that had to be monitored, but that CND 'on its own' was of no interest to the security service and was never investigated by it. A wafer-thin distinction if ever I saw one!

In the event the phone tap, requested in April 1983, was not authorised by the Home Secretary until after the June election, so information from it could not have been used in the campaign. Indeed Michael Heseltine insists, as he did at the time, that no information 'not in the public domain' was ever used in political propaganda. Given the continuous close links between DS19 and MI5, that cannot have been easy. While Cathy Massiter has confirmed to me that her own report to the MoD unit did not include secret material, she added that copies of other reports which *were* based on secret sources, 'assessing subversive influences on CND', were also supplied to DS19.

For the MoD civil servants, this was a delicate operation. DS19 was in contact with MI5 every week or two, when various highly classified reports on individuals the service had investigated were handed over. If the material was relevant – and much of it was not – it would be shown to the Defence Secretary, but crucially, not to other ministers. For example, the Armed Forces Minister Peter Blaker, who had close links with the Conservative central office, was deliberately excluded from the 'secret' loop. In this way the full resources of the security service were available to the Defence Secretary and his civil service team, but raw data from secret sources was not used in campaign speeches or anywhere else, and was not disseminated to the Tory Party spin doctors. Thus was civil service propriety preserved.

DS19 had a short life but a highly productive one so far as Heseltine was concerned. It was this committee, he recalls, which produced the idea of re-naming unilateral nuclear disarmament 'one-sided disarmament'. It proved to be something of a public relations masterstroke: 'That was absolutely the heart of the argument, encapsulated in just those two words.' His advisers calculated that while there was little public enthusiasm for acquiring expensive new nuclear weapons like the Trident submarine system, the idea of giving up existing weapons – with no guarantee of anything in return – would be rejected.

Labour dismissed this attack as just another smear. Many years later, I asked the Opposition leader Michael Foot (who strongly supported the Greenham women, and visited their peace camp with his wife Jill Craigie) what a policy of unilateral nuclear disarmament would really have meant, had he won the 1983 election. He insisted that 'the charge that we were just going to throw away the weapons without any kind of bargaining was always false'. This is no doubt true, especially as Denis Healey would have been in his Cabinet, but the charge stuck (not so surprisingly, since Labour's manifesto specifically promised to 'Cancel the Trident programme, refuse to deploy Cruise missiles and begin discussions for the removal of nuclear bases from Britain, which is to be completed within the lifetime of the Labour government').

DS19 came up with another slogan to ridicule the nuclear disarmers – 'woolly minds in woolly hats' – which the Defence Secretary said was so good that he would save it for the party conference. This could well have been a jibe at women blockading the Berkshire airfield, many of whom certainly wore woolly hats to keep out the cold, but one cannot be sure, because Heseltine seems to have regarded both the Greenham women and CND as facets of a larger entity he referred to as 'the protest groups'. Describing them to me in retrospect, he said they were:

> Anyone who lined up and shouted at me. They were a very curious mixture – and there was a serious element of rent-a-mob about it. That's not in any way to suggest that all the people who marched were of that persuasion – there were a lot of perfectly sensible and reasonable people who took a different view of defence strategy to the government. But behind them, if you went to these demonstrations, you could always

see the shadowy figures – rather well dressed often – at the back, with walky-talkies, or moving about and obviously in charge.

Heseltine's opportunity to confront the Greenham 'mob' came on 7 February 1983, when he fulfilled a long-standing engagement to address the West Berkshire Conservative Association in Newbury town hall. It was a gloomy evening. He was late. The women were waiting for him, some of them lying down on the steps of the town hall so that the man responsible for the cruise missiles would have to step over their 'dead bodies'. When he finally arrived, there was a noisy crush as the women rushed forward and a phalanx of police forced a way through for the visitor. Heseltine was dragged almost to his knees in the press of bodies – and photographed, just afloat in a sea of helmets.

It was an evening that had something for everyone. The women were pleased with a chance to vent their feelings at a government minister in person (though some were concerned that the demonstration was so chaotic). The press had a wonderful story: 'Angry Peace Girls Rough Up Heseltine'; 'Tarzan's War – Heseltine Felled in Peace Demo'; 'Peace Camp Women Mob Heseltine'; and so on. The Defence Secretary had the unruly reception he needed to justify his calculated refusal (announced just before the meeting) to debate the cruise missile deployment with the movement's leadership, especially the charismatic CND chairwoman Joan Ruddock. 'This has reinforced my judgement', he said pointedly as he left the town hall. 'These people don't want a debate. They want to stifle it.'

Whether or not to accept CND's invitation had already been discussed in DS19, where officials, and other ministers, had urged the Secretary of State to take on the peace movement in public. He said he preferred to do his debating in Parliament – a political judgement John Ledlie feels, in retrospect, was correct. The official line was that as an elected representative, a government minister should only debate with other MPs. But of course it also avoided dignifying campaigning experts like Bruce Kent and Joan Ruddock as worthy political opponents (just as Heseltine's predecessor John Nott had snubbed the original Greenham marchers when they demanded a television debate). Joan scornfully recalls being hustled out of Jimmie Young's radio broadcast studio so that the ministerial team waiting outside would not have to encounter her.

In a direct attempt to get the Greenham women's voice heard in the general election campaign, Rebecca Johnson stood against Michael Heseltine

Photo: David White

Rebecca Johnson exchanges boots, jeans and anorak for some Edwardian glamour at Henley during her general election campaign against Defence Secretary Michael Heseltine, May 1983.

in his Henley-on-Thames constituency – not that far from Newbury. Her 'Women for Life on Earth' candidacy was announced the day she came out of Holloway prison after the silos action, giving the Greenham Common peace camp as her official address. Here again the Defence Secretary avoided any face-to-face meeting. She feels she made some headway with her arguments about the nuclear threat, defence spending, and alternative solutions to the country's economic problems, but only 580 people were sufficiently impressed to vote for her. One who may well have done so – at least according to the wildly excited schoolgirl who canvassed him on Rebecca's behalf – was the Beatle George Harrison.

Battle joined

With the June 1983 election out of the way and a Conservative government consolidated in power, preparations for the climactic phase of the Greenham battle began – inside and outside the wire. It was public knowledge that the cruise missiles were scheduled to arrive towards the end of that year. In Whitehall, they hoped the protests would begin to subside as NATO's determination to deploy the weapons became absolutely clear. The women, on the other hand, were already thinking ahead. They saw fresh opportunities for protest as missile convoys left the base on dispersal exercises they were bound to conduct as part of their operational concept.

First signs of tightening military security appeared early the next month when a British battalion of the Queen's Own Highlanders was drafted in to strengthen perimeter patrols. The soldiers formed an additional layer in a multiple security structure intended to keep intruders out, though it seems to have been acknowledged from the start that in the absence of a completely new fence (like the one built round the other cruise missile base at Molesworth) the women could never be excluded altogether without applying a politically unacceptable level of force.

The outer layer consisted of MoD police, augmented as necessary by ordinary police from Newbury or the Thames Valley. Then came British soldiers, also confronting the women through the perimeter wire. Inside the base the RAF regiment was in overall control (since this was still technically an RAF base). The Americans were not supposed to touch the women, just call the MoD police. However, within the ultra-secure area housing the missile silos with their nuclear warheads, the rules changed completely. A USAF officer was in command of a mixed force (two-thirds US and one-third UK personnel), armed, and prepared *in extremis* to shoot intruders.

For a while there was a fourth layer: an imaginative scheme to take advantage of the way geese rush up to any stranger, honking aggressively. Three Chinese Geese (a species particularly prone to this irritating habit) were purchased and let loose in the base at night. To begin they were highly effective, but then people started overfeeding them and soon they were so fat they stopped honking. For Americans, especially, I feel there is a moral in that somewhere.

The possibility of shooting 'peace women', as even the USAF sometimes called them, was a serious matter indeed. The mere thought of it was enough to give government ministers and their public relations officers nightmares. In the House of Commons on 1 November 1983, with the missiles' arrival only weeks away, the Defence Secretary was duly challenged by the Labour Opposition to assure MPs that it could not really happen. When Heseltine refused to do so, there was uproar.

'I categorically will give no such assurance', he told the House. 'It has been the absolute duty of all governments to defend nuclear weapons in this country and to defend all military bases of this country's defence forces. To suggest we should now abandon that policy is reckless.'[19] When Denzil Davies, a Labour defence spokesman, protested at this, Heseltine retorted that every Labour government since the Second World War had operated a similar policy. And at Prime Minister's Question Time Mrs Thatcher made a point of publicly backing her Defence Secretary.

In a television interview later that day, Heseltine suggested that troops guarding nuclear weapons might have difficulty distinguishing between a peace protester and a terrorist, 'if the terrorist has taken trouble to try and make himself look like a peace protester'. In the last resort, it might be their duty to open fire, albeit 'under the clearest rules of engagement' (that is, those governing when and how force could be used). Whether this last claim was completely true is doubtful. The following year the Commons Defence Committee published a report on physical security at military installations in the UK in which MPs expressed concern about several anomalies in the Greenham rules.

One worry was that whereas British troops had their rules of engagement printed on a 'blue card' they could consult at any time (similar to the 'yellow card' used in Northern Ireland), the Americans did not – at least at that stage. In the Greenham context, where almost everyone was acutely aware of the political sensitivities, this probably did not matter much. When I asked the US base commander Colonel John Bachs how his armed guards would respond if the women tried to break into the nuclear citadel, he said they would be removed with minimum force (which is essentially what it said on the blue card) and handed over to the police.

At the time, I accepted this reassurance, but having recently seen something of the USAF's obsessive concern with UK base security in the wake of the 9/11 attacks on New York, I would say the Greenham women were fortunate not to be operating in today's climate of fear. Even in those more innocent days, as Rebecca Johnson was to discover for herself, the knowledge that the cruise missiles were ultimately protected by armed guards with permission to shoot could never be altogether dismissed.

For those women who believed that public opinion could be won over to their cause by rational argument, the rejection of unilateral nuclear disarmament in the June 1983 election must have been disheartening. In July they organised a week of blockades, primarily aimed at stopping construction workers entering and leaving the base. The *Guardian*'s Paul Brown, a friend and colleague who did a lot of the paper's reporting from Greenham, went down to assess the mood now it was clear the missiles were on their way. He found that although delegations had come from all over the world to join their heroines for the event – from the USA, New Zealand, even Argentina – overall numbers were a disappointment all round. The women stuck to their task day and night, singing to keep up their spirits, gloomily discussing where the protest should go next. Paul concluded that, in spite of their disappointment, they had no intention of giving up:

> The women will not miss the chance to confront the British troops when they shepherd the missiles, and the Americans try practice firing them around the wooded shires of England. They believe that when people see cruise missiles in their own backyard, the tide will turn their way again.[20]

Meanwhile the US military community inside the base was frantic with its own preparations. Basic construction work on the GAMA (GLCM Alert and Maintenance Area) to house the missiles and their nuclear components was complete. The unit that would operate them, the 501st Tactical Missile Wing – motto 'Poised to Deter, Quick to React' – had been formally activated the previous year and was now ready to receive the weapons from the USA. It was working towards what it called an 'initial operating capability' (the first 16 missiles ready to fire) on 31 December.

The number of American military personnel involved in all this was building towards an eventual total of more than 2,000. As on all major US bases in Britain, then as now, they formed an essentially self-contained community, which nevertheless tried to establish friendly contacts with the surrounding natives (for example, new arrivals are taught, in 'culture class', that British people's reserve does not mean they are hostile). In effect, the base operated rather like a Western oil company compound in the Middle East, or, to a limited extent (because it would be wrong to push this tempting comparison too far), like an outpost of the former British Empire.

Greenham never developed its home-from-home atmosphere to the level of the long-established US Third Air Force headquarters at Mildenhall, Suffolk, where the main facilities are clustered around 'Washington Square' and where you can find yourself turning off 'Texas Avenue' into 'Missouri Road'. At Greenham they just had numbered streets (a scheme to rename them in memory of US military personnel who died in a World War II glider accident ran into trouble because the names tended to be spelt with lots of unpronounceable East European consonants). Still, the Berkshire base did gradually acquire some US-style comforts: PX (post office), BX (supermarket), eventually its own school with appropriate American sports facilities, and several satellite housing estates.

The significant difference at Greenham was that while the base community relations staff did their usual best to foster friendly contact with the people of Newbury, they pointedly snubbed the 'ladies' protesting outside the gates. US personnel were under strict orders not to talk to the women, driving past them with a stony avoidance of eye contact.

In other respects, US airmen no doubt reacted to this foreign environment more or less as British soldiers based in Germany used to behave, a majority content to serve out their posting within their familiar military community, a minority eager to take advantage of every opportunity to see something of another country. The tourist sights of London were not far away. There were plenty of characteristically English pubs in nearby villages. Some of the air force wives even rode with the local fox hunt.

Besides which, the Americans were re-creating a bit of what looked like Olde England within the military complex itself. The Baxendale manor house, just across the Burys Bank Road opposite Blue Gate, had been commandeered by the 101st Airborne during the Second World War, then lain unused since the 1950s. Now the missile warriors were carefully restoring it as an officers' club, in their words 'unmatched by many clubs anywhere'. It is not an Elizabethan mansion (Norman Shaw designed it in 1879), but, glimpsed from a distance, with its heavily mullioned windows and tall chimneys, it certainly gives a good impression of one.

Photo Astra Blaug

Women deploy their bolt cutters ('black cardigans') to get down – or in this case up – to some serious fence demolition.

On the other side of the road, the women were plotting a last big surprise demonstration before the missiles' expected arrival. A countrywide invitation went out to attend a Hallowe'en party equipped with 'black cardigans' – the code name for bolt cutters. On 29 October more than a thousand women, many dressed as witches, vented their frustration at the failure to stop the weapons by cutting and pulling down several miles of perimeter fencing. In the process there were some absurd, generally good-humoured tugs-of-war as guards tried to prevent their wire being flattened. However, others responded angrily with batons, resulting in a lot of damaged fingers. Half-a-dozen policemen were also injured, by barbed wire.

By the end of the afternoon 187 women had been arrested for criminal damage, or for a crime that made them sound like Dickensian burglars – 'going equipped to cause' criminal damage. Even at this late stage some still thought cutting the fence was wrong in principle, because it involved unnecessary violence. Most just waded in with the bolt cutters, exhilarated by the spectacular results, and from that day on cutting and entering seems to have become routine.

The fence was not just a physical barrier. It also symbolised the women's inability to communicate their fears about nuclear weapons to the missile crews inside the base, training to launch them. Hence the deep satisfaction in cutting it down.

As the Hallowe'en demonstration ended, several written statements were left behind on coils of barbed wire behind the demolished fence. One declared: 'This fence is our Berlin Wall. We can only begin to tackle the concrete and barbed wire that divides our world when we start with that on our own doorstep.' A policeman responded that, in his book, wrecking someone else's fence was criminal damage, whether it belonged to your neighbour or to the MoD.

Deadline

At about 6.00 p.m. on Friday, 21 October, the *Guardian*'s duty editor called me at home to say that an unsolicited brown envelope had just arrived containing two classified MoD documents laying out detailed arrangements for the long-awaited arrival of Greenham's nuclear missiles. There was no covering letter, nor any other indication as to who had sent them. (It turned out to be a civil servant in the Foreign Office.) It was a classic leak, and a politically explosive one at that.

My first reaction was inwardly to curse the fact that here was one of the best stories of the year (for a defence correspondent), but, because I had chosen to take that day off, I would have to write it without actually seeing the raw material. I took down as many details as I could over the phone, together with a description of the documents, references and so on. One was a straightforward military plan; the other was a political, public-relations strategy for handling it (from what we should nowadays call the spin doctor's perspective), which is the one we used. They both sounded genuine, so it was agreed that I would start writing the story for the paper's second edition while simultaneously authenticating their MoD provenance.

That took a while, but we made the edition and by next morning every Greenham woman who bought the *Guardian* – and there were a few – knew exactly what Michael Heseltine was cooking up for them. We already knew the Americans were likely to bring key equipment in by air. A first huge Galaxy transport aircraft had arrived back in May, as unobtrusively as 40,000 lb of jet engine thrust would allow it, carrying initial deliveries of support equipment. This early omen had been followed in October by a Civil Aviation Authority notice warning civil aircraft to keep well clear of the Greenham airfield from the 14th of the month because it could be busy with military air traffic 24 hours a day. Now, the arrival of the actual missiles and their nuclear warheads had been fixed for 1 November – ten days' time.

The weird twist in the story was that the moment the *Guardian* published the arrival date, it ceased to be valid. The essence of the Heseltine plan was to take the women by surprise – especially so far as the actual nuclear weapons were concerned. These would be in the first aircraft to arrive, so they could be safely tucked away in their heavily protected silos before protesters had time to react, thereby minimising the awful possibility of nervous armed guards confronting women rushing across the runway. But since this surprise was no longer possible, my initial story acknowledged that the planned arrival schedule would now probably be changed – as indeed it was.

From the MoD's point of view, there were other complicating factors, such as a forthcoming debate in the German Bundestag, where the extent of any British protest could affect the deployment of cruise and Pershing II missiles over there, and the need for US missile crews at Greenham to meet NATO's operational target date of 31 December. It was also feared that Soviet negotiators might use the British deployment as an excuse to walk out of arms-control talks in Geneva intended to reduce the numbers of weapons on both sides. Under the original plan for handling this complex situation, Mrs Thatcher was briefed simply to stall any parliamentary questions until 1 November, when Heseltine would make an announcement followed by a press conference justifying NATO's strategy.

That plan was reversed. Under the revised schedule, deliveries of the missile launchers by vast Galaxy transporters began on the original date, and were officially acknowledged, while the nuclear weapons' arrival was delayed for 14 days – then brought forward by 24 hours in a last bid to outwit the protest organisers.

The moment the women had been dreading for more than two years finally came at 9 o'clock on a Monday morning. A much sleeker aircraft, a C-141 Starlifter, touched down on the Greenham runway and taxied straight towards the silos. As helicopters clattered overhead and military Land-Rovers were positioned to prevent press and television cameras recording the event, two long tarpaulin-covered crates emerged from the aircraft's belly and slid quickly behind heavy steel doors.

Protesting women were notable by their absence. My *Guardian* colleague Martin Wainwright found the various gate camps even emptier than usual on a weekday: 'Many of the women were at court hearings in Newbury and others had gone shopping. It was not until midday that the women began to take rumours of the missiles' arrival seriously. A dozen were gathered round a broccoli and carrot stew at a side gate when the radio announced that Mr Heseltine was returning to London to make a statement. 'He ought to come and make it here', said one of them, hitching a lift to the main gate to spread the news. One of her friends was visibly upset and disbelieving: 'I really didn't think they would fly in the face of world opinion.' Several others were close to tears.[21]

Government spokesmen attempted to portray the Defence Secretary's statement to the House of Commons as just a routine confirmation (the absent Mrs Thatcher, normally meticulous about attending such events, was said to be too busy preparing her speech for the Lord Mayor's banquet). Heseltine reminded the House that on 31 October a majority of MPs had supported NATO's 'twin-track' decision to deploy the missiles in Britain by the end of 1983 unless the 'zero option' to destroy all such missiles in Europe, on both sides of the Iron Curtain, was agreed. The deployment could be halted, modified or reversed at any time if the negotiations in Geneva warranted it, and meanwhile NATO had unilaterally decided to make drastic cuts in obviously superfluous short-range nuclear weapons in Europe – nuclear artillery and battlefield missiles.

The Defence Secretary did not get away with this unchallenged. He immediately came under fire on precisely the same issue that was at the centre of the earlier debate: why did the British Government not have direct control over US nuclear weapons whose launch might well precipitate catastrophic Soviet retaliation? It is a question that has dogged the Anglo-American military relationship ever since it first cropped up after the Second World War, and has implications for the broader political relationship which still governed, for example, the American-led campaign to depose Saddam Hussein.

In the context of Greenham, the argument turned on what became known as a 'dual key': that is, a physical system to prevent the Americans launching their missiles without specific British permission. And for Mrs Thatcher, still smarting from Washington's failure to consult about the invasion of Grenada, a member of the British Commonwealth, it touched a raw nerve.

A nuclear veto

The idea of a dual key for the joint control of nuclear weapons was not new. On the contrary, it was a thoroughly familiar device among NATO commanders at that time, especially on the North German plain where most of the soldiers were based. This potential East–West battlefield was crowded with nuclear artillery, much of it jointly operated, and here the boot was on the other foot. It was the Americans, not the British, who wanted a physical veto. Without some such device, the Pentagon would certainly never have allowed Britain's Rhine Army to operate US-manufactured howitzers and Lance missiles with American atomic warheads.

Shortly after the Greenham protest began, conscious that the dual key was becoming a serious bone of contention, I visited the gunners of the 50th Missile Regiment in Germany for the *Guardian* to see exactly how the system worked on Lance. There I met the two people each carrying one of the 'keys' needed to unlock it: the regiment's commanding officer, Lieutenant Colonel George Morris and, more intriguingly in this context, the Pentagon's representative in the British unit, Lieutenant Rebecca Katz.

Lieutenant Katz stood there under the beech trees, blinking through her rather large spectacles, a tiny woman with a few wisps of mousy brown hair visible beneath a camouflaged steel helmet; 25 years old, just three years in the US Army, her home town Oklahoma. I decided to start with the big questions, rather than the nuts and bolts. Did she ever worry about her military role? Specifically, did she worry about the huge responsibility of being the one who would actually unlock the atomic warhead if the regiment suddenly found itself in a nuclear war?

'Not really', she said. 'I do my job, and I don't worry about it. It's good experience.'[22] It was straight professional answer I had heard before in similar circumstances and would hear again inside the Greenham base. It may simply have been prompted by the presence of her boss and several other senior officers, but I suspect she would have said that anyway. It was the sort of military response that always used to send a chill down my spine.

Colonel Morris – realising where I was coming from – chose to represent his unit as just a small, though clearly vital, cog in a vast politico-military machine. He probably assumed, as most British soldiers did, that nobody would ever be stupid enough to start a nuclear war in Western Europe. Yet he also accepted the paradox of nuclear deterrence: that its success in preventing war might depend on demonstrating a plausible intention to use such awful weapons. 'If I'm ordered to fire them', he said, 'I fire them.'[23] As soldiers, neither he nor Lieutenant Katz felt a personal moral responsibility because they knew the decision to go nuclear would be taken way above their heads.

During that same trip I also met a US general, someone sufficiently senior for his judgement to matter had NATO gone to war. He was in Hanau conducting a big exercise rehearsing the defence of what was then West Germany, so I put the nuclear question to him. After giving it some thought, he replied that the Germans were an understanding people, and he felt sure that if nuclear devastation were the price of freedom, they would accept it. It made a great quotation, but I made a point of not naming him in the paper. There was just no telling whether he believed a word of it. Such ambiguity is the essence of nuclear deterrence strategy.

Back at the Lance missile battery, I discovered that the dual 'keys' were actually codes, given to the unit to activate its weapons only after a senior field commander's request had gone right up the NATO chain of command and down again: that is, up to the British Corps commander, on to the Northern Army Group (which included German units), then to the Supreme Allied Commander Europe, a straight-talking American general called Bernie Rogers, who would make his own wider assessment before initiating the political decision-making process – collective consultation in Brussels, and a bilateral decision from Washington and London. That was the theory, believe it or not. By the time a decision came back down this long chain, the wretched members of 50th Missile Regiment would probably have been wiped out, in spite of having dispersed to pre-surveyed woodland hideouts (exactly as the cruise missile launchers planned to disperse from Greenham).

The British batteries might even have been given advance 'permission to mate' – that is, to bolt a warhead on to its liquid-fuelled rocket motor. But no missile could be fired until both keyholders had received specific orders to do so on their own secure radio nets. Only then could Rebecca Katz use her code to take off the safety catch, while her British counterpart selected the explosive yield (probably a small fraction of the Hiroshima bomb), adjusted the height fuse and armed the warhead.

Colonel Morris assured me that even if he went mad, like the US general in the *Dr Strangelove* movie, he could not possibly launch a nuclear strike that had not been properly approved. And if by the time he received his executive order the target had moved, it would be no use just backing up a few miles, or swivelling the launcher round. Under NATO's meticulous selective release procedure, a new request would have to go all the way up the chain and back down again (one of several reasons why so many professional soldiers regarded battlefield nuclear weapons as virtually useless).

All this caution was reassuring as far as it went. However, the US nuclear missile system most often quoted as an example of a dual key during the Greenham debate, particularly by the SDP leader David Owen, was the more primitive, but much longer-range Thor, brought to Britain under NATO's auspices in the late 1950s. And the launch safeguards on this system were about as secure as the locks on the average family car.

My private briefing on Thor's dual key came in a telephone call from a former RAF technician who often practised launching the missile with his US counterparts. In that system, he explained, there were two real keys, one for the missile and another for the American-controlled warhead. The switch arming the megaton-sized bomb offered a simple choice: 'war/ peace'.

Then came the moral of his story. If a practice alert was called at night, rather than waking up a tired US airman holding the warhead key, a sympathetic RAF missile crew would complete the launch drill by opening up the American half of the dual mechanism with a screwdriver and bypassing it with a jump lead. Starting World War III required little more ingenuity than starting that family car with a flat battery!

Politically, though, whether the dual-key mechanism was crude or complicated was of secondary importance. At Greenham, the mere existence of such a device would have forced the Pentagon to treat the cruise missiles in a quite different way. Washington could not have taken their availability for granted, subject only to a vaguely defined process of consultation. Before the USAF wing could launch them, a positive British government decision to release the safety catch would have been required, just as Rhine Army's missile regiment required positive US clearance to fire Lance. If one did not know otherwise, the idea of any supposedly sovereign nation accepting foreign nuclear weapons on its territory without such positive control would seem almost inconceivable.

Hallowe'en 1983, two days after the women's fence-cutting extravaganza, was the occasion of a major Commons debate in which every aspect of the cruise missile deployment was discussed (a couple of the women also joined in, shouting 'Women from Greenham – no cruise' before being ejected from the public gallery).

The Defence Secretary opened by announcing that the missile launchers would shortly be arriving, and restating the basic NATO position: that the first weapons would become operational at Greenham by the end of the year unless the Soviet Union agreed to the 'zero option' of no intermediate-range missiles on either side.

Ranged against him were Labour's shadow Foreign Secretary, the formidable Denis Healey, and David Owen, who had been fascinated by the arcane workings of nuclear deterrence since becoming Navy Minister in the 1970s. Encouraged by at least one opinion poll suggesting that an overwhelming majority of the electorate would welcome some direct control over the American weapons – especially after President Reagan's invasion of Grenada – they both concentrated on this vulnerable aspect of the government's position.

The SDP was in formal Alliance with the Liberals. Together, they tabled an amendment to the Government's motion calling on it to 'negotiate immediately on the basis of the United States offer for the installation at British expense of a dual-key system for any cruise missile based in the United Kingdom'.[24] They also demanded a fresh initiative in the Geneva arms control talks before the missiles became operational at the end of the year.

The crux of Owen's argument was that all US nuclear weapons operated by British forces, or based on British territory, like the Thor, back in the 1950s, had been equipped with a dual key. Why should this crucial precedent now be abandoned?

Heseltine might have responded by pointing to the cost of purchasing the missiles (which he estimated at £1 billion), but the main thrust of his case was the need for mutual trust between two NATO allies who had evolved a common defence against a common threat. If Britain did not trust the Americans without a dual key, why should they allow Britain to operate an 'independent' nuclear deterrent force (the Polaris submarine missile, purchased from the USA) without a similar device?

Healey argued strongly for a dual key, especially after the experience of Grenada, and he wanted an altogether more flexible approach to negotiations with the Soviet Union – either to limit or to eliminate intermediate-range weapons. (The possibility of eliminating such weapons, on both sides of the Iron Curtain, had first been raised by Michael Foot and Denis Healey during a visit to Moscow back in 1981.) The shadow foreign secretary also pointed to the cruise missile's physical limitations – its three-hour flight time to reach Soviet targets, and its vulnerability while trundling through the Berkshire countryside. And he dealt with the underlying implications of NATO's strategy of deploying such weapons in Europe. The Americans might imagine, he warned, that they could fight a nuclear war in Europe while keeping the United States as a sanctuary.

Such parliamentary debates do on rare occasions change government policy, but this was not one of them. Although Mrs Thatcher seems to have been rattled by the suggestion that she was careless of British sovereignty, this concern was evidently overridden by the requirements of the 'special relationship'. Her Defence Secretary had to fall back on the lame assertion that the government had reviewed the longstanding arrangements for 'joint decision … in the light of the circumstances prevailing at the time' and found them satisfactory. In any case it was too late to start demanding a dual key when the missiles' arrival was only days away. In these circumstances, we had little choice but to trust our American allies.

The Greenham women felt no such trust. That year's December 'gathering' was the protest's largest single demonstration – 50,000 women who shared the campers' sense of disappointment and frustration that, in spite of all their efforts, the NATO deployment was still rolling ahead. They symbolically equipped themselves with mirrors, to force the American missile crews inside the base to reflect on what they were doing there. But it was also a bad-tempered occasion on both sides, with large sections of fencing pulled down, posts and all. Life at Greenham was about to get a lot tougher.

The Orwellian year in prospect would be a period of well-coordinated mass evictions of the peace camps. It would also be the year when Newbury's simmering resentment of the women's presence boiled over into open hostility.

The town strikes back

Newbury is the sort of place a guidebook might describe as 'a bustling market town'. Sadly, much of the bustle is attributable to horrendous road traffic. The town is half-strangled in its own one-way system. As a stranger, one has only to attempt its navigation in the rush hour to realise why residents fought so hard to get a bypass in the 1990s. There is a market, certainly, yet hardly commensurate with the visual importance of its setting – a neoclassical Corn Exchange on one side (built 1862, now an arts centre) and a tall neo-Gothic town hall on the other.

To enjoy the town, and sense more of its history, one needs to dump the car as quickly as possible and explore the canal-side paths and wharves on foot. The waterway runs right through the centre, under the main street of the old borough. It acquired enormous commercial importance in the eighteenth century when the meandering river between Newbury and Reading was made navigable for barges, some of them under sail, and renamed the Kennet Navigation (as opposed to the Kennet and Avon Canal, which now extends all the way to Bristol). Newbury suddenly became an inland port, linked to the Thames at Reading, and hence to London. On the Essex coast we associate Thames spritsail barges with the sea, so I was astonished to learn that some of those working the Upper Thames – the sort of craft Whistler painted from the windows of his Chelsea house – were actually built in Newbury. It seems they even built lifeboats there – hardly credible when one sees the quiet water flowing in the canal.

The Berkshire town has two historic heroes, one a human being, the other a coat. The first of them, known simply as 'Jack of Newbury', was an immensely wealthy but unpretentious cloth merchant whose career symbolises the town's dominant position in the fifteenth-century wool trade. He once entertained Henry VIII and his first queen, Catherine of Aragon, in his Northbrook Street house, which still stands there on the corner of Marsh Lane.[25] The town's metaphorical hero, the 'Newbury Coat' of 1811, represents a last desperate effort to demonstrate that the newly mechanised woollen mills at Greenham were still a match for their Yorkshire competitors, which had by then captured the bulk of the trade. The coat was the result of a 1,000-guinea wager by a local grandee, Sir John Throckmorton, on whether local craftsmen could produce such a garment in a single day, starting with the raw wool. A copy of a contemporary poster celebrating this feat of 'manufacturing celerity' – worth a look just for the printer's exuberant use of every typeface in the box – can be seen in the local museum down by the former canal basin.

Bold Sir John won his wager. At Greenham, he duly paraded in the coat – dyed a fashionable 'Wellington' blue – and later took dinner at the George and Pelican with forty friends. The two Southdown sheep that had given their wool were slaughtered, roasted and consumed, along with 120 gallons of ale. The local wool industry's fortunes, however, were not restored.

In those days, the old borough still contained various pockets of common land scattered amongst its houses, inns and workshops. These were gradually absorbed for new building during the nineteenth century, with land elsewhere provided as compensation. A riverside area known simply as 'the Marsh' became the town's Victoria Park. The wilder heaths of Greenham and Crookham commons, just outside the town, survived untouched until the RAF arrived.

For all its rich history, Newbury has never settled for a heritage role. After the Second World War it became a dormitory for the cutting-edge atomic research establishment at Aldermaston, and more recently provided a base for the booming telecommunications industry. Socially, however, the community playing host to the Greenham protest throughout the 1980s remained essentially conservative, conscious of its respectability and concerned to maintain it. For women arraigned before the local magistrates, it was ominous that this should be the last town in England to put one of its petty criminals in the public stocks.[26]

The town first found its angry voice in May 1983, when thousands of leaflets were distributed calling on local people to march to the Market Place at lunchtime under the banner 'Greenham Common Women Out'. The leaflets took a swipe at the women by pointedly adding: 'No silly hats, toys or flowers please'. Then they laid out their argument:

> We accept that everyone has a right to their opinion and belief, but we do not accept that anyone has a right to subject an entire community to their continual presence, to the point of being a nuisance. Their verbal aggressiveness is a constant source of unpleasantness to the public, to the

point of fear for some people. To say nothing of the cost to ratepayers. They have made their point. We therefore request them to leave, returning only for one day demonstrations, which is their right, just as it is our right to protest at their continual presence.

About 300 people turned up for the short march, plus a fair number of journalists, including the *Guardian*'s Gareth Parry. He heard the protest's organiser Miss Sheila Sheddon, a retired nurse and charity worker, complain of the 'tide of human excrement' washing around the peace camp. The way the women let their children roam around in the mud, she declared, was a disgrace to womanhood. Another marcher referred scornfully to the 'filth, smell and immorality' of the women.[27] Two large banners at the head of the procession spelt out their message: '"Peace Women" You Disgust Us', 'Clean Up and Get Out'.

The women's supposed dirtiness was a familiar complaint whenever local residents vented their anger and shopkeepers, restaurants or pub landlords refused to serve them – as many eventually did. Newbury shunned the protesters rather as other communities shun Gypsies. But of course this was the result of a vicious circle in which the authorities' determination to evict the women by removing any permanent structures, toilet or cooking facilities made it extremely difficult for them to stay clean and dignified. If they were more or less permanent campers, they either had to live rough, sleeping in the open and digging their own latrines like soldiers in the field, or fall back on the support of a few local people like Lynette Edwell, who opened her house to them as well as joining some of the actions.

Lynette is small and talkative, the sort of person who knows her rights and is determined to obtain them. She boasts of being 'the only woman to be thrown out of Holloway'. During the active Greenham years, the front door of her house in Priory Road was never locked: 'It was a good place to hold a meeting, a good place to telephone, a good place to leave messages, to meet somebody for an interview, to do banners, to sit and write.' She fed Greenham women – along with her own children, three of whom were still at home – and cared for them when they were sick. She offered the rare luxury of a bath and a proper bed, something especially appreciated before a trial: 'Women could have a bath, wash their hair, and be in court early with their wits about them.'

Yet bath and wash as they might, the women could not shake off the caricature their opponents increasingly used to discredit them – the burly, surly lesbian smelling of wood smoke, stomping around in muddy boots, scruffy jeans and a woolly hat (Karmen Cutler recalls trying to redress the balance by turning up in a pinstripe suit she wore for trade-union conferences). But like any caricature, this one did reflect a certain reality, albeit in a highly selective way.

Many of the women were indeed lesbian, and when threatened with eviction by the bailiffs or turned away from restaurants they were sometimes understandably surly. Cooking day by day over an open fire, their clothes were inevitably impregnated with wood smoke (Rebecca Johnson remembers suddenly realising this when she turned up late for a London theatre date after being unexpectedly arrested down at Greenham). As for the boots and jeans, they were practical necessities as well as a matter of personal choice. Scrambling through barbed wire on a winter's night, you would not get far in high heels and a frock.

None of which rationalisation made any impression on the indignant resident who wrote to the *Newbury Weekly News* shortly after the missiles arrived to suggest that the women were lucky not to be ejected from his 'once nice, clean town and be given the good thrashing they deserve'. Local people were as disgusted and repelled by their presence as they were by the arrival of cruise, he claimed: 'At least cruise is clean.' However, the same page also carried a letter from an elderly correspondent who said that unless her beloved Newbury had the sense to reject military plans for its extinction in nuclear warfare, she would never voluntarily set foot in it again.[28]

On big occasions during 1983, such as the Easter demonstration with CND and the vast December gathering which followed the missiles' arrival, the caricatured image that so incensed many residents was in any case blurred and softened by the presence of thousands of visitors, including some men. Intense national publicity and a general election also made it difficult for the authorities to confront the women head-on either at local or national level (though Mrs Thatcher made clear her personal irritation by suggesting they would do better to link hands along the Berlin Wall than on the road to Greenham or Aldermaston).

Early in the year Lady Olga Maitland, at that time a *Sunday Express* columnist, established a small group of 'Women and Families for Defence' (Ann Widdecombe, a London University administrator, later to become a Tory MP and Home Office minister for prisons, was an early member) to persuade anxious wives and mothers, that in a wicked world, cruise missiles were a necessary evil. Newbury District Council confined itself mainly to preparing the legal ground for future action by changing the common land bye-laws so that named women – the supposed ringleaders – could be banned, structures removed and fires extinguished.

Local residents made their next move on 12 February 1984 when about three dozen of them met at the home of Anthony Meyer to form a resistance movement whose title, Ratepayers Against Greenham Encampments, spelt out the word RAGE. In a series of newspaper advertisements, several of them adorned with drawings of a butch, spike-haired peace woman sitting astride a cruise missile, the new campaign spelt out its agenda.

First, it carefully distinguished between CND, which it 'neither condoned nor condemned', and the 40 or so 'squatters' permanently camped outside the base. Its declared aim was to use every lawful means to remove this 'small group of selfish and lawless women'. Its tactics were to put pressure on the relevant authorities – the DHSS, Thames Water, the Post Office and the police – to deprive them of financial support, water supplies, postal deliveries and electoral registration. And if these official bodies neglected their duty, one strident advertisement warned, 'WE WILL ACT'.

The RAGE campaign to prevent women using their peace camp as an address from which to vote in Newbury was more symbolic than practical, but it led to a series of arcane, expensive challenges in the courts. The issue first arose back in January 1983, when nine women managed to get themselves formally registered as living at 'The Peace Camp, outside the main gates, Greenham Common'. Setting an important precedent, West Berkshire's electoral registration officer Jim Turner had overruled objections by a prospective Conservative district councillor, taking the view that if there was any doubt, it had to be resolved in favour of the would-be voters.

The case was typical of the way the women used every legal device and manoeuvre open to them, and it infuriated local Conservative Party officials. As far as they were concerned, a peace camp was not a proper address, and, even if it were, the women's purpose in living there was to mount a protest, not to take part in the conventional political process.

Two years later battle was resumed in the electoral court by RAGE chairman Anthony Meyer and another local resident – by which time thirteen women had registered. This time Mr Turner took the view that although the women were 'in ordinary language' resident at the airfield gate, they could not vote from there because the residence was unlawful. The women appealed in the County Court and won (Judge Peck pointed out that convicts were only disqualified while actually in prison). Meyer refused to give up, however. The issue was finally decided after a three-day hearing in the Court of Appeal, when the Master of the Rolls and two other judges ruled that the 'Greenham ladies' were indeed 'resident' at the peace camp and were entitled to vote from there.[29]

Other residents took the law into their own hands, launching what the women called 'paramilitary' attacks. They would creep around at night, cutting off the peace camp's water supply, loosing off with air guns, and on one occasion dumping pig's blood and maggots in Rebecca Johnson's bender, which had to be burnt.

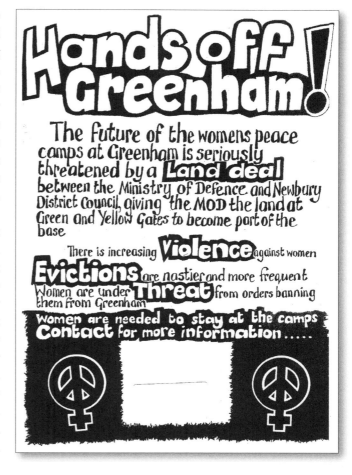

Against this background, and under pressure from the MoD on the USAF's behalf, the local authorities began planning a concerted effort to rid the base of its peace camps once and for all. Their timing was dictated by the 501st Tactical Missile Wing, which had scheduled its first public road test of a missile convoy for the night of 8–9 March. Unfortunately for the Americans, their operational concept depended on dispersing the missile launchers to camouflaged hideouts as far as possible from their main base – which was obviously prominent on Soviet target maps – and as military professionals they were not going to neglect this aspect of their training. So sooner or later they had to confront the women outside the seclusion of the Greenham gates. The job of police and bailiffs was to minimise the political embarrassment this confrontation was bound to cause.

Evictions from all the gates on the north side of the airfield began a few days beforehand, in fact several times a day, with every movable object, including personal possessions, hurled into the bailiffs' 'munchers'. On the eve of the test run, the military made ostentatious preparations to leave by the main Yellow Gate, then slipped out through the northern Blue Gate in the early hours of the following morning.

In his autobiography, Michael Heseltine records his satisfaction at the success of this diversionary tactic: 'To this day I am amazed that we got away with such a simple device. Cruise missiles had been deployed for the first time. We had shown it could be done, and the propaganda victory was ours.'[30] However, the women also reckoned they scored a victory that night, and set an important precedent by tracking and exposing the vehicles' subsequent movements.

Evelyn Parker, a cool-headed Quaker who at the time was running an organic smallholding on the outskirts of Newbury, remembers the sheer excitement of that first encounter with a convoy. It had been seen leaving Blue Gate, and a 'telephone tree', mainly connecting CND groups, was already in place to report its progress over about a 20-mile radius. In the event someone spotted this line of unusual camouflaged vehicles trundling along the A4 near Lyneham:

> He phoned back – I think it was to Lynette – and she phoned a few of us in Newbury, and we were all at the police station roundabout when it came back. And everyone shouted out: 'You've been to Lyneham.' We were surrounded by police, and you should have seen the look on their faces – they were absolutely astonished. We'd caught it. That was really exciting.

It was the first of hundreds of such carefully planned interceptions in a new form of protest that came to be known as 'Cruisewatch'.

The official response was an intensified campaign of daily evictions and a warning from the Department of Transport that even the main camp at Yellow Gate would be permanently removed on 2 April so that the access road could be widened. Di McDonald, who had usually just visited Orange Gate with her kids, spent much of this critical period permanently at the base. She remembers sleeping out in the late spring snow, wrapped 'like a cocoon' in her Gore-tex waterproof sleeping bag: 'It was a very weird time. Not only did we live in the mud, we had to be mobile. So we had these prams – one for food, another for pots and pans, and so on.'

Fearing that the destruction of their main camp might indeed mean the end of the protest, the women put out a desperate appeal for reinforcements during the period 22 March to 2 April. Unusually, the leaflet was not decorated with symbolic cobwebs or playful drawings, just sombre, black, almost funereal sans-serif lettering on a violet background. The message was stark: 'FINAL EVICTION OF GREENHAM WOMEN'S PEACE CAMP. THE SURVIVAL OF GREENHAM COULD DEPEND ON YOUR PRESENCE.' The leaflet warned:

> This is the most urgent Greenham Appeal so far. There is a court injunction for the final eviction of the camp from March 22nd till April 2nd.
> The signs that this country is on a war footing are becoming increasingly obvious. After stripping GCHQ workers' union rights from them, Thatcher's government is now depriving the people of their basic democratic right – the means of effective protest. Heseltine has repeatedly declared that the existence of the G.C. Women's Peace Camp is proof of, and a tribute to British democracy. This has been no more than soft-soaping before the iron heel descends brutally in the last week of March.
> We are appealing urgently for all women to support Greenham at this desperate time. Please come for as long as you can from March 22nd, but particularly from April 2nd, when the eviction is supposed to be completed.
> Your response to this appeal is crucial. The survival of Greenham hangs in the balance. Thousands of women are needed to support our sisters, who have endured enough already. Together we must prove to this government that women are saying NO! to Nuclear Weapons and Military Dictatorship.

The appeal was at least partially successful. Enough women gathered to persuade the authorities to hold back from Yellow Gate – but only for a couple of days. On 4 April, when many women were away at a big Crown Court hearing in Reading, leaving Newbury supporters to hold the fort, a large team of bailiffs shielded by hundreds of police moved in to strip the Department of Transport land of everything it contained. Lynette remembers Di and herself crawling in thoroughly undignified fashion through the policemen's legs to recover what personal possessions they could for the absent campers. Passports and letters were rescued from the very jaws of the munchers.

To make things even more difficult, the road from Newbury had been coned off (official reasons being quoted included an overturned lorry and a jewel robbery). But as news of the eviction spread, women came rushing back to resume their old game of hopscotch: shifting what was left of their belongings on to common land not covered by the latest eviction order, right against the fence. Not that there was much comfort there, since under the new bye-laws fires could be, and were, repeatedly doused with extinguishers. Still, the camp survived – just – and from the women's perspective something positive did emerge from all this misery.

Evelyn Parker's fellow Quakers decided they must do something to help the women. Though wary of becoming politically involved, they agreed it was their duty to provide practical assistance. This they did in generous fashion by installing a shower, a washing machine and a pay telephone in their meeting house near Newbury railway station. There was also a room where women could make a cup of tea and relax. These facilities were well used – and occasionally abused, as some disgruntled members complained. It was one instance of the wider support provided by Quaker meetings throughout the country. Another was a remarkable invention known as a 'Getaway': a simple triple-hooped tent with integral groundsheet that could be scooped up over a woman's arm as the dawn bailiffs hit the camp. The final touch was a label announcing that the Getaway was the gift of such-and-such a support group in Manchester or wherever, so that it counted as a personal possession (which the bailiffs were not supposed to confiscate) rather than a structure (which could legally be bundled straight into the muncher). It was yet another example of the resourceful way the women wriggled through the tiniest gap in the law, as well as the wire.

A kind of missile

'Poised to Deter, Quick to React.'

Motto of the 501st Tactical Missile Wing

'Poised with the Truth, Quick to Stop Pretending.'

Greenham women's riposte

My first experience of a cruise missile was as a 10-year-old in wartime Clacton-on-Sea, walking home from school with a couple of my mates. Like all boys at that time, we knew the distinctive sound of the various German aircraft: the drone of a Dornier, the higher-pitched whine of a Heinkel. The small aircraft approaching from the north-east – not 'one of ours', so far as we could see – made a quite different sound, with an emphatic rhythmic beat to it. It was a VI, a pilotless 'flying bomb', a 'Doodlebug'.

The vital thing we already knew about Doodlebugs was that if that distinctive throb stopped, you were in trouble. But this one flew safely over our heads. We relaxed. Whoever it was destined for, it wasn't us. Seconds later the engine suddenly went quiet. We turned back to watch the bomb glide silently down, sending out a massive crump as a ton of high exposive detonated on the outskirts of town.

Doodlebugs were the first cruise missiles. Had they carried a nuclear warhead like the ones at Greenham, they could have destroyed London many times over. After the Second World War, equipped with captured German technology, both the Americans and the Russians experimented with them, while concentrating increasingly on the development of ballistic missiles, which were in many ways more effective. The Soviet Navy persisted long enough to produce a 20-foot delta-winged cruise missile called a Styx, which could be launched from small, fast patrol boats it sold to various client states, including Egypt. And it was the Egyptians who laid on a fresh demonstration of the devastation such weapons could cause.

At about 5.30 in the evening of 21 October 1967 the Israeli destroyer *Eilat*, an ex-British Z-class vessel, which first saw service in 1944, was gently steaming through a quiet sea about 15 miles off Port Said. She was alone, without air cover. But nobody worried much about that. After their brilliant 'blitzkrieg' victory over the Egyptians only a few months earlier, the Israelis were supremely confident. This was just a routine patrol of the Egyptian coast. Most of the *Eilat*'s crew were relaxing in the forecastle.

The first warning came from a lookout who had sighted the exhaust trail of a missile coming in fast from the south. The watch on deck just had time to attempt an evasive manoeuvre and open up with their Bofors anti-aircraft guns. It looked as if the missile would miss, but when it was quite near they noticed it change course (its radar guidance had locked on) and head straight for them. Seconds later it struck the destroyer amidships. Two minutes later a second missile smashed home in almost the same spot.

The explosions wrecked boilers and the engine room, started a fire, and left the elderly Israeli vessel wallowing in the gentle swell without power or radio communications. Rather than drift inshore, her crew dropped anchor and spent the next two hours fighting the fire, treating their wounded and struggling to establish a radio link with their base. They were just too late. The message got through at last, but at 7.30 a third Styx struck the destroyer's stern and she slowly capsized. The final missile exploded in the water among the survivors. Fifty-four members of the crew had been killed.[31]

As a piece of technological propaganda, the sinking of the *Eilat* could hardly be equalled. It was a shock to navies all over the world – and especially the Royal Navy, which had just been told by Denis Healey that the defence budget would not stretch to replacing their four ageing aircraft carriers. Cruise missiles were soon back in naval fashion, as a French-built Exocet was to demonstrate to British sailors' cost on 4 May 1982, by sinking HMS *Sheffield* during the Falklands campaign.

The American Tomahawk cruise missiles, by then on their way to Greenham, evolved only in the broadest sense from these predecessors. Conceptually they were in the same family of 'flying bombs'. But their 1,500-mile range, and the addition of a nuclear warhead several times more destructive than the bomb which obliterated Hiroshima, made them suitable for strategic deterrence rather than war-fighting – or so one might assume. In fact, NATO's leaders seemed suspiciously uncertain about the strategy that underlay the European deployment.

At the simplest bean-counting level, they suggested that the 464 American Tomahawks (plus 108 Pershing II ballistic missiles in Germany) were intended to match Soviet SS-20 and other missiles increasingly deployed in eastern Europe. If this balance-of-terror approach failed to impress, there was a second argument. The Tomahawks' presence on this side of the Atlantic was supposed to reassure Europeans that Washington was committed to deter attacks, not just against its homeland, but also the rest of NATO. The intermediate-range cruise missiles over here would provide a 'linkage' with the intercontinental missiles back in the United States.

However, for many people, including the Greenham women, this forward deployment conveyed quite the opposite message: that the Americans were preparing if necessary to fight a nuclear war in Europe, while preserving their own territory as a sanctuary. It was a point Labour's Denis Healey had made in the parliamentary debate just before the missiles arrived at Greenham.

Perhaps equally relevant, as it turned out, was an argument attributed to James Wade, the US Undersecretary of Defence who launched the programme in 1971: that a long-range cruise missile would prompt the Soviet Union to waste vast military resources creating specialised air defences that would not otherwise be needed. Because, in truth, here was a classic case of advanced military technology – in this instance computer guidance, a highly efficient turbofan jet engine and a miniature nuclear warhead – looking for a strategy to justify its manufacture. Some clever engineer in the US aerospace industry realised that with these components he could build an exciting new toy for the Pentagon – in fact three variants of the same basic toy – with big development and production contracts attached.

The ground-launched version of the Tomahawk was known to the USAF as the Gryphon. In Britain, the main force of 96 missiles (six 'flights' of 16) was based at Greenham, with a further 64 planned for Molesworth in Cambridgeshire, the last of all the European bases. Each flight consisted of four brutally named Transporter Erector Launchers (TELs) and a pair of Launch Control Centres (LCCs), plus sixteen supporting vehicles. So when a complete unit emerged on to Berkshire's country roads, it was difficult to miss.

The vehicles that attracted most attention from the women were naturally the TELs – monstrous 50-foot articulated 12-wheelers with a payload of four missiles in sealed canisters. These were raised into the firing position by a hydraulic ram, rather like a tip-up truck preparing to dump sand on a building site. In the field, fibre-optic cables connected the TELs to their launch control centres, which were in turn linked to the NATO command chain by secure radio commications (rather more technically sophisticated, one assumed, than the crude jump-lead electrics of the Thor missile based here in the late 1950s).

The Tomahawk was an astonishingly versatile system. It was originally designed for the US Navy, to be launched if necessary from a standard submarine torpedo tube – hence its 21-foot length and 21-inch diameter. The Gryphon variant was boosted off its ramp by a rocket motor, unfolded its short wings, switched on a miniature jet engine and set off under inertial guidance in the general direction of the target.

The really clever bit – or so it seemed in those early days of computers and satellites – was an additional guidance system known as TERCOM (terrain contour-matching inertial navigation). This used an altimeter to plot the contours of the ground beneath the missile and compare them with a computerised map stored in its memory. By flying over a series of pre-mapped TERCOM 'fields', the missile could update its position and plot a course to the next waypoint. After final course adjustments over the last field, it would drop to about 50 foot above the ground, more or less invisible to radar, and arm its 50-kiloton warhead.

Launched from Berkshire, a Gryphon Tomahawk could just about have reached Moscow. Leningrad was a little bit nearer. Suppose, in a hypothetical nuclear conflict, the Greenham unit had been ordered to destroy the Soviet naval base at Kronstadt, not far from Leningrad. The missile would first climb to an economical altitude to cross the North Sea, then perhaps transit the southern tip of Norway so that its TERCOM computer could make use of the steep mountainous contours, fly on across neutral Sweden, with maybe a last guidance check on the Finnish coastline before the final dash to the target, just feet above the Gulf of Finland. Once launched, the missile could not be recalled.

In theory, the warhead would have detonated no more than a hundred or so feet from the chosen target. In reality, nobody outside the US cruise missile programme really knew how accurate these Mark I Tomahawks were. This was one of the factors (along with the so-called 'Moscow criterion' – the need to convince the Soviet leaders they would not be safe, even deep in their Kremlin bunkers) that prevented cruise missiles being seriously considered instead of the Trident ballistic missile chosen as Britain's strategic deterrent in 1980. Could they make a successful transition from their Nevada test range to the featureless, often snow-covered plains of northern Russia?

These early versions were certainly far less precise than the upgraded Tomahawk we all saw on television during the first Gulf War, flying down a Baghdad street preparing to turn left at the second traffic lights. The modern weapons make use of GPS, an extraordinarily accurate global satellite positioning system nowadays familiar to every yachtsman and many motorists, plus close-quarters television guidance – though, like all bombs, they still sometimes go astray.

However, there was another feature of the ground-launched cruise missile far more immediately important to the Greenham women than its accuracy. In the event of war, the USAF planned to disperse its launch and control vehicles to camouflaged sites over a wide area to make them less vulnerable. This made obvious military sense. It was also good public relations to suggest – wrongly – that Newbury would be much less of a target for Soviet retaliation. In the words of Michael Heseltine, or at any rate in the words often quoted back at him by the women, the missiles would 'melt into the countryside'. The next phase of their campaign – Cruisewatch – was devoted to ensuring that, in peacetime at least, this was never possible.

The odd thing about the years of inconvenience Cruisewatch caused the US Air Force is that the Americans need not really have bothered. All the operational components of a cruise missile flight could be, and were, assembled and tested inside the Greenham base. If there had ever been a war alert, convoys could have smashed their way straight out of the gates and hurried to their secret, pre-surveyed launch sites across the South and West of England, guarded by armed British and US troops. No rehearsal was needed. But of course that is not the military way of doing things.

Soldiers often say that 'no plan survives contact with reality'. But if there is time, it is obviously better to practise manoeuvres in as much realistic detail as possible so as to discover the unexpected snags – and in peacetime soldiers usually have a lot of time on their hands. They practise over and over again, way beyond the point of boredom. The 501st Tactical Missile Wing, certainly, were absolutely intent on exercising their dispersal concept. Quite apart from their personal survival, how they performed out in 'the field' was an important aspect of NATO's periodic tactical evaluations. Promotions, salaries and status depended on the outcomes.

Then there was the little matter of public relations. Local people sufficiently interested to take a look at the massive, blast-resistant silos that housed the missiles (hardened to withstand 2,000 lb per square inch, according to Duncan Campbell[32]) were already concerned that they might well be a nuclear target. Had the Americans made no effort to disperse their weapons, it would have been absolutely clear that Newbury was just a couple of miles from ground zero.

Cruisewatchers therefore felt that if they could disrupt the convoys, they could make some claim to having invalidated the USAF's operational concept. This was not a strong argument, because wartime alert conditions would have been so totally different. However, they were on stronger ground in seeking simply to expose the convoys' movements. Deterrence in peacetime is all about perceptions, about demonstrating political resolve

so as to prompt uncertainty in an adversary's mind (merely ordering the missiles to disperse on alert, for example, would have sent out a powerful signal).

So it was undoubtedly a deep embarrassment for the Americans to have the military seriousness of a 'Nighthawk' nuclear dispersal exercise held up to disruptive public scrutiny. At the very least it made people throughout Britain aware of what was going on. Cruisewatch certainly took this view, as one of its publications explained:

> Monitoring Cruise convoy dispersal exercises shows that the USAF cannot achieve the declared objective of Cruise 'melting into the countryside'. Simply by the witnessing and frustration of its movements, this military plan has been made impossible. This has increased public awareness of the dangerous situation that these preparations for nuclear war represent.

Greenham women were heavily involved in this new campaign. They were its frontline troops, blocking the airfield gates with prams, fires, chains or their own bodies. But the movement deliberately spread itself wider, to include 'a network of people from all walks of life, including CND members, Greenham women and other peace campaigners from across the South, South West and Midlands of England – part of the international campaign against Cruise missile deployments'. In other words, the men were back. They were invited to rejoin the protest, provided only that they did not interfere with the women's activities immediately around the base. The rules about this were remarkably strict.

Male volunteers were instructed not to approach any of the Greenham gates even when accompanied by a woman; they were not allowed to watch for a convoy by parking opposite the main Yellow Gate; they had to keep clear altogether of the A339 running along the southern edge of the airfield; and they were told to take care not be arrested anywhere near Greenham, so as to avoid confusing publicity. 'There are miles of road elsewhere to get arrested on', their instructions tartly pointed out.

Over the next few years, a contest of political will played out across southern England like a long-running war game. The Americans' aim was to achieve their training objectives (which they did with some professional distinction, even being mentioned in the US central command's 'Scroll of Honor'). Cruisewatch volunteers worked tirelessly to ensure (also success-fully, so far as I know) that not a single convoy emerged from the base without at some stage being tracked and publicised.

Former Cruisewatchers will probably be appalled by my suggesting they were involved in anything resembling a 'war game'. So let me concede immediately that the comparison is a superficial one. In advertising for supporters (I nearly wrote 'recruits') they themselves emphasised the fun-damental differences between their approach and that of the military:

> Above all, this is not a clandestine or paramilitary organisation – there are no leaders or official posts. Cruisewatch is completely open, the aim is always publicity, not secrecy; blowing the cover on the secrecy and security which are essential to these rehearsals for nuclear war.
>
> This broadsheet may give the impression of efficiency and organisation – but in fact what Cruisewatch has achieved is the result of the spontaneous actions of many diverse individuals. Its methods are often haphazard and reliant on luck – and certainly perseverance – everyone simply keeps their eyes and ears open.

Yet, for all these disclaimers, I still feel sure the SAS – if not the Household Cavalry – would applaud the combination of ingenuity and determination Cruisewatchers displayed. As for their reconnaissance organisation, by military standards it was wildly eccentric, but it worked. It was based on what Di McDonald, whose secluded late-Victorian house on the outskirts of Southampton was the organisation's local base, calls the 'peanuts' system. Unless a convoy was out on exercise, the Greenham base was monitored every night from parked cars. And, as if to emphasise the improvised, non-military nature of the exercise, suitable vantage points were originally plotted on a map not by pins, or little coloured flags, but by a handful of peanuts.

In those days before mobile phones, communications were provided by a telephone 'tree' and the few expensive Citizens' Band radios they could afford. As in warfare, there were long periods of boredom interspersed with sudden excitement: 'Sometimes when there was a big alert, and a convoy was seen moving, over the CB radio we would hear the message "Calling all herbs, calling all herbs!" And that was a real alarm call. Start the engine; don't know where we're going; just get ready.' Using herbs or plants as code names was another characteristic touch. Di's was 'Bracken', because

Photo: Bob Naylor

A success for 'Cruisewatch', 30 April 1985. One of the 501st Tactical Missile Wing's launch control vehicles is halted on its way back from a nuclear alert rehearsal on Salisbury Plain, its windscreen smeared with white paint.

she owned a battered old brown car at that time. A Newbury couple who operated a CB radio went by the name of 'Cauliflower Cheese'.

The convoy might head west for Lyneham or south-east for the army camp at Longmoor in the Woolmer Forest. The most frequent destination was Salisbury Plain, where there are thousands of acres of military land, scattered with copses in which the missile launchers could be hidden. 'To begin with,' Di recalls, 'they just turned into some bushes and hoped for the best, but they soon found they were inundated with protesters, tripping over them in their foxholes. So then they started putting barbed wire round, and the British Army had to set up a reception area for them – and that of course alerted people, who by now were familiar with the Plain.'

The Cruisewatch symbol was a human eye. Drawn large on a card, it could be held up in the headlights of an approaching missile launcher to show that its nuclear manoeuvres had not gone unnoticed. If the women could actually halt a convoy, by blockading the airfield gates or sitting down across the road, so much the better. On one occasion they managed to get white paint under the windscreen wiper of a launch vehicle, temporarily paralysing the whole convoy and producing spectacular pictures for the next day's newspapers. There were plenty of arrests. And, almost inevitably, things sometimes got rough, as when Di's van was tipped into a ditch, or when women were held in a muddy pit at the Longmoor army camp.

The possibility of a major road accident was never far away, though everybody was conscious of the danger. For example, the women took care not to jump out in front of vulnerable police motorcyclists, and the American drivers were bound by their own safety rules to have eight hours' sleep before taking to the road. Nevertheless, Di recalls a typical near miss on a roundabout near Amesbury:

> In front of us were lines and lines of police with their backs to the convoy, and their intention was to protect it. But it was all very dodgy, with a rush of air as the big vehicles went round. I can remember pulling policemen towards me, out of the way. It was always dangerous, particularly for the British police.

For the American airmen, trips to 'the field', albeit only a few miles down the road to Salisbury Plain, were a testing climax to the training cycle. They meant a week away from base comforts, going through their drills and attempting as instructed – though never quite succeeding – to avoid contact with the protesters. According to the Wing's own solemn record of the Greenham mission, *The Last Crusade*, each dispersal was distinctive, yet somehow they all ended up being dubbed 'the dispersal from hell'. It was a love–hate situation:

> Sitting in a muddy firing position with rain pouring down and no sleep, with only MREs (pre-packed emergency rations) to eat, isn't glamorous. Yet after the challenges of a dispersal were met, many of those who had labored through it would return to base with a sense of accomplishment and pride. It was a test that set GLCM flight members apart as warriors.

In other words, the USAF took this aspect of its operations every bit as seriously as the Cruisewatchers hoped and believed it did – which helped to justify the years of effort they put into their protest.

Snakes, paint and bolt cutters

While Cruisewatch staked out Salisbury Plain, Greenham women intensified their activities around the perimeter of the base. Mass evictions in the spring of 1984 failed to kill the protest. On the contrary, incursions through the fence became more frequent, almost routine. A few women actually camped inside for days at a time.

'Actions' ranged from the playful to the plain destructive, from floating symbolic cobwebs on helium balloons to simply pulling down the fence, from rushing to paint 'Greenham Women are Everywhere' on the runway to a carefully planned commando-style operation to occupy the airfield's control tower. For Jean Hutchinson, who must have spent more time at Greenham than almost anyone, the way in which serious protest was often dressed in fanciful, even childish clothes, made it all the more effective: 'We were able to do things, in an apparently gentle way, that were actually hard as nails. Teddy bears, snakes, splashing holy water on gates – it terrified the Americans.' One only has to imagine earnest male members of CND dressed as teddy bears to realise that men could not have got away with such tactics.

Jean recalls one peculiarly surreal occasion when she found a group of off-duty Americans line-dancing in a hangar, with the cruise missile launcher she was really interested in parked at the back. On an impulse, she joined the dancers. They pretended to ignore her, following standing base instructions to avoid all eye contact. She felt she had to keep on dancing until the MoD police arrived, which took an exhausting half-hour: 'It nearly wore me out.'

The American response to the control tower action, deliberately planned to demonstrate that women could penetrate sensitive areas of the base, was rather more alarming. Rebecca Johnson and two other women went in from nearby Violet Gate under cover of darkness. They climbed the 40-foot tower without being spotted, broke in and spent some time exploring, and reading classified technical documents, before realising that they could be there all night unless they did something to attract attention. So they started switching lights on and off. At which point an armed US serviceman burst in, 'shaking like a leaf' from the shock of finding them there. 'We had to calm him down by talking to him and telling him to keep cool.'

It was the nearest they had so far come to testing the Defence Secretary's recent warning that if intruders went too far, they could be shot. A much more serious test occurred 11 months later, on a November night in 1984, when the women finally tried to penetrate the nuclear core of the US operation. Rebecca was once again involved:

It was the idea of a good friend from Gravesend, who drove for a living. She didn't live at Greenham, but used to come and stay frequently – her name was Jan. And she talked to me about this idea of hot-wiring an American bus and driving it to the silos from inside the base.

We had already been into the hangars – in fact three of us had disturbed an emergency exercise in one of the hangars when everything was supposed to be dead. But although we'd done that kind of thing we hadn't managed to get to the silos, where they actually kept the warheads. It was from there that the real nuclear menace emanated. And Jan had the idea that, with all the security facing outwards, if we approached from inside we would take them by surprise.

I thought it was a great idea. She went in with a couple of friends and checked out the trucks in the hangar – checked out that she would be able to hot-wire them. But then I had a court case and thought I wouldn't be able to do this action. So I hadn't prepared myself mentally, even though I had talked to her about it months before. Also I'd had at least a couple of glasses – or paper cups – of wine, because it was Rose's seventieth birthday and we had a party at Orange Gate. Rose was a wonderful woman from the Camden Greenham support group, ex-Communist Party, used to wear bright red lipstick no matter what.

And Jan came to me and said: 'I know you were expecting to be in prison, but we really need you because there's quite a lot of women who want to do it and we're thinking of going in two groups. Can you lead one of the groups?'

This was one of those actions that was planned by women – every inch Greenham women – who had come down for the weekend. There were Camden women, there were Hackney women, there were Kent women. And of course, although it really was Rose's birthday, the big party up at Orange Gate was a cover for a lot of them. It made the police less suspicious. So at the last minute I said: 'OK, we've got two groups.'

Jill headed off round to the right with her group and I headed off to the left with mine. The point was, we knew we were always being watched at the fence, so when we got up to start this action we made a big show of kissing each other goodbye, and some of the women were slamming car doors, and a few of the others who knew about the action but weren't taking part made a great show of driving off (then sneaked back) so police or soldiers watching would think the party had broken up.

I headed down with my group towards the quarry, and out came the bolt cutters, and we cut our way in. As you climb up from the fence there's the inner road, and then you have to cross the runway to reach the silos. My group of women was supposed to get to a designated 'bus stop' at midnight. However, we'd been having such a good time at Rose's party (and Jan had gone in late) it was now nearer one o'clock. And as we started up this steep bank we suddenly realised there were two police cars waiting at our bus stop – so clearly they were expecting something. And then we saw the bus start to come through, and we thought: 'Oh God, they're going to get stopped.' And we watched the bus drive slowly past the police, and not get stopped.

But I'd got some stragglers, we were in full view of the police, and I was thinking: 'No, we can't do this yet.' And as the bus moved past I realised that one of the police cars was detaching itself, with not only its headlights but some kind of high, swivelling beam of light. So I shouted, in a stentorian whisper: 'Everybody, get down!' And everybody ducked down along the slope. And then I heard Rose's voice, as if from a crouching bush – 'This is as low as I can get.' (Rose was seventy, and about six feet tall.) And of course we all burst out laughing. But the police car didn't see us. It carried on round, and it didn't even chase the bus. It was weird.

Anyway, the bus looped round and started to come back, quite slowly. So I led the women up and over this ridge thing, and we just streamed on to the bus, bolt cutters in hand. The police car still at the bus stop didn't seem to notice. So the bus carried on round, went right up the runway and then veered off towards the silos.

As we got very close to the silos, a British squaddy jeep pulled up, to get the bus to stop, to see what it was doing there. And it was kind of chaotic, and I just said: 'Look, we go for it.' So Jan opened the doors of the bus and we streamed off the bus and headed for the fence – cutting, cutting, cutting – and behind me I was aware of this chaotic radioing going on from these soldiers, who just hadn't a clue what had hit them.

So we were very very quickly cutting through the first fence, cutting through the second fence – by which time I was vaguely aware of lots of soldiers behind me, and women were getting arrested, and sitting down, and being dragged away. And at some point I realised that I only had one fence to go. And I looked across and there was one other woman, Carola from Violet Gate; and she and I were both starting to cut at this fence. It may have been the third; it may have been the fourth; I know it was the last.

Suddenly I look forward, and realise that what initially looked like beads all along the top of the silos – and I'm cutting, and orange lights on everything – I realise that they are heads, soldiers' heads, and they are right across the top of the silos. And in the shadows the silos are casting I see there's all these American soldiers, mostly standing up. The ones at the top appear to be lying down. But they all have rifles, and it seems that every one of those rifles is pointing at me.

It's such a strange moment because it's completely silent on the inside – that's how it feels – and there's this incredibly distant melee, shouting, and things like that, going on behind me as I'm cutting. And I remember thinking: 'Oh God, if I do go through this fence, they're going to shoot me.'

Everything went into slow motion. I was still cutting the fence and it was one of those moments – it probably only took a second or two – that was completely elongated. And suddenly I was wrenched backwards by somebody – it turned out to be a squaddy – and I remember I just managed to throw my bolt cutters over the fence. So at least *they* got into the silos.

The last thing we saw was all these utterly silent soldiers, with their heads picked out in the lights, just standing in front of the silos.

As a result of the bus action, 28 women later appeared in court. Rather to their amazement, because the judge seemed decidedly hostile, an all-women jury acquitted them. The accused had exercised their right to challenge jurors, accepting any woman, 'even if she was carrying a copy of the *Daily Telegraph*', and objecting to any man, 'even if he looked like a card-carrying member of CND'. But the acquittal was not an expression of sisterly love (one juror told them afterwards: 'I didn't do it because I agree with you'). The military authorities, rather as the women had hoped, were just thoroughly confused about what happened that night – who stole the bus, who took a ride on it, who simply cut through the fence and walked across the airfield. The prosecution therefore produced the wrong evidence, the women understandably declined to clarify matters, and in effect the case collapsed.

I am embarrassed to admit that as I listened to Rebecca's account of this escapade, absurd military comparisons sprang to mind. I visualised her in some old British Colditz-type war movie, playing the head of the escape committee – the difference being that her lot were devising ways of cutting their way in, rather than out. And that in turn reminded me of a story from someone called Liane in the camp's professional-looking news magazine, *The Greenham Factor*. She recalled a woman standing on another's shoulders at the perimeter fence, furiously cutting away at the wire as a panic-stricken soldier watched from the other side. Suddenly the woman with the bolt cutters smiled at the soldier and called out: 'Don't worry, we'll soon get you out of there!'

For her part, Rebecca pointed out that had the bus action been a military operation, her group would have arrived at the designated bus stop right on time at midnight, instead of lingering over the birthday party, and probably been arrested by the waiting MoD police – because she was fairly sure someone had tipped them off beforehand.

All the Greenham women to whom I have spoken assumed that in some degree, their movement was infiltrated by the security services, whether it was MI5, the American CIA, or just plainclothes police (from time to time female journalists would also disguise themselves as 'peace women' for a few days to provide their readers with the 'inside story'). MI5's infiltration of CND is well documented;[33] although according to that service's former intelligence officer Cathy Massiter the Greenham women were not officially regarded as subversive, they were certainly part of the wider protest movement monitored by Heseltine's DS19 unit in the Ministry of Defence, which had regular contact with MI5. In her judgement, most of the surveillance that did occur was the work of the police Special Branch.

Di McDonald reckoned they could usually spot a Special Branch plant because they would turn up in a car and take a pristine pair of wellies out of the boot. And she is quite certain the CIA took a close interest – close enough to know the registration number of her white VW van – because while in the United States she saw documents recording the story of how it ended up in a ditch off the Swan roundabout near Greenham. The van is now in a Bradford peace museum.

Many women seem to have taken the view that if the security services were not keeping an eye on the camp's activities, they certainly should have done. To ignore the protest altogether would have been almost insulting. Moreover any secret agent who spent any time at Greenham might have learnt something: that this was a non-violent, democratic movement with nothing to hide and nothing to be ashamed of.

The women drew the line, however, at suggestions (in the authoritative periodical *Jane's Defence Weekly* (*JDW*), reporting from Washington) that up to six female members of the Soviet Spetsnaz special forces recruited in east and west Europe had infiltrated their camp. Trained in remote areas of the USSR using mock-ups of the Berkshire airfield, it was claimed, the role of the Soviet agents was threefold: to incite protests so as to test the USAF defences, to sabotage the missile units in the event of war, and to act as 'beacons' for other Soviet forces.

'Although the agents are not now outside the perimeter wire', wrote *JDW*'s correspondent Yossef Bodansky,

> the Soviet Union still maintains a presence in the area which can be mobilised at short notice. Defectors and informants have given details to *Jane's Defence Weekly*. They are not being identified because they fear their lives are at stake and some still have relatives in their country of origin.

> After extensive inquiries in Washington, London and Greenham Common, *JDW* can exclusively reveal that:

> - There has been a regular rotation of agents to enable a large number to gain field experience. The operation is controlled by the GRU, the main intelligence directive of the Soviet General Staff. They are attached to the Western Theatre Military Command, headed by Marshal of the Soviet Union Nikolai Vasilevich Ogarkov.
> - The women agents are trained in camps situated in the Rovno–Lvov–Lutsk area of the Carpathian military district and the Ural and Volga military districts. They contain mock-ups of elements of the Greenham Common camp like the heavily guarded inner defence zone. There the women are trained to attack the missile sites under war or surprise conditions in a pre-emptive strike. They will act as 'beacons' for other Spetsnaz and airborne troops who would be used to attack the missiles in war.
> - These Spetsnaz women receive emergency cash via 'dead drops' when needed, or they travel abroad to meet their paymasters. The members of the network 'holiday' overseas to meet a controller – those who go to Austria go on to Czechoslovakia for a meeting; others who reach Yugoslavia, enter Bulgaria.[34]

Stories like this, quoting unnamed sources describing secret operations, are almost impossible to confirm or deny. But because of its political implications I felt obliged to follow this one up for my own newspaper. The Greenham women reacted with angry disbelief, dismissing the report as 'a ludicrous slur'. For my part, I pointed out that although in wartime both Spetsnaz and the SAS would no doubt be up to all kinds of tricks, the Soviet special forces were trained primarily as saboteurs, not spies. In wartime, defences around the Berkshire airfield would also be a lot more robust – unless, as planned, the missiles had already dispersed. Any agents provocateurs sitting round the Greenham campfires were more likely to be from Special Branch or the CIA (or just journalists looking for an inside story) than Communist assassins trained in the Urals.

Meanwhile the *Guardian*'s Alan Rusbridger (now the paper's editor) went down to investigate. After spending a wintry day with the Greenham women, he judged that for all her rigorous training, your average Olga from Spetsnaz would have been hard put to cope with such operational conditions:

> Supper might, if she was lucky, have been a slightly soiled Marmite sandwich. Bed would have been a plastic sheet and dampish sleeping bag. The night might well have been disturbed by agents from a crack unit of Newbury District Council's bailiffs. Around closing time, further crack units might have spilled out of the local pubs to kick down a tent or urinate on a sleeping form or two.[35]

Women and the law

For most of us, getting involved with 'the law' is something that only happens to other people. And no doubt most Greenham women saw it that way before the protest began. But such attitudes could not long survive the first arrests for breaching the peace or causing criminal damage. Not only were women facing the grim possibility of imprisonment. The whole purpose of their allegedly criminal acts was to draw attention to what they saw as a 'greater crime' inside the base, and to publicise that protest in the theatrical setting of a court of law. A crash course in court procedure and legal jargon was essential. And some women soon went way beyond this.

They found that if they understood the legal system, they could occasionally beat it. A few of them – women like Sarah Hipperson, herself a former magistrate and a long-term resident of the Yellow Gate peace camp – actually began to relish a legal challenge. They realised they could turn the law to positive advantage in their battles with the military establishment. Two of them, Jean Hutchinson and Georgina Smith, eventually spent four years contesting MoD bye-laws right through to the House of Lords – and won. And this case proved to be of crucial importance not just to the hundreds of women who had been wrongly convicted under those same bye-laws, but also to Greenham and Crookham commoners fighting to retain their ancient rights.

At the airfield, the representatives of the law were of course the police. Women cutting their way into the base might be spotted by US servicemen, or grabbed by British squaddies, but under the rules they had to be handed over to the MoD police and eventually to the civil constabulary. At certain periods, for set-piece demonstrations like 'Embrace the Base', for blockades and evictions, police were there in their hundreds. Local officers were reinforced from the neighbouring Wiltshire force, Thames Valley and London's Met, with occasional support from rapid-response units. Arrests were numbered in thousands (probably 4,000 in the first five years). Newspapers delighted in calculating for their readers how many millions of pounds it was all costing 'the taxpayer' (£3.7 million in 1983 alone, according to one report).

For individual bobbies it was a pretty thankless task, especially in winter, even if some found consolation in substantial overtime payments, and the realisation that soldiers patrolling the inside of the fence were working and living in much worse conditions. Nor could they pretend that forcing the passage of a nuclear convoy through a crowd of frantic women at midnight was 'just another traffic job', in spite of exhortations to this effect. How they coped, and how they dealt with the women they had to manhandle, was down to individual personality and experience, as it always is in these situations. Some were detached, others sympathetic. One or two of the older men were made the more cautious by knowing that their own daughters could be taking part in the protests. Some adopted the women's survival tactics, building shelters in the woods and warming themselves with camp fires – until these too were banned under Newbury's bye-laws.

In general, the women reckoned the local police were more friendly than those bussed in from further afield, though this generalisation did not always hold good. It was a local policeman, Sarah Hipperson recalls, who told her: 'There isn't anything anyone can do to you lot I would consider criminal.'

For women arrested and charged, the next stage in the legal process was usually Newbury Magistrates' Court. (In supposedly more serious cases they could opt for a jury trial in the Crown Court, but experience showed that if found guilty, they risked heavier penalties.) At first, bewildered lay magistrates made an effort to treat this new breed of defendant courteously, and to listen patiently as women explained the motives behind their protests. As the cases multiplied, however, attitudes hardened. Legal aid was often denied. Women who insisted on telling 'the whole truth and nothing but the truth' – which meant expounding their views on the dangers of nuclear escalation at length before admitting, incidentally, to having damaged the Greenham fence – were cut short, or warned they were in contempt of court.

Women responded either by talking on regardless, or perhaps breaking into song. The solemn rituals of the law were being mocked, or at least ignored. There was pandemonium in court, not silence. And, to cap it all, guilty women would refuse to pay fines or be bound over to 'keep the peace' (on the grounds that they were already trying to do just that), leaving magistrates little option but to send them to prison.

Looking back in 1986 on her own early experience of the law, Rebecca Johnson felt that this suffragette tactic – refusing to pay fines or be bound over – was 'one of the most powerful instruments in our dealings with the courts'. Taking responsibility for their actions was central to their approach: 'We admit the facts of cutting fences or painting if that is what we have done, and claim that the law entitles us to take such actions if it is to save life. We argue passionately that to commit technical offences by non-violent actions to alert people to the genocidal deployment of nuclear weapons is justifiable if one genuinely believes one is in real danger.'[36]

As pressure on the Newbury court intensified, full-time stipendiary magistrates (nowadays known as district judges) were called in. The women found their professional approach preferable in some respects. They would not be bullied by their clerks. They had the confidence to question police evidence. But in other ways they were tougher on the women. For example, it was the stipendiaries who began the practice of refusing to accept the peace camp as an address, chiming in with the RAGE demand that women living there should not be allowed to vote in local elections. And, predictably, they seemed to prefer to keep proceedings within the narrowest legal confines. Attempts by women to argue 'lawful excuse', by explaining their personal fears of nuclear war, were quickly interrupted.

'Virtually the only consistent aspect in Greenham's changing relationship with the law', Rebecca concluded at that time, 'has been the courts' adamant refusal to recognise the political purpose of what we are doing.' She noted, in this context, that the authorities hesitated to use the Official Secrets Act.

In the end, all legal roads led to Holloway. The women's first experience of prison was inevitably a shock – the confinement, the noise, the strip searches, the general atmosphere of claustrophobia and depression – however well they had prepared mentally. But in dealing with it they had several big advantages. Their sentences were short and fixed (typically 14 days, although some did get several months), so the threat of lost remission or parole could not be held over them. They had numerous supportive contacts outside, sending letters and flowers. Above all, they never regarded themselves as criminals, and nor did the warders, whatever the law might say.

Helen John recalls deciding during her second stay in prison that she would try not cooperating – refusing even to speak to the staff. Next morning she was examined by an Indian doctor, who was told that this prisoner wouldn't speak. 'Ah', she said, 'so she's a political prisoner.' Like other Greenham women, Helen did her best to engage with other inmates and to help them, tackling the prison authorities on their behalf, sharing her flowers and her ideas. 'The story of Greenham and prisons was not a negative one,' she insists, 'it was very positive.'

Rebecca expressed similar concern from a different perspective:

> I quickly found out that most of the 'real criminals' were there for reasons as political as mine, and I lost the exalted notion that I was in a special category as a political prisoner. No account was taken of the context of their crimes either. Lawful excuse does not cover poverty, racism, sexual discrimination, male violence, unemployment and the lack of alternatives or opportunities.
>
> I learned a lot in prison. I listened a lot. I was appalled by the conditions some women, especially the mentally ill, endure. When I came out I could not stop telling people about the kindnesses I had received from women shut away 'for society's protection'.

Di McDonald remembers the kindness of a woman called Pearl, who took her under her wing as she tried to cope with the initial shock of imprisonment. Pearl was curious as to why anyone should in effect choose prison – by refusing to pay a fine – and alarmed by Di's further refusal to work assembling war toys. As predicted, this refusal led to serious trouble. 'I was taken to a kangaroo court; frog-marched along with two guards in front, two behind, a prison officer on each arm, into a little room to face the deputy governor. And she said; "You'll be punished for not doing as you're told."'

While Di was inside, the prison authorities organised an 'Easter Parade'. She decorated her hat with the suffragette colours of purple white and green. Rebecca came in singing, sporting a pirate's hat made from newspaper. There was a lot of singing. They all knew the Greenham songs. 'Yes, this episode of the kangaroo court. I was put in what was called a strip cell (a very bare room, with a cardboard table and chair, and a mattress on the floor). And there was another woman in a nearby cell for the same reason – refusing to pack war toys – and we sang ourselves hoarse, for hours and hours.'

Georgina Smith, who was later to turn the law back against the MoD in spectacular fashion, tried to convey the anxiety of her first prison experience (Pucklechurch in her case) in a poem she wrote on returning home:

Dizzy lying down
Sitting up squeamish
Cold hands, I need the cat on my lap
Looking at my cards
Remembering my friends remembering me
Why am I panicking?

She recalls the deliberate humiliation of the reception procedure, rattling keys and invading cockroaches, miserably barred windows, improvised scrabble, the cheery women who ran the workroom, with its bales of furry material from which she once made a kitten:

They finished off the kitten for me when I was put in solitary (for refusing to let the M.O. examine me because he wouldn't say what form the examination would take). Solitary didn't matter. I had the *Guardian*, which one of our daughters, Lucy, always got the newsagent to send in. And a tiny radio without an aerial. Prison was for sleeping and making plans, drawing and writing.

Over there

No one could accuse the Greenham women of parochialism. Having failed to persuade Newbury magistrates that nuclear cruise missiles were potentially genocidal as defined by the Genocide Act of 1969, and therefore illegal, they decided to challenge the President of the United States.

Stripped of its heavy politics the plan was simple: to obtain a judgment from the US Federal Court that Ronald Reagan's action in deploying the missiles in the UK was contrary to the international laws of war; and in the process (though even they could barely stretch optimism this far) persuade the US court to halt the deployment while the issue was resolved.

In the summer of 1983 they made contact with the Center for Constitutional Rights in New York (originally established to fight for civil rights in the 1960s), and it was agreed that thirteen women calling themselves 'Greenham Women Against Cruise Missiles' would act as plaintiffs, supported by as many organisations across Europe and America as could be mobilised in the time available. Time was extremely short – at least as time is measured by lawyers – because they already expected the missiles to arrive at Greenham in November.

In the event the request for an injunction halting the deployment was scheduled for 9 November, more than a week after the original arrival date chosen by the USAF and only five days before the missiles actually did arrive. To heighten the drama, and widen the publicity, an overnight candlelit vigil was held on the New York courthouse steps, while back in the UK 24-hour protest camps were organised outside every one of the 102 US bases or military facilities existing at that time, from St Mawgan to Scatsta, Brawdy to Mildenhall.

Judge Edelstein was unimpressed. He refused to grant the injunction, suggesting in explanation that the deployment was still probably a couple of weeks away. Instead, he promised to consider US government arguments for dismissing the case outright (presented by Rudolph Giuliani, later Mayor of New York at the time of the 9/11 attacks) on 22 November. His judgment

was not delivered until July 1984, when he ruled that contrary to the government's opinion, his court *did* have jurisdiction, but that unfortunately the
issue was far too complicated for this or any other court to resolve. It was a
disappointing outcome for the women, but it did at least mean they could
mount an appeal, for which they assembled a large team of experts. These
witnesses were then able to explore every aspect of the missiles' technology,
strategy and physical effects. They argued that such vastly destructive
weapons were inherently genocidal (recapitulating on this much larger stage
the arguments raised in the women's first Newbury Magistrates Court trial
for breaching the peace) and that the use of slow-flying 'first-use' missiles
like these violated the principles of the United Nations.

Of course they still lost the case. It did not stop the Greenham deployment. No one ever really expected that it would, notwithstanding all that
legal argument, all that intellectual effort. If history is written by the victors,
so too are the laws of war. And if they prove inconvenient, a state as powerful as the USA will surely ignore them – witness Guantánamo Bay.

Jane Hickman, who was involved in the US case as a solicitor, and on
whose account of it I have relied,[37] nevertheless rejects such a counsel of
despair. Writing in 1986, she argued passionately that the women's effort
was worthwhile, first because it forced the US government at least to some
extent to answer their case, and second because it raised public awareness
of the international laws governing warfare. And she made the added point
that if, as some claim, the laws of war are unworkable or irrelevant, why
do we so readily accept the concept of a 'war crime'?

The case was an example, she wrote in conclusion, of the steps even
small groups of people can take to bring the law to others' attention:

> It is ironic that in discussing both branches of the law of war the onus
> apparently rests on individuals, the mere subjects of sovereign states,
> acting alone or collectively to develop and enforce international laws.
> Yet this is the situation we are in. A consciousness of this fact is growing
> in this country.
>
> It is for this reason that the peace movement has grown so
> dramatically in the past few years. The establishment of the peace camp
> at Greenham Common has, in the minds of many people, led to a
> radical reassessment of the law, the way it operates, and its importance
> both domestically and internationally.

Since those Greenham days, there have been some vicious wars, but
also one or two encouraging developments so far as the law is concerned.

New international courts have indeed indicted military commanders and political leaders for war crimes, including genocide. In Britain, much to the government's embarrassment, the Iraq invasion revealed widespread public interest in whether that war was legal, as well as a sharp professional concern among the military top brass to have the Attorney General's judgement on its legality in writing before British forces were committed.

The Greenham women's audacious venture into the US Federal Court was just one aspect of a sustained effort to disseminate their message worldwide and to build mutually supportive contacts – especially in the United States, where the missiles were made, and in the Netherlands, Belgium, Germany and Italy, where they would also be deployed. Foreign visitors were constantly turning up at the camp, to ask questions and to answer them. A Polynesian delegation came literally from the other side of the world to stand under umbrellas outside the main gate, explaining the impact of French nuclear testing in the Pacific. And with the visitors came return invitations. Helen John had barely settled into her new life at the camp before she was off to Amsterdam for a conference, which she recalls involving twenty five different nationalities. She relished the opportunity to widen both her own experience and the scope of the protest.

Whether they were flying off to some European capital or – much more likely – talking to the Nottingham Women's Institute, the women had their own term for spreading the word in this way. They did not 'address meetings' – they 'did speaks'. The blunt language conveys a determination to communicate as directly as possible, rather than through the filter of academic or political convention. Women were not chosen to do speaks because they were already accomplished public speakers, or recognised as leaders – though obviously some were quicker to volunteer, while others always held back. Youngsters were not barred by their age.

Nor was there any need, at least as Di McDonald remembers it, to dress up for the occasion: 'We made it acceptable to turn up at a conference in mud-covered boots, thick socks and bright colours. The clothing was part of a statement of positive life, in complete contrast to the death machine of the military.' When she told them about Greenham, there were two typical questions: why was the peace camp women-only, and why did they have to live in such appalling conditions? And her typical response was no doubt to accentuate the positive, just as she did in conversation with me, lest I should think the Greenham experience was nothing but mud and evictions: 'It wasn't a drab or miserable place; we didn't reject having a good time. One of the things about Greenham was the colour, and the verve. We weren't martyrs – we were celebrating life. Many said they had never had such a wonderful time in their lives.'

It was two friends from the original Greenham march, Ann Pettitt and Karmen Cutler, who conceived the idea of taking their message to Moscow. They were near the end of another protest march at the time – to Brawdy in South Wales. Not for the first time, a passing motorist catching sight of their banners yelled out: 'Why don't you tell that stuff to the Russians?' Ann was sitting minding some of the kids in the tiny Pembrokeshire village of Maenclochog when it dawned on her that far from this being just a meaningless jibe, it might be an excellent idea – 'to go and find out whether there were people like us there'.

They starting searching for any information they could find about the Russians, and the practicalities of organising such a trip at a time when obtaining a visa for the Soviet Union was a monumental exercise in diplomatic bureaucracy. By chance Ann came across an American, Jean McCallister, who spoke fluent Russian (having worked on a Soviet fishing boat, apparently). The American was attempting to address a meeting in North London called by European Nuclear Disarmament (END), the campaigning group trying to break down barriers between East and West, but was being shouted down by Communist Party women. Afterwards Ann managed to track her down and she agreed to join the trip as their interpreter. What is more, she put them in touch with Olga Medvedkova, a dissident Muscovite from the Group for the Establishment of Trust between the USSR and the USA.

It was arranged that the three of them would make a week's visit in May 1983, using the old name 'Women for Life on Earth', and try to arrange for a larger group of perhaps 30 women to visit in the following autumn. Their accommodation was in the decayed grandeur of the Metropole Hotel in central Moscow, the sort of place, Karmen recalls, 'where there are fountains in the dining room but you have to bribe the waiters to give you any food'. They did make some contacts with interested, hospitable people, talking late into the night. With some of them they held a 'peace picnic' in the Lenin Hills above Moscow, sticking posters on the trees and watched by curious passers-by – plus a bunch of heavy-set men who seemed to follow them everywhere.

As far as the Soviet authorities were concerned, the formal climax of their trip was supposed to be a meeting between 'the heroines of Greenham' – assumed by the Russians to be anti-American rather than just anti-nuclear weapons – and the official Soviet Peace Committee under its vice-chairman Oleg Khakardin. It had been arranged through a Quaker group back in England. But it did not go at all smoothly. As my colleague Jonathan Steele, the *Guardian*'s Moscow correspondent, reported: 'It must have been one of the most difficult encounters the Peace Committee has ever had to endure.'[38]

The three women took along their 'Moscow representative', who introduced herself, in front of the television cameras, as Olga Medvedkova. She was of course known to Khakardin as a member of a dissident group the KGB had been trying for years to suppress. Her unexpected presence left the Russians 'completely stunned'. They turned to their boss, waiting for his reaction. Feet were shuffled, cigarette packets tapped, fingers drummed on the table 'like an army of mice'. Eventually the tough old Stalinist vice-chairman pulled himself together. If Medvedkova had anything to say to them, he declared, it was not at that table and not at that time.

However, the women stood their ground. Ann and Karmen explained that Olga was a woman for peace. She was with them, and should be allowed to speak. Khakardin interrupted to say that, on the contrary, her presence was a provocation. Yet the meeting did continue, and the Greenham women tried to explain that they weren't 'anti' anyone – just the danger posed by the escalating nuclear arms race. They were hoping to organise further visits, to make contacts with ordinary Russians in their homes and workplaces, perhaps make a documentary film to show people back home what life was really like in the Soviet Union, and so on.

There *were* further visits, though not in the form they had envisaged. Karmen went back but Ann could not get a visa. Some months later Olga was arrested for assaulting a policeman, though not finally imprisoned, thanks in part perhaps to strong protests on her behalf from Greenham women. The last Karmen heard of her she had apparently emigrated to America, where her son later joined the US Marines.

At the wire

'This is Our Berlin Wall'

Greenham women's notice

Fences are natural to military organisations, anathema to those fighting to preserve public access to common land. So the wire fence erected round Greenham and Crookham commons for the benefit of the US Air Force was bound sooner or later to be contentious. For Greenham women, it was the immediate focus of activity.

The protest had begun when four women chained themselves to the fence outside the main gate and refused to 'move on' when requested. As the campaign developed, cutting through the wire was the prelude to most of their 'actions'. Big demonstrations sometimes involved pulling down long stretches of the fence. It was both a symbolic barrier to communication with an alien military force and the specific piece of MoD property whose destruction so often led to a court appearance. Eventually, when it was already clear the missiles were on their way out, the women discovered to their delight that the modern fence was technically unlawful, a discovery that was also crucial for commoners just beginning their own battle with Whitehall.

The original RAF airfield was not fenced in. The runway was simply laid out across the commons, as if to emphasise the temporary nature of the military occupation. When the Americans returned after the war, however, most of the perimeter was enclosed with wire mesh, though with just wooden posts and rails at the western end. Over the years rust and rot did their work, gradually opening up gaps local people, walking their dogs or whatever, would occasionally use.

Chris Austin, a local huntsman who was later to lead the commons restoration campaign, recalls broken places where he could jump his horse in, ride across the airfield and jump out again: 'I remember once a fox cut the corner of the base and the whole hunt went across.'

The new fence confronting the women consisted of plastic-coated chain-link wire strung between concrete posts about 10 foot high. At the top the

The fence still standing at the women's 'Green Gate', patched, re-patched and patched again after their many incursions.

posts were cranked outward, threaded with three strands of barbed wire. A small length of this structure still survives around the missile silos in the south-west corner of the former airfield, by what the women called Green Gate. The wire mesh is patched, re-patched and patched again where a long succession of bolt cutters went to work.

To a remarkable extent, it was the physical nature of this barrier that determined the protest. Had there been no fence at all, or just the simple railings over which Chris Austin jumped his horse before the airfield acquired such strategic importance, demonstrators would of course have been able to overrun the base and disrupt its operation without difficulty. Had there been a solid wall, or even the modern weld-mesh fencing which surrounded the missile silos and bomb storage 'igloos' – much harder to cut through – human contact between the two communities, inside and out, would have been largely precluded. The protest would have taken a different form.

Given the vast sums of money the British government poured into the cruise missile programme and the years of unwelcome publicity the women's campaign generated, I have always been puzzled as to why Michael Heseltine did not build a more formidable barrier round Greenham – welded mesh, alarms, razor wire, the works. It seems all the more strange when one realises the quite extraordinary enthusiasm with which he organised the fencing operation at Molesworth – the second British cruise missile base in Cambridgeshire:

> We planned it on the basis that in the war they planned the Mulberry harbour – that was where the idea came from. We had to assemble all the kit, and all the people, so that after the Press had gone to bed, and the last broadcast had taken place, we moved. And by six o'clock the next morning, before any newspapers could be changed, and before anyone had listened to the radio or television, we had completed the eight-mile fence. It was the single biggest thing the Royal Engineers had done since they crossed the Rhine in 1944.
>
> And it was done immaculately. Not a word leaked. Just think of it – the numbers of people, the amount of kit, all heading towards Molesworth, collected up and deployed, without a single journalist hearing about it. I mean, it was utterly miraculous.

The enclosure revealed that next morning consisted of triple coils of razor wire, within which the contractors could build a permanent fence. Although there was no runway to protect, it enclosed an area not far short of the Greenham airfield. The protest camp site was cleared in the process, though I remember noticing that the Cambridgeshire police – who seemed to have a more tolerant approach than their Berkshire colleagues – had left the half-built 'peace chapel' standing in its own wire circle, like some primitive do-it-yourself Norman chancel.

It was during his dawn inspection of the triumphant Molesworth operation that the Defence Secretary was photographed, and subsequently ridiculed, for wearing a camouflaged combat jacket. Heseltine insists it was simply offered to him by an RAF officer to keep off the rain. Fair enough – though I notice he was wearing a similar outfit when my colleague Ian Black accompanied him on a tour of the Greenham construction site some time before that. But as a long-term observer of defence secretaries, let me nevertheless offer future incumbents a piece of public relations advice: it never pays to adopt military dress. The press photographers will rush to take your picture, but in next morning's newspapers it will always strike the wrong note (Malcolm Rifkind later fell into the same trap when he donned combat kit to drive an armoured vehicle.) If necessary, just get your pinstripe suit muddy.

When I asked Michael Heseltine why he did not call in the Royal Engineers to repeat their Molesworth operation in Berkshire he pointed out, reasonably enough, that Greenham already had a fence, albeit an inadequate one hopelessly vulnerable to bolt cutters. But it was not as simple as that, and the full story is instructive.

One problem was obviously the cost, which in 1984 the Commons Defence Committee estimated at £3.5 million. In fact that was probably a serious underestimate, but, as the MPs pointed out, policing the protest had cost £3 million over the previous year, and there was still no end in sight. So the other explanation Heseltine offered me – that the Greenham airfield was common land – is more plausible, and much more significant than most people then realised.

By the time MoD civil servants gave evidence to a second Defence Committee inquiry, they were already treading warily round the legal quagmire that ancient rights of common were opening up. They admitted they were conducting confidential negotiations with the district and county authorities about a land swap that would help eliminate the main Yellow Gate camp, and create a buffer zone between the perimeter and the missile silos. But this tactic was inhibited by the fact that their combined holdings of common land could not be increased. Another idea was to shrink the airfield perimeter so as to make it easier to patrol, but that would have left more common land on which the women could camp.

Looking back at all this from a political world in which New Labour's ministerial thugs seem to have few qualms about sacrificing ancient legal rights in the name of security, it seems to me to the credit of that earlier generation of civil servants – and of the Defence Secretary they served – that they were so fastidious. Prime Minister Tony Blair's lot, one suspects, would have sent in the bulldozers first and tried to dodge the awkward questions afterwards.

However, there was one extraordinary proposal doing the rounds in the 1980s which was not in the least fastidious: to deter the Greenham women's incursions by electrifying the perimeter fence. I have not been able to discover from which dark corner of officialdom this crackpot idea emerged, but emerge it certainly did, as Heseltine has tacitly acknowledged. Notwithstanding his passionate determination to win his propaganda war with the anti-nuclear movement, he must instantly have realised that such a draconian measure would be counterproductive. His advisers simply pointed out that, commoners' rights or no, it was an impossible idea. It might be lawful under some circumstances to shoot the women, but not to electrocute them.

The MoD was forced in the end to fall back on an unsatisfactory compromise: leave the outer fence as it was, with a few extra rolls of barbed wire, watchtowers and so on, and accept that the women would break in without much difficulty. Serious physical security would be concentrated around the nuclear citadel, with its new multiple fencing and armed guards.

The authorities were encouraged in this approach – falsely, as it happened – by the knowledge that a comprehensive set of new bye-laws was in preparation, to come into force on 1 April 1985. These would make it illegal to enter the base, regardless of the damage caused in the process. Women could be charged with trespass (rather than criminal damage or breaching the peace), a charge against which there was little obvious defence.

So for the women, the fence remained much as it was when they first arrived, to be alternately decorated with ribbons or attacked with bolt cutters. It formed a sort of semi-permeable membrane through which a limited amount of movement and communication was possible. Helen John remembers one woman, a visiting German who had lost her family in a Nazi concentration camp, for whom the grim symbolism of the fence was overwhelming. As they walked round the perimeter one evening, her visitor turned to address the young policeman following them with a guard dog just inside the wire. Last time men built anything like this, she told him, the people they intended to kill were on the inside. Here at Greenham the potential victims were on the outside, but it amounted to the same thing, and, so far as she was concerned, he was the same as those concentration camp guards.

Helen was impressed by how the German woman's words struck home: 'He was very upset, in tears, and said he was not that type of man. But she patiently pointed out to him that he was, because he had made a choice, to support what was behind him.'

A statutory instrument

In the spring of 1985, having failed to remove the women from Greenham by direct physical eviction, the MoD launched a fresh attack on the legal front. Its big idea was that the Defence Secretary should use the century-old Military Lands Act 1892 to draft new bye-laws for the regulation of RAF Greenham Common. This would make it a criminal offence to trespass on the airfield, regardless of whether the fence was damaged in the process, or whether there was some associated 'breach of the peace'. It looked simple and effective. One foot inside the wire and a woman could be done for trespass. No arguments in court, virtually no defence.

The new bye-laws came into effect on 1 April. And at the stroke of midnight more than a hundred women – determined to make an April Fool of this new tactic – broke into the base to test them. Sarah Hipperson, the Scots grandmother who was developing a taste for legal argument that would carry her through many subsequent challenges, remembers the official discomfiture this caused: 'We were throwing down the gauntlet. It took all night to process the women. They had to bring police from all sorts of places.'

Initially, the women wanted simply to swamp the new system and see how the authorities reacted. But 17 days later, two of them unknowingly set up a test case that would preoccupy the MoD's lawyers for years to come. In Greenham protest terms, it was a small, routine event. Somebody had been holding a 21st birthday party, and afterwards Jean Hutchinson and Georgina Smith took a walk along the perimeter wire to see what the Americans were up to. From one of the hangars they heard a sound they recognised: the powerful diesel engine of a cruise missile launcher being revved up. Perhaps a convoy was preparing to leave for Salisbury Plain, in which case it had to be challenged. They slipped through a gap in the wire cut by women from Blue Gate the previous night and ran across the airfield.

In the prohibitive words of the Defence Secretary's statutory instrument, the two women 'did enter, pass through or over, or remain in or over, the

Protected Area without authority or permission given by, or on behalf of, one of the persons mentioned in bye-law 5(1)'. Georgina put it rather differently, in a poem she called 'Trespass':

After the party I'm ready to drop
The hangar door squeaks open at the favourite hour
We're waiting for the revving up
The hole, the barbs, the bank, the run
The long wall we peep round
The long launcher set there
Familiar, evil.
The ranting, the running round
The feel of taking over
The satisfaction of shouting out
It's worth another charge.

They were indeed charged and convicted at West Berkshire Magistrates Court on 23 July 1986, and promptly set about preparing an appeal, assembling as many different defences as they could conjure up. This was not an easy task in such a simple, clear-cut case. Lawyers they consulted could see 'no legal merit' in the appeal, and advised that it would be 'unprofessional' to proceed. Disillusioned but obstinate, Georgina remembers jointly deciding with Jean that there was only one way forward: 'Well get the buggers on our own.'

One obscure point they came across in the 1892 Military Lands Act used by the MoD to support its new bye-laws was a reference to 'rights of common'. The late-Victorian legislation had evidently been drafted to enable the War Office to commandeer land where local yeomanry or militias could practise their drills (in time for the second Boer War). In fact the Newbury heaths had in the past been used for such military manoeuvres. But, crucially, the Act stipulated that any bye-laws made to keep people safely clear of the army's firing ranges should not 'take away or prejudicially affect any right of common'. And the women realised there were about 60 local people who still possessed archaic rights on Greenham and Crookham commons – to set pigs loose in search of acorns, to graze cattle, dig peat or whatever. These 'commoners' had of course been unable to exercise their rights on the airfield for the past 50 years, and all but a few had not the slightest intention of ever exercising them in the future. But if that was what the law said, it might provide a defence.

One of the people with whom they talked it over was Leslie Pope, a retired National Insurance inspector living in Newbury. Leslie was both sympathiser and supporter. By an appropriate coincidence, his original wartime boss when he worked in Bethnal Green, London, had been a Miss Gertrude Fishwick, an ex-suffragette credited by Christopher Driver as the original instigator of the Campaign for Nuclear Disarmament.[39] Leslie's wife Wendy was among the hundreds of other women who deliberately flouted the new MoD bye-laws, arguing in her own defence – to the evident boredom of the magistrates who subsequently convicted her – that the Military Lands Act and the bye-laws it spawned were both unnecessary and undemocratic, especially since not a single woman had voted for the parliament which produced the original legislation.

Leslie Pope had a civil servant's sharp eye for detail. With the help of the National Council for Civil Liberties, he had already thwarted Newbury Council's attempt to ban meetings on common land around the airbase by pointing out that the relevant statutory instrument merely authorised them to 'regulate' assemblies, not to prohibit them. Now he was watching the MoD developments and working with Wendy on her appeal.

Their painstaking study of documents at the Public Record Office in Kew showed no evidence that the MoD had ever revoked the public right of access to Crookham Common (the bit of heath on which Wendy was supposed to have trespassed) granted by its original private owners. This was going to be the basis of her appeal. But they had also heard from Elizabeth Abraham, an eccentric Greenham woman who was fascinated by the history of the commons and the historic rights attached to them, that they might find some legal ammunition there. So they also searched the county's Commons Register, which showed there were about 30 commoners who still held rights at Greenham and about the same number at Crookham. Accordingly, when Georgina explained that she and Jean were thinking of adding the rights of common argument to their defence case, Leslie was all for it: 'I said "I think you've got a point; put it in." And a good thing I did, because all their other points went down the drain. Judge Lait dismissed them. But he accepted this last one.'

His Honour Judge 'Josh' Lait, who sat in the Crown Court, is a pivotal figure in this story. The women actually liked him. He was courteous. He took them seriously. He even appreciated their legal jokes, as when they would carefully list the number of pigs or geese that were entitled to roam the airfield. 'You mean to tell me that twenty pigs could stop World War III', Jean Hutchinson remembers him saying. For Sarah Hipperson, he was 'an independent, fair-minded human being who always listened to our evidence even if he didn't agree with us' – a remarkable accolade from someone who felt that the local Magistrates Court merely reflected Newbury's collective hostility towards the Greenham women, its atmosphere 'poisoned by prejudice'.

Precisely what Josh Lait made of the women I cannot say. I did track him down in retirement, but he was as discreet as only a lawyer or a priest can be, explaining carefully that 'our approach was to listen to both sides patiently and courteously, then decide what the law was, and what the facts were'. In other words, he tried to do a thoroughly professional job, and the clarity of his judgments in this case bear that out. They vindicated the women's decision – at great financial risk in some instances – to take on the legal might of Whitehall. They also laid the legal foundations of the separate campaign which was to recover the commons from military occupation.

The crucial importance of commoners' rights became clear as soon as Judge Lait began hearing the trespass appeal on 2 April 1987, behind the forbidding baroque frontage of Reading Crown Court. The government's counsel realised the women were on to something, and immediately asked for a three-month adjournment to consider the MoD's response. It made no difference. When the hearing resumed on 17 June, the judge declared that the two women not only had a case; it was 'of substance'. But to their dismay, he went on to explain that since the outcome of the appeal had such wide implications (there were dozens of other trespass cases in the legal pipeline), he needed to check with a higher court as to whether a relatively lowly Crown Court judge should rule on it.

Alarmed that the appeal might after all be lost, Sarah Hipperson and a group of other women attending the Reading court rushed straight back to Greenham where they openly cut down sixteen sections of the airfield fence and deliberately courted arrest, watched by a bunch of Americans playing baseball. The women feared their understanding judge might have been nobbled. They wanted to be sure there would be another test case. They even painted their names on the bolt cutters to record their personal involvement.

They need not have worried. Josh Lait was told to go ahead, and on 25 February 1988 he finally gave his ruling: that the Defence Secretary had exceeded his authority under the 1892 Act by making the bye-laws – in legal terms they were *ultra vires* – because in doing so he had prejudicially affected commoners' rights. It followed that those bye-laws, under which Jean Hutchinson and Georgina Smith had been convicted, were invalid.

Their convictions would therefore be quashed. And if they were wrongly convicted, so were more than a thousand other women charged with trespass since the bye-laws supposedly came into force.

At this stage, the two women might reasonably have thought they could claim victory. But the state was not ready to concede defeat. On the contrary, it was determined to drag out the legal argument as long as possible while MoD officials worked out what to do next.

The Director of Public Prosecutions therefore asked the Divisional Court for its opinion on whether Judge Lait's ruling was correct. And in this arcane legal world you do not get an opinion just by picking up a telephone. Two judges in the Queen's Bench Division spent seven days listening to the arguments all over again, and in October 1988 came up with a contradictory new judgment, whose verbal contortions were worthy of Gilbert and Sullivan. They acknowledged that the Defence Secretary Michael Heseltine had unfortunately been labouring under the mistaken belief that he was empowered to make certain bye-laws. But in their view this did not invalidate the two women's convictions, because had he realised his mistake, he would not have made it. Exceptions would have been made so as to protect the commoners' rights while still penalising the women for trespass under those parts of the bye-laws which remained valid.

From the women's perspective, this looked like a shameless reversal of the old principle that ignorance of the law is no defence. Their lawyers accordingly sought permission to appeal to the highest court in the land, the House of Lords – which was granted. But bear in mind that the case had already been under way for more than two years, during which the situation at Greenham Common had totally changed.

The appeal was heard by five law lords on 13 November 1989. Leslie Pope was there to support the two women, as he had been at all the previous hearings. He was struck by the way this final court of appeal dispensed with the theatrical hierarchy of the lower courts, where judges look down sternly from their benches on the accused awaiting judgment. Here in the House of Lords, paradoxically, everyone was on the same level: the five judges arranged in a horseshoe facing the two legal teams, with a couple of rows of chairs at the back for interested members of the public. The atmosphere was altogether less formal, almost conversational. But Leslie also noted the disparity between the small legal team on the women's side, all of them female, and the massed ranks of dark-suited male lawyers opposite – 'they had come to win'.

In this they were disappointed. On 12 July 1990, just eleven days short of four years since the original conviction, their lordships delivered their judgment in favour of the two Greenham women. First, they reaffirmed Judge Lait's ruling that Jean Hutchinson and Georgina Smith were wrongly convicted, because under the Military Lands Act the Secretary of State was not permitted to make bye-laws which prejudicially affected rights of common. Then they dismissed the Divisional Court's notion that the Defence Secretary's lawyers had inadvertently failed to notice this bit of the Act so that the women, who were not themselves commoners, were still guilty. Their judgment pointed out that five other sets of bye-laws made by the MoD under the same section of the Act between 1976 and 1980 all contained careful, express provisions to safeguard commoners' rights. In short, the MoD must at some level have known it did not have the legal authority to create the 1985 Greenham bye-laws.[40]

It was a famous victory. Two Greenham women had realised the importance of ancient rights of common foolishly ignored by the MoD, taken on the state, with its virtually unlimited financial and legal resources, and won. Yet sadly, the outcome was in some ways an anticlimax. Of the many hundreds of women who were wrongly accused of trespass, only a few took the trouble to have their convictions formally quashed. As soon as the House of Lords judgment was published, some local women like Wendy Pope did go back to the Crown Court. Josh Lait duly reimbursed the £320.57 she had spent obtaining a legal opinion for her appeal, travelling back and forth to the court, and so on. But most of those involved had long since left Greenham. Any compensation for their wrongful arrest and conviction was apparently a matter for the Home Office rather than the courts, and the Home Office did not think it was appropriate.

Most of those who would eventually benefit from this legal challenge were not Greenham women at all, but residents of Newbury, who generally regarded the protest as a public nuisance. The bye-laws case began to expose the surprisingly shaky legal foundations on which the military presence at Greenham was built, and the real power embodied in rights of common. Both discoveries would prove invaluable when the time came to reclaim the town's lost commons.

Just another job

Dawn Hewitt, scarcely 5 foot tall in her boots, corn-coloured pigtail tucked under her hat, was another of the Greenham women. The difference was that she lived and worked inside the wire, not outside. I met her in November 1986, when the Pentagon and the Ministry of Defence took a major policy decision to allow the news media to see for themselves what went on inside the base.

By then, all 96 of the 501st Tactical Missile Wing's weapons were operational (Greenham was the only cruise missile base where this was achieved). More than 2,000 USAF personnel and their families were established in and around the airfield. Facilities on the base itself, though modest by American standards, were more or less comprehensive – a food mall and a bowling alley had recently been opened. The women's protest against the nuclear presence continued, but both sides in the argument had to some extent come to terms with one another. Although the missile convoys never went unchallenged as they left the base, by now their crews were accustomed to running the gauntlet of protesting women. As one USAF officer put it: 'the siege mentality was fading'.

When the airfield gates were finally opened to a small group of press and television correspondents, there, as if deliberately to ram home the symbolism of the occasion, was this quite different kind of Greenham woman (the *Guardian's* sub-editor could not resist calling her a 'blonde bombshell'[41]) with her finger literally on the nuclear button. Twenty-four-year-old First Lieutenant Hewitt volunteered for duty at Greenham while she was still doing her USAF-sponsored degree in computer science. She had heard then about the NATO plan to deploy ground-launched nuclear cruise missiles throughout Europe. In the American world of nuclear deterrence, the US-based Minuteman intercontinental ballistic missile had more status than the humble GLCM, but Dawn said she particularly wanted to come to England, because her home town of Boston, Massachusetts, had strong – if not always harmonious – English affiliations.

Dawn's post with the 501st was launch-control officer. Her wartime role was to sit in a mobile control centre hidden somewhere in the English countryside (the kind of vehicle the Cruisewatchers regularly pursued across Salisbury Plain), waiting for the order to send her flight of nuclear missiles on their way to the Soviet Union. When I asked her how she coped with this awesome responsibility, she said she had no intention of discussing her emotions in public. As it was, nobody would ever take her seriously after all this attention from the press cameras. And, no, she had not spoken to the women outside the gate – indeed she was under orders not to do so.

Given the elaborate, artificial secrecy that had surrounded this young woman's working life, perhaps it *was* rather daunting to stand there, watched by her senior officers, answering a string of journalists' questions. Finally she took refuge in the verbal formula that has comforted many others charged with mass destruction for reasons they do not fully understand – 'I do my job.' And I remembered that I had heard those words before, five years earlier, from US Army Lieutenant Rebecca Katz, when I visited the British Rhine Army nuclear artillery unit to which she was attached.

In Germany, the US lieutenant was operating a 'dual key' controlling the use of an American warhead attached to a British missile. Here at Greenham there was no such oversight, but for other security reasons the flight lieutenant did work in tandem with another junior officer. Inside the control vehicle they sat at identical consoles, in air-conditioned comfort that would coincidentally protect them from nerve gas or nuclear fallout.

It was the other half of the team, First Lieutenant Mark Carter, who explained the final launch procedure. Looking back, it reminds me of the step-by-step process many of us use these days when ordering a budget airline ticket on the Internet, culminating with a reminder, before you finally confirm the booking, that you will not get a refund if you cancel.

The US President's orders would be passed down through the USAF and NATO chains of command. With the orders would come weapons-release codes (some of which had to be punched into the launch-control computer by both officers simultaneously) plus targeting data he would use, but not understand. Finally, a simple message would flash up on the screen – 'RECOMMEND EXECUTE'. If he was satisfied the computer knew what it was doing, he would follow its recommendation by pressing the small green button on the left of the console. There was no recall button.

The missile launch team's boss, and base commander, was Hungarian-born Colonel John Bachs. Unlike his subordinates, he was prepared to talk about the women's protest, so as to emphasise – for the purposes of this set-piece press occasion – that their presence outside the gates had if anything increased his men's determination to demonstrate their professional readiness. He also pointed out something I felt the women were inclined to forget: that a real nuclear alert would be 'a different ball game'. The missile convoy's route would be forcibly cleared and its launchers protected by an armed force of 44 men, of whom a third would be members of the RAF regiment.

The new openness and confidence with which the Americans showed off their nuclear hardware that autumn can largely be explained by just one word – Gorbachev. In March the previous year Mikhail Gorbachev had become General Secretary of the Soviet Communist Party and had almost immediately decided, among the many fundamental reforms he introduced, that his country could no longer afford to be crippled by the East–West arms race. After long years of virtual deadlock, during which arms control negotiations between the two superpowers had inched only grudgingly forward, they began to leap ahead with almost embarrassing speed.

As Michael Heseltine had often reminded his political opponents, it was explicit in NATO's 'twin-track' decision of 1979 that its new European missile deployment would be modified or reversed if parallel arms control talks with Soviet Union succeeded in establishing lower limits. Since then Ronald Reagan, who became US President about a year later, had dramatically increased the prospects for disarmament with his offer of a 'zero option' – the Americans would scrap all their new Tomahawks and Pershings if the Russians would get rid of their SS-20s and other similar missiles threatening western Europe.

Against the background of recent experience, the zero option looked like pie in the sky. Good public relations, perhaps, but not a serious proposition so far as NATO's strategists were concerned. From their perspective, eliminating these new 'intermediate' forces would break the chain of graduated nuclear deterrence linking the USA with Europe at precisely the place where they had been planning to mend it. At most, they were prepared for negotiations to produce an East–West balance in this category of weapons at a lower level. However, since no one expected the Kremlin hardliners to take up Reagan's offer, they could afford to keep their doubts more or less to themselves.

Gorbachev had no such doubts. He regarded his predecessors' provocative deployment of SS-20s in eastern Europe as 'an unforgivable adventure', and fully understood NATO's reaction to it.[42] His determination to make a start on nuclear disarmament was strengthened in April 1986 by the catastrophic explosion of the nuclear power station at Chernobyl, a disaster he described as 'one more tolling of the bell that warns us that the nuclear epoch needs new political thinking'. The Soviet leader decided to call NATO's bluff, to take Reagan at his word about the zero option, which was soon expanded in scope to turn it into a 'double-zero option'. At allied military headquarters, they began to talk fearfully of the possibility of a 'triple-zero option', under which Western Europe would be completely de-nuclearised, and dangerously reliant – in their view – on conventional forces for its defence. As one senior official NATO official put it: 'People have become comfortable with their nuclear weapons. The prospect of losing them makes them feel as if their underwear has been removed.'

Nevertheless, the pace of the negotiations accelerated. By the time the Pentagon decided to open the Greenham gates, Reagan and Gorbachev had met in Reykjavik and come close to shaking hands on a disarmament deal so drastic that it left old campaigners in the arms control community catching their breath in disbelief. Only a residual dispute over Reagan's beloved 'Star Wars' programme prevented agreement. Later that October, when NATO defences ministers and military officials met at Gleneagles, Scotland, they had already coalesced into two main groups: those who wanted above all to take the zero option while it was going, and those, including the Supreme Allied Commander (SACEUR), US General Bernie Rogers, and his German deputy, who still advised caution. General Rogers rushed between Brussels, Washington and Gleneagles, warning any who would listen against 'decoupling' Europe from the US nuclear deterrent and leaving West Germany in particular vulnerable to short-range Soviet nuclear weapons not covered by the proposed deal on intermediate weapons.

At the end of the first day at Gleneagles, the new British Defence Secretary George Younger emerged from the meeting to declare that if the zero option was finally chosen, and all the cruise missiles were removed from Greenham, 'we could live with that'. Down in Berkshire, the Yanks knew they were probably on their way home.

After two decades of reporting painfully slow progress in East–West arms control, dogged by mutual suspicion, crippled by worst-case analysis, this sudden burst of positive disarmament negotiation was a wonder to behold. Until then there had been precious few successes to celebrate. In 1963 the Americans and Russians did stop the near-suicidal practice of testing atomic weapons in the atmosphere. Nine years later they managed to agree on an antiballistic missile treaty which indirectly slowed the numerical escalation of long-range nuclear weapons. Then there were the so-called SALT agreements, which limited their total numbers – but set the limits so high they were almost meaningless. Now suddenly, for the first time, an entire category of nuclear weapons would be eliminated.

The INF (Intermediate-range Nuclear Forces) Treaty was signed in Washington on 8 December 1987. It provided for the destruction of 2000 weapons – seven types of land-based missile, three American, four Soviet, with ranges from 300 to 3000 miles – under the scrutiny of both sides' inspectors to avoid any possibility of cheating. Included in these totals were the 96 Tomahawk cruise missiles at Greenham and the 16 missiles which had by then arrived at Molesworth in Cambridgeshire.

The treaty did not take effect until June 1988 and would then take three years to implement. So, for the time being, the military ritual of missile convoys dispersing to Salisbury Plain continued almost as if nothing had happened. The protesting women were not counting their chickens. But everyone understood that the terms of reference had totally changed, both for the USAF and for those campaigning against its presence. The residents of Newbury also woke to the realisation that their long fight to recover the two commons for the local community would shortly be resumed.

An unexpected welcome

On 19 July 1988, British air traffic controllers were suddenly asked to squeeze an extra flight plan into their overcrowded schedules – an Aeroflot Ilyushin 62 specially cleared from Moscow to Greenham Common. With the red flag of the USSR blazoned on its tail fin, the Soviet aircraft landed at the Berkshire airbase at 1.00 p.m. – an hour early because of a misunderstanding about British Summer Time – and two teams of Russian inspectors stepped down onto the US Air Force equivalent of a red carpet.

Among the unprecedented features that made the INF Treaty such a remarkable achievement were the tough provisions for what the diplomats call 'verification' – making sure both parties keep their word. In this case either party could descend on the other's nuclear bases with only a few hours' notice to count the weapons, search for any that might have been hidden away, or watch them being ritually destroyed. And that is what the Russians were now doing.

The irony of the resulting situation ran deep. After years spent trying to prevent access by the women protesters, worrying lest they had been infiltrated by Spetsnaz or the KGB, the Americans had actually invited NATO's potential enemies to crawl all over their base with cameras, tape measures and Geiger counters. Military secrets were not so much grudgingly disclosed as laid out for inspection. Indeed it occurred to me at the time that one of the unacknowledged forces driving the arms control process was the fascination this form of mutual legitimised 'spying' held for military professionals who had spent half a lifetime vainly striving to uncover the same secrets by conventional espionage.

For the British military establishment, where mindless secrecy was endemic, especially in nuclear matters, the culture shock must have been bewildering. The MoD's instinctive approach to nuclear deterrent forces – I'm caricaturing, but not much – was to pretend they did not exist. Whereas their French allies, in logical Cartesian fashion, would proudly show off their missiles to a foreign journalist and explain in detail how the President would launch them, the British liked to keep the other side guessing.

This uncertainty principle had its own logic (as Israel's dogged refusal to admit to possessing nuclear weapons has shown) but it sometimes led to absurdity. For example, MoD spokesmen were always trained 'neither to confirm or deny' the presence of nuclear weapons on any particular base, or warship, or aircraft – so as to deprive anti-nuclear campaigners of a clear target for their protests. The MoD could hardly apply this formula to the demonstrative NATO deployment at Greenham, but the habit reasserted itself at Molesworth, the second cruise missile base. As a result, the arrival of the first flight of cruise missiles at the Cambridgeshire base was reported in the *Guardian*, and no doubt elsewhere, for some time before it was officially acknowledged, even in Parliament. Only when the INF Treaty's database was about to be published in Washington was the Defence Secretary George Younger forced to own up (in response to a question from Labour MP Joan Ruddock), narrowly avoiding an embarrassing situation where MPs were the last to know what was happening in their own country.

When the 501st Missile Wing first realised what was in store for it in terms of inspections, as its official history records, it was not at all sure how to deal with the Russians: 'Did you treat visiting inspectors as hostile, or as dignitaries?' Eventually, it was decided to accord them diplomatic status, and in the event the whole process was conducted in a courteous, cooperative spirit on both sides.

This first visit involved two ten-man teams, one for a 'baseline' inspection at each of the British bases. Their leader, Vysacheslav Lebedev, promised they would abide by both the spirit and the letter of the Treaty, which he said 'paved the way to a de-nuclearised world'. His hopeful sentiment was echoed in a pamphlet prepared by the Greenham women for distribution to the visitors. 'We are glad you are making a start on dismantling these terrible weapons', it said in Russian. 'We hope it is the beginning of total disarmament.' What the Soviet inspectors would have made of this unofficial endorsement is not known, because seven women who slipped into the base that night to deliver the leaflets were arrested, Evelyn Parker among them. She admitted later that they had been surprised by a missile convoy rushing back from dispersal, and felt obliged to reveal their presence by mounting their usual Cruisewatch demonstration.

Under the Treaty's rules, the inspectors had to give at least 16 hours' notice of their arrival (the Americans had in any case been preparing for weeks). Having announced which base or bases they wanted to inspect, they had 24 hours to conduct their survey of the silos, hangars and training areas – anywhere a missile might be parked – then four hours to write their report. Curiously, they were not allowed to count the actual nuclear warheads, because, much to the Greenham women's disgust, these were not part of the deal.

The Russians were accommodated in part of a barrack block cleared for their use. According to their hosts, they really liked the American food served up in the Crusaders Inn – 'never missed a meal and always on time'. According to the *Newbury Weekly News*, they also slipped out for a pint at the Coach and Horses down at Midgham.

All six Soviet visits to Greenham before the USAF departed went equally smoothly, without a single complaint being filed. This was of lasting significance, because the INF Treaty model for 'challenge' inspections was then carried over to the much more extensive process of conventional, non-nuclear disarmament by NATO and the Warsaw Pact that began in 1990. And it worked well there too.

Under the Conventional Forces in Europe (CFE) agreement, thousands of tanks, guns and aircraft were systematically destroyed as the Cold War's military tide began to ebb away from the Iron Curtain that had divided Europe. Again, it was sometimes difficult to believe that such a rational process of mutual disarmament was really happening, and that both sides had their inspection teams hard at work.

By the winter of 1996 the Russians were sufficiently relaxed to allow a few journalists to accompany a British team paying an unannounced visit to a fighter airbase 200 miles east of Moscow, enabling us to see something of the procedures that had been pioneered at Greenham. The chief British inspector Major Margaret Roberts processed down the line of Su-27s, not merely counting the aircraft, but even noting the serial numbers stamped inside their wheel bays. Under the treaty, the Brits were allowed to open any door measuring more than 2 metres – one suspicious-looking aperture turning out to contain the pigsty where the Russians reared their own supplies of pork.

The trip was memorable for several other reasons: for the biting Russian cold, for the wolves Michael Evans (my opposite number on the *Times*) claimed in his story to have heard howling in the surrounding forest, and for the seemingly endless toasts drunk in excellent vodka – starting, as is the custom, with a toast 'to the ladies'. The base commander General Gennady

Mukhamedyarov declared that former enemies were now 'more like col-leagues'. For the base also to have chosen George and the Dragon as its symbol seemed at first to be carrying this new-found fraternity a bit too far – until I was told that for some implausible historical reason Russia shares Saint George with England. He is also the patron saint of Moscow.[43]

For the American cruise missiles in England, it was a case of last in, first out. By the time the INF Treaty was ratified in 1988, the second US base, at Molesworth in Cambridgeshire, was still not fully operational. Only one batch of missiles had been installed, and on 8 September the first of these were loaded into a droop-winged Starlifter at nearby RAF Alconbury for the 12-hour flight back to Arizona, where they would be destroyed under the eyes of the Russians.

The missiles' departure was an essentially cheerful occasion for all con-cerned. One almost expected the Defence Secretary George Younger and CND's Meg Beresford to shake hands on the tarmac as the Starlifter's smoke trails disappeared over the western horizon, while in the background the dedicated local Cruisewatch group exchanged bouquets with members of the 550th Tactical Missile Wing. It did not happen – not even metaphori-cally – because although both sides in the nuclear debate had indeed turned up to celebrate, they were celebrating different things. While Younger at-tributed success to NATO's 'firmness', the CND general secretary insisted that but for the peace movement, the missiles would still be in place. Besides which the anti-nuclear campaigners were still only watching from outside the gates, holding up banners that carried a distinctly sceptical message. 'Bye bye Cruise. Now what about the warheads?' said one, referring to the fact that the warheads' fissile material was not being destroyed. 'No new nukes' said another, with reference to talk of 'adjusting' and 'modernising' NATO's remaining nuclear arsenal once the cruise missiles had gone.

At Greenham, the USAF operation was of course on a much larger scale, and the programme for closing it down and flying the weapons back to Arizona was spread over two years, starting on 1 August 1989 when the first 16 missiles left, with wide international publicity. Even when all the missiles had gone, the massive empty silos where they were hidden remained subject to Russian inspection for many more years – until May 2001– an important fact governing the airfield's eventual redevelopment.

But from the moment the Treaty was signed, and it became clear the missile warriors would soon be on their way home, rumours as to who would replace them began to proliferate. Among the more dramatic possibilities being touted around the Newbury pubs were that the new American B-2 'Stealth' bomber would be based there, or that the central headquarters of the whole USAF operation in the UK would transfer from Mildenhall in Suffolk. The question was partially answered early in 1990 when it was announced that the base would revert to 'standby' status in June the following year, but that still left its long-term future in doubt.

According to Rebecca Johnson, who later made many US military contacts in the course of her arms-control work, American planning was seriously influenced by the women's protest. One USAF colonel said that the women's sheer persistence, in the face of constant harassment and evictions, had both surprised and demoralised Americans inside the base. A different source recounted Margaret Thatcher's indignant reaction when presented with a list of US bases to be vacated at the end of the Cold War. 'You can't withdraw from Greenham', the Prime Minister apparently exclaimed. 'We can't let them think they've succeeded.'

So far as Newbury people were concerned, the Pentagon's plans were only part of the problem. Many of them were increasingly determined that this time around, almost half a century after the end of the Second World War, they would find a way to rid their commons of all military occupation, under whatever flag. They turned their attention back to their own defence department, newly armed with the knowledge that the men from the ministry had unaccountably failed to extinguish archaic rights of common, which seemed to confer quite extraordinary power on those who possessed them.

PART TWO

New Alliances

A common heritage

The law doth punish man or woman
Who steals the goose from off the common
But lets the greater felon loose
Who steals the common from the goose.

Anonymous eighteenth-century verse displayed on Greenham fence

One only has to visualise England without its village greens, London without Hampstead Heath or Clapham Common, to see the deep historical
imprint left by the concept of common land. When parts of the West
Country moors, Snowdonia, the Lakeland fells and the North Pennines are
added in, there are more than 2,000 square miles of common land throughout England and Wales. That might sound a lot – about 8,000 individual
commons covering a total area the size of Lincolnshire – yet in truth this
is no more than a remnant of the vast tracts that existed before they were
eroded by the demands of private landowners, modern agriculture and
urban development.

The term 'common land' contains a confusing paradox. We tend to
think of it as a place where by definition we are all free to walk the dog
or have a picnic. In fact it originally acquired that description not through
public ownership, but because people other than the owner – that is, the
'commoners' – had ancient rights over it to graze cattle or collect firewood,
and if a legal right of public access was granted, it was probably done more
to control that access than to welcome it. Greenham and Crookham commons are a case in point. Both were privately owned until shortly before the
Second World War, when Greenham Common was acquired by Newbury
Borough Council as a public space. At Crookham, the right of public access
had already been established. More importantly as it turned out, various
rights of common were attached to nearby properties and these survived
the wartime upheaval, albeit dormant and ignored, until the 1980s.

A general right of public access on foot to all registered commons has
only just been established, after decades of campaigning by the Open

Spaces Society and others, under the Countryside and Rights of Way Act of 2000. We do at last have a so-called 'right to roam', albeit still heavily circumscribed. It took a long time partly because the law of commons is hideously complex, but more importantly because powerful competing interests were at play.

For centuries, English commons were obstinately, sometimes even violently, contested between ambitious lords of the manor and the peasantry, private landowners and their tenants, city developers and local residents. However, the contestants did often share a common concern. They did not want some stranger, just any old member of the public, wandering across their land.

Perhaps the new right to roam will change this attitude. If so, I fear this too will take a long time. Whether it derives from our feudal ancestry, or the combative, class-ridden nature of our overcrowded communities, we English seem burdened with an obsessive sense of property.

Only in England, surely, could one find a suburban house with its gravel drive neatly laid out for cars to turn, yet fenced off with absurd little white posts and chains, and a notice saying 'PRIVATE DRIVE — NO TURNING'. Even in supposedly open countryside we tacitly acknowledge a basic rule: never go anywhere until you establish a specific right to do so, for example from a signpost indicating a public footpath. Whatever the law of trespass may actually say, the truculent farmer with his shotgun conveys a blunt message: 'Keep out!'

They order these things differently elsewhere. Danish law establishes a fundamental principle of free access, even to privately owned fields, woodlands or beaches – provided of course one does not damage crops. The Swedes have *Allemansratten* – freedom to walk or ski across private land, pick bilberries or gather mushrooms. The Norwegians are also typically sensible. Under their Open Air Recreation Act you can walk anywhere on uncultivated land, and even across cultivated land when covered by snow. Perhaps my view of France is distorted by a holidaymaker's rose-tinted spectacles, but although there is certainly a strong sense of property in that country, somehow the shotguns are less in evidence. Even in the desperately overcrowded Netherlands there is a basic freedom of public access unless specifically prohibited by a notice quoting the relevant law.

English law of commons derives from the medieval, manorial system of rural land management which survived until the 1920s. Lords of the manor owned much of the land, but others were granted 'rights of common', which for the poor were vital to their survival. They could gather firewood ('by hook or by crook') and put their geese or pigs out to feed, if only on the less productive, unfenced 'waste land of the manor' – such as Greenham's heath. Some 'stinted' land might be enclosed by mutual agreement, for communal use – hence by a roundabout route the phrase 'to do your stint'.[44]

It was a bargain of sorts, dating back in legal principle to the thirteenth-century Statute of Merton. Since then it seems to have been generally accepted, albeit grudgingly, that if land were enclosed, the wretched peasant who had nowhere else to put his cow should somehow be provided for. And it followed that if rights of common were extinguished, the commoners deserved appropriate compensation. But in practice the scales were weighted heavily in favour of the big landowners.

At the end of the English Civil War the 'Diggers', a radical reforming group on the Parliamentary side (and a movement from whom some of the Greenham women drew inspiration) tried to redress the imbalance. In fact the situation soon got worse, driven by the economic imperative to rear sheep for their wool, and grow corn for an expanding, increasingly urban population. Fields were enclosed to protect both crops and animals, and the favoured legal device for this purpose was the Inclosure Act, passed by a Parliament which was itself, as objectors pointed out, 'a committee of landowners'.

During the eighteenth and early nineteenth centuries several thousand such acts were passed, in many cases without local people knowing about them in advance (later, a warning had to be posted on the church door, rather like today's planning notices). Land was gathered into efficiently or-ganised estates to finance elegant country houses set in landscaped grounds. We admire them now, yet their immediate social impact could be devastat-ing. 'When farmers become gentlemen,' wrote William Cobbett, himself a farmer-turned-journalist, and acquainted with Greenham Common, 'then labourers become slaves.'

In 1845 the process of land enclosure was codified in a general Act. Those who lost rights through enclosure were compensated with freehold land elsewhere, and a certain (in practice small) amount was also set aside for communal purposes and for the benefit of the poor – which could just mean building a workhouse. Another dodgy bargain. By now common land was being threatened as much by explosive urban development, especially round London and across the Midlands, as by changes in farming methods. Appropriately perhaps, given Mrs Thatcher's political priorities, a survey of common land conducted by the Countryside Commission towards the end of her premiership showed that her home town of Grantham in Lincolnshire was more deprived in this respect than almost anywhere in the country. Just one old sheepwash remained, measuring a tenth of an acre.[45]

London's especial need for open spaces, lungs through which it could breathe, had been recognised as long ago as the reign of Elizabeth I. The enclosure of common land within three miles of the city gates – areas like Smithfield – was forbidden so as to preserve some open recreational space. But of course that did not long deter the builders.

By the mid-nineteenth century not only was London a vastly bigger city; the last remaining patches of green were in danger of being bricked over. To prevent this was an early campaigning objective of the Commons Preservation Society (CPS) founded in 1865 and now known as the Open Spaces Society. Among its prominent backers was the philosopher John Stuart Mill, who is linked to the causes fought for at Greenham in another way, through his support for women's suffrage.

The CPS emerged as a heroic organisation, not averse to the sort of direct action the Greenham women would undoubtedly have approved – like pulling down a couple of miles of illegal iron fencing on Berkhamsted Common. It is thanks to the Society's campaigning that Londoners can still walk their dogs on places like Hampstead Heath. The local lord of the manor, Sir Thomas Wilson, planned to build on the heath, but the CPS mounted a legal challenge which lasted so long that he died before the issue was resolved. His successor handed the land over to Metropolitan Board.[46]

By the end of the century the National Trust had been established, eventually becoming a major owner of common land, along with national park and local authorities. Another key date was 1925, when the ancient copyhold system of land tenure, based on manorial records, was replaced by the modern concepts of leasehold and freehold. The Law of Property Act passed in that year was amended, thanks to pressure from the Commons Preservation Society, to provide public access to all urban commons (access to rural commons could also be granted by the owners in return for some control over public activities, which is what happened at Crookham). A second provision of the Act, controlling fences and other structures on common land, later became crucially important in the Greenham story. Building permission had to be obtained from the Secretary of State for the Environment – another legal requirement the MoD's lawyers somehow forgot about until it was too late.

A major struggle to preserve what was left of our common land, and to transform the widespread custom of public recreational use into a fundamental legal right, began in 1955, when a Royal Commission was established to review the whole situation. This led to the clumsily drafted 1965 Commons Registration Act, which at least established a national database, even if it did not stop the steady leaching away of common land for housing development and other private purposes. A crucial factor in a common's subsequent survival turned out to be whether commoners' rights, as well as the land itself, were recorded in the county council's register – which eventually leads us back to Greenham, the women and the Ministry of Defence.

Whereas for a Cumbrian hill farmer an ancient communal right to graze sheep on the fells could be essential to his livelihood, most rights of common on the Berkshire airfield had long since ceased to have any economic value. With their archaic names, they merely served to add some historical colour to the title deeds of local properties. If a modern household did happen to keep a pig in the back garden, the right of *pannage* would entitle them to let the animal loose around the heath to root for fallen acorns or beech mast (though shaking trees to bring the acorns down would be forbidden). The right of *turbary* means digging peat or turf. Collecting firewood, bracken or the gorse that proliferates in the poor Greenham soil is *estovers*. Fishing rights are *piscary*. And *common in the soil* is the right to extract sand, gravel or stone, for example to repair a rough country road.

Quaint though they may sound, the ancient lineage of such rights of common, and their association with a system of land tenure and agriculture stretching back thousands of years, gives them a quite extraordinary legal clout. Defence officials, used to getting their bureaucratic way in the interests of 'national security', just as their Home Office counterparts later found justification in the 'war on terror', were slow to realise this. One of the first to sense what Whitehall was up against, whether it was dealing with protesting women or the burghers of Newbury, was a certain Mr A. Ward, head of Defence Secretariat 9 (Air), who gave evidence to the Commons Defence Committee on 16 May 1984, as it investigated the security situation at RAF Greenham Common.

The MoD man began – in open session – by explaining to the Select Committee's chairman Dr John Gilbert that it was not considered either 'sensible or necessary' to make the airfield perimeter totally secure, or to deploy sufficient British troops to prevent any possibility of a confrontation between the women demonstrators and US servicemen: 'Our policy is that occasional incursions by demonstrators are of no real security significance; they are not likely to get very near at all to secure areas' (an opinion shown to be overoptimistic later that year, when the women came close to cutting their way into the high-security missile storage area).

In response to further questioning by the Conservative MP Winston Churchill (grandson of the wartime prime minister), Mr Ward then turned to new MoD bye-laws which he hinted were under consideration (and were subsequently introduced at Greenham in April 1985). He warned that they involved a process of consultation which might have the effect of 'raising the public profile undesirably' – a problem on which he offered to elaborate when the Committee went into closed session (i.e. with no journalists or members of the public present).

The private explanation he later gave MPs[47] showed that the Ministry already knew it was in trouble with the ancient law of commons, but was hoping that if it kept quiet about it in public, others would not notice. 'There is not a lot to say', the discreet Mr Ward told the Committee,

> but one problem with the application of bye-laws under the Military Lands Act is that the process of public consultation that is required can give rise to a greater knowledge about little-known commoners' rights and rights of way across Ministry of Defence establishments, which do seem to exist, for reasons I do not fully understand. They are very long in history, and some such rights are very hard to extinguish – but as the commoners die, then perhaps the commoners' rights die.

Mr Churchill, who seemed rather better informed, interrupted to say he was sure that was not the case. 'I do not know', continued Mr Ward. 'Either that, or they are passed on to the successor householder.... There is very little known about them. The process of consultation about bye-laws runs the risk of spreading knowledge about their existence.'

It was a remarkably revealing exchange. Mr Ward admitted he was no expert in the law of commons, but his bureaucratic instincts warned him of danger and, in true Whitehall fashion, his response was to go to ground.

The scent of danger

Looking south from Greenham Common, the low escarpment on the horizon about four miles away is Watership Down. In 1972, an extraordinary book of that name was published, written by a civil servant called Richard Adams, then nearing retirement from the Department of the Environment. The book was extraordinary because Adams managed to transform such unlikely material – the adventures of a group of rabbits – into a runaway bestseller.

In the story, a rabbit called Hazel and his hypersensitive brother Fiver, who has a premonition of impending danger, are among a small group who escape just before man-made disaster strikes their warren at Sandleford – a real place, beyond the western end of the airfield, where the author had lived as a boy. The danger Fiver senses is painted on a noticeboard he cannot read, its posts reeking of creosote, advertising the development of an 'ideally situated estate' of new houses. Before the builders move in, the warren is cleared with gas.[48]

Twenty years later, by which time almost everyone in Newbury had heard of their celebrated local author, commercial development was threatening not just a couple of fields at Sandleford, but the whole tract of former heathland about to be vacated by the US Air Force. If there was to be a battle over the future of the airfield, Richard Adams was an obvious patron of any campaign to save the commons as a public space, and he quickly took up the challenge, promising to 'fight to the bitter end'.

By now the initial, quite natural assumption that one kind of American weaponry would simply be replaced by another had given way to a realisation that the Cold War was ending, and that the whole scale of the US military presence in Britain would diminish. In January 1990 it was announced that the Greenham airfield would revert to standby status in June of the following year, when the 501st Tactical Missile Wing disbanded. And since the RAF too was expected to scale down its operations, the airfield seemed poised at the top of a familiar, slippery slope: surplus to

MoD requirements, sold to the highest bidder for a respectable mixture of housing, industrial estate, shopping mall and leisure centre.

In fact it began to look worse than that. Greenham was known to be one of the best runways in Europe, prompting alarmist talk of its becoming London's third airport. When that idea was scotched (Newbury's road traffic was already horrendous, a rail link was difficult, and Aldermaston's nuclear laboratories lay under the eastern approach path), planners came up with a proposal for a complete twentieth-century 'new town' alongside the medieval one, supposedly to take the pressure off the local countryside.

To prevent this descent from the frying pan of military occupation into the fire of wholesale commercial redevelopment, an informal campaigning group began to form, drawn partly from local supporters of the women's protest such as Evelyn Parker, Lynette Edwell and Leslie and Wendy Pope, partly from among Greenham residents who wanted to preserve their rights of common, such as Jim and Jackie Langdon. The Langdons had bought a cottage not far from the main gate of the airfield, on the edge of birch woodland facing south towards Watership Down, and immediately registered rights to gather firewood and dig gravel attached to the property. Now they realised, as the Greenham women had before them, that the authorities were peculiarly vulnerable where common land and commoners' rights were concerned.

The legal challenge to the MoD trespass bye-laws mounted by Jean Hutchinson and Georgina Smith – on the grounds that commoners were harmed by them – was in its final, ultimately successful stages. Meanwhile sharp-eyed Leslie Pope, alarmed by military plans to erect a 200-foot radio mast, had made a startling new discovery: that because the airfield was built on common land, recent structures such as the perimeter fence and hangars required permission from the Secretary of State for the Environment, which had never been obtained. The very fabric of the base appeared to be unlawful.

A first attempt to rouse the sixty or so Greenham and Crookham commoners into action on this basis was something of a disappointment. The OSS expert on the law of commons, Paul Clayden, and a Hampshire commoner who had previously tangled with the military authorities, agreed to address a meeting at the Newbury United Reform church hall to discuss 'Our Common Heritage', but only half-a-dozen local commoners turned up, and the whole audience was barely twice that number. Yet within a few weeks, the government had publicly acknowledged that it was indeed in an extremely weak legal position.

The admission came on 29 April 1988 through a parliamentary device government departments used to 'bury bad news' long before that phrase was made notorious by one of New Labour's spin doctors – a written answer to a planted question from the Newbury MP Michael McNair-Wilson. Replying on behalf of the Secretary of State, defence minister Roger Freeman admitted that once its wartime emergency powers expired, at the end of 1958, the MoD was required by the 1925 Law of Property Act to seek permission from the Secretary of State for the Environment (in addition to the normal planning consents) before building on land subject to rights of common. No such permission had been obtained for the renovated fences and other extensive structures erected on the airfield in preparation for the US cruise missiles; 'Consequently, doubts about the legal position have been raised.'

The minister further announced that more construction work would be needed 'in connection with the inspection arrangements under the agreed verification regime once the INF treaty is ratified' (an implausible explanation that made no mention of any radio mast). 'Steps therefore need to be taken', he continued, 'to remove a legal obstacle to further construction which could impede this and other work.' The ministry had therefore decided – and here was the real sting in the tail of his answer – 'that the appropriate course would be to negotiate fair compensation for the legal extinction of the commoners' rights, which we propose to pursue under the provisions of the Defence Act 1854'.

It was an extraordinary situation. The seemingly all-powerful Ministry of Defence was now facing two serious legal challenges, over bye-laws and planning consents, both based on rights of common. For all its talk of being merely 'doubtful', it was in fact sufficiently alarmed to warn its American tenants to stop building. According to the Missile Wing's own account of events in 1988, 'The situation caused such an uproar that all new construction was restricted on the base.'

However, Whitehall was still far from admitting defeat. The INF arms control treaty had only recently been signed, so, notwithstanding any longer-term plans, the US nuclear base was still a going concern. Accordingly the MoD's lawyers were given orders to attack on both fronts. While continuing to contest Judge Josh Lait's ruling on the bye-laws, they called meetings of the Greenham and Crookham commoners to explain how they proposed to get rid of those annoying, archaic rights of common. In doing so they carefully followed the procedure laid down in the Victorian legislation they had finally decided to use, the 1845 Land Clauses Consolidation Act. The assumption was that the commoners would obediently form committees to negotiate compensation, without further argument, for the loss of their rights. But things did not go at all according to plan.

The Greenham meeting was held on 8 August in the St Mary's parish church hall, with the RAF Wing Commander who was notionally in charge of the base acting as self-appointed doorman. In spite of his best efforts to restrict entry to actual commoners (who had their own Commons Association), a number of people whose agenda went way beyond fixing the price of cooperation talked their way in. They included Sarah Hipperson from Yellow Gate, Leslie and Wendy Pope, and a maverick representative of the Open Spaces Society, all of whom correctly saw rights of common as a powerful lever with which to control not only current construction on the base but also the airfield's eventual redevelopment. They were intent on persuading the commoners not to sell out, and their message was evidently received and understood. A five-man committee was elected, not to negotiate terms of surrender, but 'to fight the MoD to the end'. At which point the three ministry officials left the platform, looking 'severely shaken' according to one witness, and hurriedly departed.

The next evening, Crookham commoners did not even wait for the Whitehall team to arrive before electing a representative committee. The men from the ministry were invited merely to observe proceedings from their seats in the front row. As it turned out, opinion at this end of the airfield seemed less resistant to the Government's offer, or perhaps the defence officials were just better prepared. No clear decision was taken. The upshot of the two meetings was that all the commoners went away, combining under the chairmanship of Dr Roy Swayne (who owned an appropriately imposing house on the south side of the airfield) to reconsider their position.

They took their time, alternately swayed by the increasing momentum of the campaign to save the commons from redevelopment, and by the tempting prospect of money in the bank. After waiting eight months for a reply the MoD came up with a compromise: it would only extinguish rights over the built-up areas of the base, provided commoners agreed not to exercise residual rights over the rest of the airfield while it was needed for military purposes.

Leaving some of the rights intact in this way was an important conces-
sion, even if they were temporarily unusable, since local residents would
retain some minimal control over what eventually happened to the land.
Dr Swayne recommended acceptance. But when it came to the point, four
of the sixty-four commoners – all of them, as it happens, from Greenham
– still refused to sign the MoD's memorandum of understanding. They
were suspicious of the military's long-term intentions; they could not see
why any of their ancient rights should be extinguished, and they were not
at all sure that it was lawful to do so. The mid-nineteenth-century Defence
Acts on which the government lawyers were evidently relying looked more
appropriate to training cavalrymen for the Crimea than conducting a
nuclear Cold War.

The response from Whitehall was nevertheless uncompromising. Just
before Christmas 1989 the MoD finally lost patience, indicating through
Newbury's MP that unless every one of the commoners signed up, the
deal was off. All rights of common would after all be extinguished, and
negotiated compensation paid (the original offer on the table was reported
to be about £700 for each household).

At this point one might have expected the last of the opposition to ebb
away. In fact, just as the flood tide will turn beneath an estuary while the
surface water still runs out, the campaign to save the commons – for Newbury as a whole, not just for the parishioners of Greenham and Crookham
– was about to gain powerful backing from a number of influential local
figures, including the author Richard Adams and his near neighbour Lord
Denning, Master of the Rolls. Sensing that local opinion was behind them
– for example from the sympathetic attention attracted by an article Adams
wrote for the *Sunday Times* – the small group of diehard commoners and
their supporters decided to seek wider public support.

They hired the Luker Hall at St Bartholomews School in Newbury for
the evening of 11 January 1990, and distributed some hastily drafted leaflets
declaring that 'NEWBURY NEEDS ITS 1000 ACRES OF COMMON LAND'. A
few hours before the meeting, Jackie Langdon was asked to take the chair
because the commoner originally chosen was not available. She remembers
little except that the school hall was crowded: 'All afternoon I'd been absolutely clammy with nerves. I'd never done anything like that before.'

The main speaker was Richard Adams. His message was simple: Newbury had lent its neighbouring common land to the government for a
wartime emergency, on the understanding that it would be returned when

the emergency was over. That was a long time ago, and now the town wanted the land back. Lord Denning did not attend, but sent a message to be read out, conveying his authoritative opinion that under the common law of England, commoners' rights could only be extinguished by Act of Parliament. A representative of the Open Spaces Society announced that it had written to the Defence Secretary Tom King urging him to abandon plans to acquire Greenham commoners' rights and ensure that the common was eventually restored to its original state.

Also on the platform was Trevor Brown, well known from his years as a Liberal county councillor. He was billed simply as a 'former councillor', which does less than justice to his tireless campaigning on everything from safety standards at the nearby Aldermaston Atomic Weapons Establishment, where he was a senior scientist, to Newbury's desperate need for a bypass. On the commons issue, he took great pride in having persuaded Berkshire County Council many years previously to pass a resolution to the effect that the heathland should be recovered for the local community when it was eventually vacated by the RAF. He had reminded the Greenham commoners of this at their first meeting with the MoD, and in the same spirit represented the county council on the airbase liaison committee (only to be dumped by the RAF chairman with a sigh of relief the moment he ceased to be a councillor).

Trevor Brown showed a rare ability to be simultaneously a respected member of the local political establishment and a sharp thorn in its collective side. Now in his eighties, he still sounds boyishly passionate about chemistry, the subject he chose to study at Oxford (where he recalls an eager young student called Margaret Roberts – now better known as Mrs Thatcher – who always sat in the front row at lectures). His particular speciality was the poisonous, intensely reactive gas fluorine – 'good fun, but bloody wicked' – which made him an excellent catch for a rapidly expanding nuclear industry processing uranium. He transferred to Aldermaston in 1961 to run a new fuel plant but never felt welcome there, not least because he persistently questioned its safety procedures. It was his whistle-blowing, he maintains, which eventually forced him into premature retirement.

Where Trevor would stand on any particular issue was never predictable. For example, he says he was probably the first resident of the town to join Friends of the Earth, but when protests arose at the prospect of driving a bypass through the adjacent countryside he told them 'the environment you have to worry about is the environment of Newbury'. He sympathised with the Greenham women's anti-nuclear protests, but as a councillor on the police liaison committee he also had sympathy for the men who were asked to control the demonstrators. About the need to recover the commons, however, he felt no ambivalence, and was quite prepared to set aside political differences to achieve this.

In the audience at the Luker Hall was Chris Austin, another familiar figure in local politics. I do not know what he was wearing that evening, but the chances are he arrived in the well-worn Barbour jacket and downward-tilted tweed cap that identifies a certain type of Englishman, as devoted to traditional country pursuits as the Greenham women were to their anti-nuclear cause. And he was among those who responded to the chairwoman's invitation to reconvene a fortnight later at the Friends Meeting House, where they formally established their campaign. One wonders what the others made of him. Some would have recognised the master of a local hunt, and a vocal critic of the women's peace camp. Trevor Brown, in a crucial intervention, recognised that he was the ideal chairman for 'Commons Again'.

Commons again?

On meeting Chris Austin for the first time many years later, I was curious to know why he had been nominated to lead the new pressure group by someone who clearly did not share his wider political views. What did Trevor Brown see in him?

> A Tory. He had enough sense to realise that if this campaign was seen as a continuation of the peace movement, it would fail. Whereas if it was led by a commoner, someone with common rights – in other words someone with a proper legal interest – and also a known local Conservative, it stood a better chance of succeeding. There was a bit of resistance to that, but Trevor Brown was well respected by people on the left of politics, so they shut up and did as he suggested.

In this crude political sense, as in other ways, Commons Again gained strength from the way it transcended familiar divisions in the Newbury community – a Conservative chairman, a Liberal treasurer, a Labour secretary, at least a couple of Green Party members. And in spite of Chris Austin's concern that the campaign should not to be contaminated by association with a women's protest many local people abhorred, several of its most active supporters – such as Evelyn Parker and the Popes – moved across quite naturally from the anti-nuclear campaign. The legal knowledge they brought with them proved invaluable, and several of the publicity stunts previously mounted by the women – such as inviting arrest for cutting the airfield fence – were readily adaptable to serve this new cause.

For the Greenham parish councillor now heading Commons Again, the symbolism of the fence was just as powerful as it was for someone like Helen John, who had started the women's protest by chaining herself to it. As a young man already passionate about horses, hunting and rearing cattle, Chris Austin knew every useful gap in the dilapidated wire structure, which was a permanent affront to anyone who realised this was common land. But whereas Helen is avowedly of Irish and Scottish descent, seeing Greenham merely as an example of a wider nuclear confrontation, Chris

Chris Austin: scourge of the
Greenham women, champion
of commoners' rights.

seems thoroughly English, and deeply embedded in this Berkshire community – joint master of a local hunt, Tory activist, part-time cattle breeder, a leading light of Newbury's amateur operatic society.

Whatever local organisation you mention, Chris seems to be the chairman. Here is a man completely at home in a public setting. Asked to describe himself, he offers a crisp summary: '48, divorced, no children'. He now lives, appropriately, on the southern edge of the town near both the racecourse and the commons. The flat's decoration is noticeably restrained except for the hunting prints and portraits. It's as if his public persona is so vivid – resplendent in masterful hunting pink, or dressed for the role of Marco in Gilbert and Sullivan's *Gondoliers* – he has little need of colour in his private life.

Regardless of his political views, Chris Austin's relationship with the Greenham women was never going to be an easy one. He so often appeared astride some vast horse – an authority figure if ever there was one. On hearing reports of a collie snapping at the heels of ponies down at Blue Gate, dangerously close to a busy main road, he rode down there and after remonstrating unsuccessfully with the women, 'nearly cut the collie in half with my hunting whip'.

Chris's most dramatic encounter with the protesters came while hunting near Yellow Gate. There, as he suspected, two foxes were lurking in a patch of gorse behind the peace camp. One found refuge across the main road. The second shot off towards Crookham, pursued by the hounds, and while other members of his hunt cautiously skirted the women's camp before following through the woods, he deliberately rode straight through it. He was not going to be intimidated by a bunch of peace women. Though by his own account it was the women who seemed intimidated, 'bemused and awe-struck' by the sight and sound of a pack of hounds in full cry.

In conversation with someone likely to be sympathetic to the women's cause, Chris makes scrupulous efforts to give them credit for their honourable motives and dedication to peace. But he admits that at the time, he just wanted rid of them:

> To those of us who live in and around Greenham, the whole of the peace camp experience was a bit of a nightmare. Most of Newbury was hostile to them, although there was obviously a minority that was very supportive. The irony was that both sides wanted the same thing.

Unlike the anxious man Helen John lodged with on the march from Wales, for whom the cruise missiles posed an overwhelming, vividly immediate danger, Chris evidently saw nuclear deterrence as an extension of normal politics – a high-stakes poker game certainly, but not a survival issue. From this perspective the women's protest appeared both politically naive and socially undesirable, a burden on the taxpayer, making local houses unsaleable, and so on. On one occasion he even joined some of the vigilantes on a midnight expedition to sabotage the women's water supply, although he always counselled strongly against any form of personal violence. Yet the dwindling band of women still camped at Greenham in 1990 almost certainly agreed with him on one point: that once the Yanks went home the MoD should be made to hand the airfield back to Newbury, rather than wait for NATO to find some other use for it. And thanks to some of those women, it was now clear that ancient rights of common might be the best instrument to achieve this.

Chris had acquired his own commoners' rights by virtue of a few acres of land his parents purchased on the western edge of Greenham Common, beyond the women's Blue Gate, where he ran a riding school. He bought his first 'suckler' cow (i.e. a cow that suckles its calf rather than providing milk for human consumption) in the late 1970s, a few years before the marchers arrived, and built his herd up to a peak of about 70 animals. So for him, being able to let them loose on the commons would be of real economic value. Whereas for most of his fellow commoners (as he himself explained, lest I should read too much history into a modern suburban situation), such rights were no more than a quaint anachronism:

> They bought a nice house on the edge of the common which happened to have commoners' rights, and the solicitor said: 'Oh, by the way, you've got the right to graze a cow, or you can collect firewood'; to which the reaction was 'But we've got all this central heating.'

Much as one might wish otherwise, such accidental commoners were unlikely to see themselves as champions of some new peasants' revolt, restoring common land to the people. It was the law, which really does have its roots in England's history, which gave them such an unexpectedly important role. One of Chris Austin's first acts as chairman of Commons Again was to take Gadsden's legal tome *The Law of Commons* out of the library and read it from cover to cover. Then he set about generating publicity in all the usual forms: letters to the editor, lobbying parliamentary candidates, and laying on visual stunts for the television cameras.

One particularly splendid event involved his horse Captain (a 'chestnut Irish hunter' to the experts). Chris rode up to the main gate of the base, with a regional television crew in close attendance, and informed the bemused sentries that he intended to exercise his rights of common.

> I rode up to the American guards, who were quite polite, and said: 'I'd just like to ride on to the common.' And when I explained who I was they didn't much want to let me on, because they said, well, it's your father whose the commoner, not you. And I explained that under commons law, close members of the family can exercise rights on his behalf. I just wanted to ride over there, turn round, and ride back again. So they said: 'Oh well.' Then the bloody horse reared up, which was uncharacteristic of him. So there was me on a rearing horse, like Zorro or something, which of course made a wonderful image for the telly.

What the Americans made of all this is not recorded. By this stage they were almost literally lowering their guard, and presumably recognised a photo-op when they saw one. Those among them with a grasp of local politics will also have realised that they were no longer the main target of protest, but merely caught up in the crossfire between competing interests within their host community.

In earlier times Chris Austin and his ilk had been reasonably happy to accommodate Newbury's US invasion – 'On my table at the hunt ball one year I think I had four lieutenant-colonels and a major, because their wives often rode with us.' Now the Americans were in the firing line, albeit as no more than political cannon fodder in a quintessentially English war.

> It was Leslie Pope – he was very anti-cruise missiles, digging away, trying to find legal ways of nobbling the Americans – who really flagged up the idea that commoners' rights were still in existence. So there were the Americans, enclosing the commons, threatening to shoot all and sundry, yet here was a group of local people who had a perfect right to walk through the main gate and go anywhere they wanted on the base. Of course the Americans – you can imagine – they went spare.

Not that the American reaction any longer signified much, one way or the other. Within weeks of the establishment of Commons Again, the operational disbandment of the 501st Missile Wing was announced for June 1991. Half the cruise missiles had already left. What mattered now was the MoD's threat to extinguish commoners' rights, using obscure Victorian legislation. If that dubious-sounding manoeuvre were to succeed, it would remove what little direct control local people had over the future of the airfield. By increasing the commercial value of the land, it might also influence Whitehall's attitude to the disposal.

In those days, government rules for disposing of property were a good deal cruder than they have since become. Essentially, the Ministry of Defence was duty bound to get the best value for the taxpayer, which probably meant just selling it to the highest bidder. It was all part of the 'peace dividend' the country was demanding in the aftermath of the Cold War. Mrs Thatcher was in No. 10 Downing Street and market forces ruled. The only caveat was that under the so-called 'Crichel Down rules' the former owners of agricultural land acquired for military purposes usually had to be given a chance to buy it back – which should have worked in Newbury's favour, since the old borough council had owned Greenham Common for forty years from 1939 to 1960, when most of it was sold to the Air Ministry.

The year 1991 was therefore critical for the future of the commons. The American airmen were packing their bags. The MoD's lawyers were alternately tempting the commoners with cash and twisting their arms to relinquish their rights. Newbury District Council was being urged and prodded by the Commons Again pressure group not to renege on its promise to recover this ancient common land as a public space.

The Ministry of Defence, for all its devious ways, was not necessarily inimical to that aspiration. Living on an overcrowded island, cheek by jowl with the civilian population, the British armed forces have long since understood that if they are to achieve their primary objective – enough room to conduct realistic training – they have to give ground in other ways. That means providing public access wherever possible to their extensive training areas, minimising public nuisance such as aircraft noise, and being seen to take environmental conservation seriously.

For example, the MoD is aware, where you or I might not be, that it is Britain's largest owner of lowland heath, an increasingly rare habitat of which Greenham Common is an important example. And it accepts that public ownership brings with it certain responsibilities. The Department has its own glossily produced conservation magazine, *Sanctuary*, full of articles spelling out the unlikely partnerships and accommodations that develop once military men become environmentally conscious – or at least politically sensitive. Every big military establishment in the countryside – even Aldermaston – nowadays has its own conservation officer.

Porton Down, that sinister chemical warfare research establishment in Wiltshire, infamous for the nerve-gas experiments conducted on volunteer servicemen during the early days of the Cold War, has turned out to be a perfectly protected habitat for butterflies, moths, orchids and ants (Sarin must be an acquired taste!). The army's scientists moved in during 1916, when British tommies started being gassed in the Flanders trenches, since when 7,000 acres of chalk downland have been spared the attentions of agricultural machinery, pesticides and the like. If you can get past the MoD police (disguised as a member of the Wiltshire Moth Group perhaps, or, more sensibly, escorted by one of the Porton Down Conservation Group's guides) you will find 46 of Britain's 55 native species of butterfly there, including such beautiful-sounding creatures as the Chalkhill Blue, the Silver-spotted Skipper and the Pearl-bordered Fritillary – also an estimated 35 billion Yellow Meadow Ants.[49]

Given the inherently dangerous nature of its activities, the MoD does a lot better than many private landowners when it comes to providing public access. The tank gunnery ranges alongside Lulworth Cove in Dorset (which not only contain three 'Sites of Special Scientific Interest' but have recently been declared a World Heritage Site) happen to lie right across a designated coastal path. The army's response has been an elaborate arrangement of 'permissive ways' whereby walkers can cross the ranges when the guns are not firing – which works out at about one day in three, including most weekends.

On the Essex coast where I sail, it is not walkers but yachtsmen who wait for the guns to go silent before proceeding. The army has been using the Foulness Sands beyond Southend since 1805, when Colonel Shrapnel asked permission from the lord of the manor to test his new invention, the exploding cannonball. The gunners value the expanse of relatively firm sands for the same reason as the local cockle fishermen: that at low tide you can walk out and recover something, whether it be shells or shellfish. For many decades, therefore, the tiny farming population of Foulness Island has been trapped more or less willingly behind military fences and dykes worthy, in their different way, of Greenham or Aldermaston (in fact Foulness became an offshoot of Aldermaston for some of its secretive nuclear weapons work). But in a public relations gesture which long predates that unsympathetic modern term, MoD bye-laws provide that the Havengore bridge blocking the creek leading out into the Thames estuary will open for barges, fishing boats or yachts for two hours either side of high tide.

At Greenham, the rough outline of a compromise over the future of the airfield that would satisfy both Whitehall and Newbury could be identified almost as soon as the Americans announced that they were off. Nobody was banking on it, however. Too many conflicting interests still had to be resolved. Newbury District Council wanted its commons back as an open space, but how much was the airfield going to cost to buy, clean up and maintain? Why not let a commercial developer do the hard work, especially when the town was in need of new jobs to replace those lost with the USAF's departure? For its part, the MoD was mindful of its half-promise to return the land, but must at the same time satisfy the Treasury that it was striking a hard bargain.

Moreover, future military requirements were still being reviewed. As late as February 1992, Newbury Council's chief executive Paul McMahon was warning people not to assume that the RAF would let go of its fine long runway: 'My personal judgment', he told the *Newbury Weekly News*, 'is that it is quite unlikely the base will be returned to the people of Newbury. The MoD will keep the base in some capacity for contingency purposes in the future.'[50]

So far as Greenham commoners were concerned, the battle over their rights reached its climax at the end of May 1991, when, having rejected the MoD's compromise proposal, they finally agreed to sell them – that is to give the government permanent control over two-thirds of the airfield, including the built-up military area, though still not including common land outside the perimeter. The vesting deed by which they accepted Whitehall's gold was dated 30 May 1991, just one day before the 501st Tactical Missile Wing formally shut down its operations. In resounding, archaic language well-suited to distract attention from any flaws in its legal provenance, it states:

> NOW THIS DEED WITNESSETH that the Secretary of State, in exercise of the powers for this purpose conferred on him by the aforementioned Acts, declares that the said land shall henceforth vest in him and his successors forever, for a legal estate in fee simple absolute in possession on behalf of Her Majesty, freed and discharged from all commonable and other rights in, over or affecting the same.

To which the twentieth century commoners replied:

> We the undersigned, being three of the committee appointed pursuant to Sections 102 and 103 of the Land Clauses Consolidation Act of 1845 by the parties entitled to commonable or other rights affecting certain land at Greenham Common Berkshire, hereby authorize and request you to draw the remittance for £90,312 50p, being the compensation agreed by us with you for the extinction of such commonable and other rights in favour of Crookham and Greenham Commoners Committees.

'It's a sad day', Dr Roy Swayne, who led negotiations with the ministry having originally opposed a sell-out, told the *Guardian*. 'We have lost in the end because of the dissenters. The only way to challenge the Ministry's decision to extinguish our rights would be to take it to court, and that would cost a lot of money' (in fact Commons Again did subsequently explore the possibility of a judicial review).[51]

There was a complex irony about all this. The 30 Crookham commoners who for tactical reasons had earlier signed the MoD's memorandum of understanding (a compromise whereby some rights inside the airfield were extinguished while others remained in abeyance) never received any financial reward. Their rights remained intact and survive to this day. It follows that in spite of the Greenham commoners' capitulation, the ministry's lawyers were never able to resolve their basic legal problem: that both the bye-laws under which Greenham women were prosecuted, and the perimeter fence they attacked with their bolt cutters, were unlawful because of the existence of rights of common.

Why Whitehall accepted this unsatisfactory situation is still not clear. Did they doubt their own legal procedure, as the women suspected and Lord Denning argued they should do? Or were they really concerned only to extinguish rights over that part of Greenham Common within the airbase? Because this included the built-up area with most obvious potential for commercial development, whereas 'Crookham Common within' consisted of concrete runways, vast underground fuel tanks and some open grassland?

Twelve months later, when consultants hired by the MoD presented their first suggestions for the airfield's redevelopment, they maintained that Greenham rights had effectively been extinguished (though not yet removed from the Commons Register), but explicitly recognised that the rights of Crookham commoners remained intact.

Meanwhile the Commons Again activists, a much smaller group than I realised at the time (fewer than ten people), had been keeping up the pressure. On 3 February 1992 Chris Austin and Jim Langdon – like hundreds of Greenham women before them – took a pair of bolt cutters to the airfield fence, taking care to have a *Newbury Weekly News* photographer on hand to record their action. They were duly arrested and charged with criminal damage. With a general election in the offing, a few USAF personnel still in residence and the government officially 'reviewing options for the future of the station', it was a timely protest. The immediate intention, Chris explained, was to test the MoD's legal position following the payment of compensation to Greenham commoners (about half the money had by then been distributed). But the authorities either could not or would not play his game:

> Of course they couldn't find a bench in Newbury to try me, because I know practically every magistrate, so it was deferred and deferred and deferred, and then eventually they sent me a tiny piece of paper photocopied so many times it was all blurred, which said: 'Your case has been dropped for the following reason (with various boxes for the Clerk to tick) – Lack of Evidence.'

When this was confirmed by the Crown Prosecution Service that October, Chris claimed victory for Commons Again. When you commit a criminal act in front of a police officer and a photographer, he told the *Newbury Weekly News,* and the case is then dropped due to insufficient evidence, you can surmise there is insufficient evidence that commoners' rights have been extinguished: 'They had the chance to test whether the rights had been extinguished and they did not use it. They were not prepared to fight.' A delighted Jim Langdon added that so far he was concerned, his rights were intact and he would be out there exercising them.[52]

Councillor David Rendel (later to become Newbury's Liberal Democrat MP) also took heart from the failure to proceed against the two men. It showed, he told his colleagues, that the government realised it hadn't got a leg to stand on, and if the airfield had to be sold with only 'common land' value, it would probably be bought by the council.

Evelyn Parker, an active Cruisewatcher and strong supporter of the women's protest, had meanwhile been doing her bit for the Commons Again cause by testing another historic right known as an 'easement', which the MoD seemed to have forgotten about entirely. An easement was a right of way across Greenham Common, belonging in this case to the owners of a patch of land near Green Gate – the 'Sanctuary' – bought by several of the women. What made this particular right of way so provocative was that it ran right across the high-security area of the base where the nuclear weapons were stored, straight towards Newbury by way of Blue Gate.

Evelyn chose to exercise her right of way by cutting through the perimeter fence, quite openly, accompanied by another woman, and starting to mark out the easement with a line of arrows, using a pot of leftover paint provided by her husband. She did not get far, but the point was made. The magistrates accepted that she was entitled to cut the fence – to the extent that her bolt cutters were returned – but fined her £7 for painting MoD tarmac!

The US Air Force finally left Greenham in September 1992, half a century after it arrived. So far as its own personnel were concerned, their tour of duty really finished 15 months earlier, on 31 May, when the 501st Tactical Missile Wing shut down operations and its commander, Colonel Richard R. Riddick, thanked them for their participation in 'The Last Crusade'. His personal farewell message provides an intriguing insight into how the Americans – or at any rate their senior commanders, writing for the official record – saw their overseas mission:

> As a wing we have been involved with some of the most historically significant issues and events of our time. The initial decision to field the GLCM mission was a landmark for NATO. The build-up tested the alliance and its determination to deter – the member nations of NATO stood fast.
>
> This resolve was especially important here as over 25,000 peace protestors laid siege to Greenham. Undaunted, the people of the 501st, in conjunction with the Ministry of Defence, made this mission work. The long years of facing down the protestors and the Warsaw Pact were stressful but you persevered and succeeded. The Intermediate-range Nuclear Forces Treaty was signed and for the first time a whole class of nuclear weapons was eliminated. Your efforts helped make this happen.
>
> Now, in drawdown, we face the difficult task of maintaining morale while disassembling and removing what we have poured so much of ourselves into. Remember your accomplishments – you helped keep the peace and promote freedom – how many others can justifiably say the same?

His message raised again the old question: Who are the 'real peacekeepers', those who campaign directly for peace, or those who prepare for war in order to deter it? In a British context, is it CND and the Greenham women, or Royal Navy submariners on deterrent patrol with their Trident missiles? Colonel Riddick, as a good NATO man, evidently put his faith firmly in nuclear deterrence. Yet even he seems to have some residual doubt, as when he acknowledges the women as 'peace protestors', a term presumably implying approbation, yet at the same time brackets them with the Warsaw Pact as something to be 'faced down'.

A similar confusion confronts British undergraduates intent on studying military affairs. Should they enrol for a course of 'peace studies' (at Bradford University) or 'war studies' (at Kings College London)? Are they different subjects? Does the name matter? From what I hear of the two departments, there is a real difference of approach – though probably much less now than during the Greenham protest – but on what logical basis, since they are both studying the same problems?

The answer has an oblique bearing on the much wider question of how far 'peace movements' of any kind, and the Greenham women's protest in particular, have achieved their declared objectives. The women began to consider this on their own behalf, individually and collectively, from the moment the INF Treaty was signed in December 1987. Was the departure of the cruise missiles (which began in 1989 and spread over two years) the right time to pack their tents, mission accomplished? Or should they wait until the last Americans left in 1992? Or was it worth continuing this extraordinary experiment in anarchic, feminist campaigning at Greenham so as to apply similar tactics at nearby Aldermaston, or lend support to Newbury's campaign to recover its common land?

The issue was complicated by the fact that towards the end of 1987 the Greenham camp split, because of bitter arguments over how the protest should be organised and what its priorities should be. When it was clear the dispute could not be resolved in the normal consensual fashion, Yellow Gate parted company with Blue and Green gates. And, as it happened, it was a small group of Yellow Gate women who stayed on after most had left, chasing legal hares they had started earlier, determined to exhaust the momentum built up during the years of mass protest on whatever causes seemed appropriate.

On a November weekend in 1993, Blue and Green Gate women gathered to discuss whether to face another winter in the open, or to pack and go. A Blue Gate banner – 'Commons are for People and Animals, not Developers' – suggested that their own campaign had already moved on to embrace the concerns of Newbury's residents. But, as one of the small band of campers explained, those invited to the meeting would provide a much wider perspective: 'There are thousands of Greenham women. Blue Gate has closed before and reopened. It doesn't have to be a final decision.'

The Yellow Gate banner suggested different priorities: 'Resist Trident – Resist Poverty – Resist War.' Nor was there yet any question of leaving. 'There's no debate here' said Katrina Howse, imprisoned 19 times for her protests over the previous decade and currently facing another charge for cutting the fence around the Burghfield nuclear bomb factory attached to the nearby Aldermaston research establishment. 'As long as there's one nuclear warhead, we'll continue our non-violent direct action. Warhead production has to stop.'[53]

A couple of months later Blue Gate was finally abandoned, leaving Yellow Gate to fight its own battles. In a last defiant gesture, the departing women pulled down a length of perimeter fence before driving off in their battered cars and vans. Local residents celebrated with champagne. 'It's what we have prayed for all these years', said one, 'but we never thought we would see the back of them.'

For Evelyn Parker, it was a sad occasion, but by no means the end of the story: 'The women's movement is still very much alive. The peace women have not died – just moved on to continue their work where it is needed. I do not think they will ever be back again on a permanent basis. They have too many causes to fight for.'[54]

Precisely how and when the protest should have ended is still a matter of debate among Greenham women. Rebecca Johnson's own plan had been to hold a party at Greenham to celebrate the signing of the INF Treaty which disposed of the missiles, and then leave, though not necessarily for ever: 'I wanted to go, to get a job, to pay back the large number of friends and family that had been lending me money for years. I wanted to get on with a different part of my life.'

Sarah Hipperson, an older woman with five grown-up children, chose to stay. Over the next few years the tiny group at Yellow Gate extended their protest to other sites, such as Aldermaston and Burghfield. They also pursued various legal challenges, including a cunning though ultimately unsuccessful attempt in 1995–96 to entice the MoD's lawyers into debating the legality of extinguishing commoners' rights in open court (during the later stages of its campaign, Commons Again strongly disapproved of this tactic, for fear the ministry really had abolished the crucial rights).[55]

By 1998, six years after the last Americans departed, even the Yellow Gate diehards began to think about packing up. Their concern now was that the Women's Peace Camp (though not of course the wider women's peace movement) should end in a dignified way that acknowledged, and if

Sarah Hipperson, long-term resident of the 'Yellow Gate' peace camp, entertains some young visitors.

possible commemorated, their long hard years of protest. But this too was, and remains, a controversial issue among Greenham women.

Rebecca Johnson, for one, is adamant that the women's true memorial is the work they are still doing around the world: 'We have taken the ideas, and the imagination, and the women's power for non-violence, and incorporated them in all kinds of way in our own life – in peace work, in human rights work, in UN work, in social work, in aid work, or in raising families.' The only physical reminder she admits to enjoying is the derelict control tower, scene of one of her favourite 'actions', abandoned to the encroaching heath.

If Sarah Hipperson, Jean Hutchinson and others associated with the memorial project were aware of such doubts, they did not heed them. Plans were made for a 'Commemorative and Historic Site' to be established immediately outside the old main gate of the airfield, where the protest had begun. The chosen design, as it now exists, is based on a garden. At its centre is a 'flame' sculpture of twisted steel, surrounded by seven standing stones – for which Jean, Sarah and the sculptor Michael Marriott scoured the Welsh quarries. Nearby, and also by Marriott, is a spiral water sculpture with a phrase from the most famous of the Greenham songs carved into its surface: 'You Can't Kill the Spirit'.

The campaign to turn such ideas into physical reality, at an estimated cost of £80–100,000, began with a presentation to the West Berkshire District Council (Newbury Council's successor), quickly followed – when it became clear that some strong opinions were flying about – by an explanatory article in the *Newbury Weekly News*. It looked as if the bitter arguments that had divided Newbury at the height of the women's protest would be rekindled by this scheme. The *Weekly News'* letters page offered both praise and condemnation. Some thought the protest worth commemorating; others wanted it dead and buried. To which the women responded, in a statement attached to their request for planning permission, by expressing the hope that the garden would promote reconciliation rather than reopen old wounds:

> We envisage the site as presenting the community of Newbury with an opportunity to heal the breach that developed over the siting of Cruise Missiles, and the divisions that were created not only between the protestors and the Newbury residents, but also by the polarisation within the community over the issue. We believe that despite years of conflict between the military occupation of Greenham Common and the Women's Peace Camp, history will record that the resistance by the women was governed by a commitment in practice to non-violence, producing a spiritual energy which eventually brings benefit to the area. We believe that this commitment should be commemorated.

In the event, the 'peace wimmin' evidently had enough closet supporters within Newbury's establishment to obtain the support they needed, not least from the Greenham Common Community Trust, which by now was making its own plans for the future of the airfield, and which owned the land on which the garden would be built. On 5 September 2000, the last of the women formally declared their 19-year protest at an end. A month later they got planning permission for the memorial. All they needed now was the money to build it.

It was rumoured at the time that the commemorative site only got planning permission because councillors thought the women would never find the necessary funds. It was certainly difficult. Sarah Hipperson co-ordinated the appeal, members of her own family providing one of the first substantial cheques. The National Union of Mineworkers chipped in with £5,000 and a message looking forward to this 'lasting testament to the courageous women of Greenham Common' (one wonders whether whoever wrote it remembered the time a male voice choir from the Welsh mining valleys was turned away, because it was by definition male). Yoko Ono, John Lennon's partner, sent a handsome donation. Letters appealing for support went to all the recently elected female Labour MPs. Most failed to respond.

About a hundred donors finally attended the inauguration on 5 October 2002, along with Mrs Thatcher's old enemy, the miners' strike leader Arthur Scargill. The air was heavy with symbolism. Circle-dancing around the sculptures recalled the old days, except that a number of the dancers were men. The following summer there was an open day, to which Newbury residents were invited. 'Some did come', Sarah recalls, 'but not as many as we had hoped for.'

A nuclear whodunnit

In February 1993, the Ministry of Defence acknowledged that the Berkshire airbase its American guests had been using on and off for half a century was at last 'surplus to requirements'. It seemed a simple enough statement of position, but nothing this labyrinthine Whitehall department says is really that simple.

In April the following year, as surviving remnants of the heathland gorse burst into flower, scientists from an organisation called the Defence Radiological Protection Service turned up at Greenham to conduct a discreet survey of the airfield. This was a special kind of survey. They were measuring gamma radiation, paying particular attention to three places: the spot where many years previously a US B-47 nuclear bomber was destroyed by fire, the area where the Americans dumped their waste, and the underground drainage system.

The aim of the exercise was to check that nothing untoward had happened during the US military occupation – in terms of radioactive contamination – that might affect the airfield's disposal. The men from the ministry knew something the rest of us did not. Back in 1961, two of their fellow scientists from the Atomic Weapons Research Establishment at nearby Aldermaston had indeed detected radioactive contamination – by fissile uranium, a crucial raw material of atomic bombs. And with the airfield now about to be sold for possible redevelopment, Whitehall could not afford to have irradiated construction workers, or a Newbury bypass that glowed in the dark (since much of the runway concrete would be sold for road building). This would definitely not be good public relations – especially since local people were already alarmed by 'clusters' of leukaemia and other childhood cancers around Newbury.

The two Aldermaston boffins, a Mr F.H. Cripps and his colleague Mr A. Stimson, had stumbled across the Greenham contamination almost by accident, following a highly secret military investigation known by the codename 'Exercise Overture'. The nuclear arms race was at full pelt, and the aim of this particular exercise was to discover whether, by analysing atmospheric dust samples deposited on the ground, our nuclear bomb makers could find out what their opposite numbers were up to far away in the Soviet Union, or wherever.

I can personally vouch that the eventual answer to their inquiry was a resounding affirmative. The evidence really is written in the dust. Years later, I was shown wide-eyed round a laboratory in Suffolk – an outpost of the Sizewell nuclear power station, as anonymous as an electricity substation – where by analysing dust collected by a sticky fabric screen on the roof, scientists could casually show you the residual constituents of last week's Chinese bomb test. If ever there was a demonstration of our environment's global interdependence – the reality George W. Bush's administration has found so hard to accept – this was it.

By 1963, the United States, the USSR and Britain (though not France or China) had of course signed a treaty banning nuclear tests in the atmosphere. But in the late 1950s and early 1960s, as the nuclear powers raced round their vicious circle, our planet's atmosphere was thick with clouds of irradiated particles, waiting to be washed down in the next rainstorm.

The Overture team were using the Aldermaston research establishment to test their theoretical calculations, because, however carefully its laboratories were sealed, the establishment inevitably discharged a small amount of radioactivity. They wanted to understand how this local contamination was dispersed across the surrounding countryside.

The study produced some startling results. Ten miles away to the west – beyond Greenham – they collected a sample of laurel leaves containing a hundred times more uranium-235 than they expected at that distance from the laboratories (U-235 is the fissile type of uranium, or isotope, which makes possible an explosive chain reaction, and hence a bomb).

Cripps and Stimson decided to investigate. And, in the carefully measured words of their subsequent report, 'it soon became apparent that a release of U-235 had taken place in the vicinity of the USAF base at Greenham Common'.[56] They also checked for plutonium-239, another bomb-making material, but found no more than would be expected from general atmospheric fallout.

Adding up the overall amount of weapons-type uranium indicated by leaf and mould samples, the two boffins estimated it was about 20 grams – more than the total discharged from Aldermaston since it opened! And when the samples were plotted on a map, and joined up to form contours, they produced what looked like a highly significant pattern centred on the Greenham runway. The contours formed two 'lobes', one extending from each end of the runway, suggesting that contaminated dust had been churned up and distributed by the coming and going of the US jet bombers based there – a theory apparently confirmed by the fact that more U-235 seemed to have been deposited at the western end of the runway, matching the direction of the prevailing westerly winds (aircraft always take off against the wind if possible).

Analysing their data, Cripps and Stimson decided that Greenham's contamination was too concentrated to have drifted over from Aldermaston five miles away (against the prevailing winds). Nor was it likely to have been caused by slow leakage, which would produce roughly circular contours. In their view, the evidence was strongly suggestive of a fire or explosion, and they knew of only one incident that fitted this description – an accident only three years previously, on 28 February 1958, when a nuclear bomber was destroyed by a terrible fire in which two US airmen died.

The B-47 Stratojet which caused the accident was known for some odd military reason as 'Granville 20'. Having completed a tour of duty on Reflex nuclear alert, it should have taken off from Greenham at 3.30 p.m. that afternoon, but was delayed by the late arrival of the replacement aircraft. Captain Harold L. Hopkins and his crew – no doubt impatient to get home – were finally cleared for take-off at 4 p.m., and sixteen minutes later Granville 20 lumbered down the runway loaded with more than 100,000 lb of volatile fuel for the long transatlantic crossing.

Just one minute into the flight, cockpit warning lights indicated fire in two of the bomber's engines and overheating in the left wing. Captain Hopkins radioed the control tower requesting an immediate emergency landing. But to do that successfully, he first had to jettison some of the fuel, carried in two drop tanks on the B-47's wings.

There was a standard procedure for this. Full tanks like these would normally be dropped off Lundy Island in the Bristol Channel. But this was not a normal situation and the aircrew chose instead to use the procedure for empty tanks, which involved flying back along the airfield to drop them on a narrow strip of land between the main runway and the northern taxiway. As luck would have it, the pilot momentarily lost sight of the airfield as he turned – not so surprising when he believed his wing was about to burst into flames at any moment – and had to make a second pass, this time approaching from the west, over Crookham. As the damaged bomber roared back, the (inexperienced) control tower operator gave the order to release the tanks, but the manoeuvre went disastrously wrong. Not only was there a 5–10 second delay before the tanks fell away, the aircraft was aligned slightly across the runway, heading for hangars on the South side where other bombers were parked, and beyond that not so far wide of the 'igloos' where their nuclear weapons were stored.

Both 1,700-gallon fuel tanks exploded on impact, one smashing through the roof of a hangar and the other engulfing a B-47 parked nearby undergoing maintenance. In desperation, the airfield covered in smoke, Granville 20 was diverted to RAF Brize Norton, near Oxford. The crew must have feared they were not going to make it, but in fact they landed safely, to discover that the engines were not, after all, seriously damaged.

Back at Greenham, there was one overriding question for Berkshire fire brigades who joined the Americans to fight the fire (and indeed for the residents of Newbury, had they but known it): was there a nuclear bomb in the burning aircraft, or in the hangar? If so, no one admitted it at the time.

One eyewitness was former USAF Sergeant Jerry Kroger, whose account I reported in the *Guardian* many years later, by which time he had married a local girl and was working as a taxi driver in Newbury. He pronounced himself '99.9 per cent sure' the burning Stratojet was unarmed. 'I was 50 yards away when it went', he said. 'There was no bomb on that aeroplane.'[57]

Mr Kroger based his belief on his detailed knowledge of US Air Force procedures. Nuclear weapons were loaded and unloaded by a special security-cleared team he recalled as '4th ADS' (though he could not be sure of the designation after 40 years). Other personnel, even including the pilots, were kept out of the way. Yet on this occasion another sergeant was sitting in the cockpit as the jettisoned fuel tank hit the plane, and one of the power units under Mr Kroger's control was standing alongside. Moreover, debris from the wrecked bomber was later dumped at the eastern end of the runway (no doubt one of the areas the DRPS survey team checked out). This would not have been permitted, according to the former US airman, had the authorities known the wreckage was contaminated by an incinerated atomic bomb.

Jerry Kroger was an extremely impressive witness. His testimony, combined with the absence of any admission by either the US or the British military authorities, seemed to put an end to such speculation. Had there been a serious accident, it should have shown up in the Pentagon's records, classified as a 'Broken Arrow'. Worldwide, there have been many such accidents. In Britain, so far as I know, the only one officially acknowledged in this dangerous category – albeit belatedly – occurred two years earlier at another US airbase, Lakenheath in Suffolk. This also involved a B-47, with no bombs on board, practising touch-and-go landings. The pilot misjudged his last landing. The aircraft slid off the runway, crashing into nuclear bomb storage igloos at the far end and starting a ferocious fire fed by its spilt fuel. According to Duncan Campbell, who investigated the accident for his book *The Unsinkable Aircraft Carrier*,[58] the American fire chief decided it was his grim duty to suppress the fire around the igloos before attempting to save the aircrew trapped in the burning aircraft – because he feared the stored weapons might explode, spreading radioactive plutonium for miles around. Judging by stories of US personnel rushing to leave the base, they were not at all confident he would succeed in controlling the fire.

The Greenham accident, horrific though the fire must have been, did not appear to be in the same nuclear league. Yet the wording of Cripps and Stimson's internal AWRE report, delivered in July 1961, shows that they distrusted the official account: 'We suggest that, in fact, a nuclear weapon may have been carried in the aircraft and burned with it.' They speculated that foam used to suppress the fire would retain loose irradiated particles, but spread them around the aircraft parking area, to be picked up and dispersed as planes came and went.

Their final conclusion could not have been more clearly stated:

> The size of the release and the nature of the distribution pattern
> suggests that damage to a nuclear weapon has caused contamination
> of the surface of the airfield by U-235 and this has been subsequently
> spread to the surrounding countryside by local atmospheric disturbance
> due to movement of aircraft. The only known incident which appears
> to have been large enough to produce contamination of sufficient
> magnitude is the fire which occurred on 28 February 1958, in which an
> aircraft, possibly carrying a nuclear weapon, was involved.

In a closed professional world where even the canteen menu was technically an official secret, it is no surprise to find that the report was originally classified as 'secret'. Politically, even then, the contents were explosive. Only six copies were authorised for distribution 'because of the sensitivity of the subject'. In a covering letter, Aldermaston's Frank Morgan said that 'other information' from a group security officer lent credibility to the Cripps–Stimson theory, but also wondered – in seeming contradiction – if it was worth checking other Strategic Air Command bases in the UK to see if they were all contaminated. Whether this suggestion was ever followed up I do not know, but it appears to raise the interesting possibility that radioactive dust might have been brought in to Greenham by visiting planes, rather than originating there – not such a far-fetched idea given the amount of bomb fallout swirling through the atmosphere in those days.

The MoD's response to all this was to sit on the Cripps–Stimson report for the next 25 years. This might not have mattered so much if the only issue was whether the B-47 was carrying an atomic bomb. It was standard Whitehall procedure 'neither to confirm nor to deny' the presence of nuclear weapons for fear they should become the target of protests or the subject of unwelcome parliamentary questions. But this was not primarily a matter of military security. Amid rising concern about the health effects of low-level radiation, particularly among those living in the vicinity of nuclear laboratories, the discovery of uranium contamination was of great public interest whatever its source.

So in the late 1980s, when the government responded by asking the Committee on Medical Aspects of Radiation in the Environment (COMARE) to investigate the increased incidence of childhood cancer in West Berkshire and North Hampshire, and whether Aldermaston, Burghfield or Harwell had anything to do with it, you might have expected the MoD to dig out the Cripps–Stimson study and say: 'Hey! Before you go any further, you might like to look at this.' Not a bit of it. COMARE was allowed to blind on with its investigation in 1989 without ever realising that the Greenham airbase might be implicated.

It was left to the Campaign for Nuclear Disarmament to blow the whistle, in July 1996 – with galvanising effect. In addition to revealing the existence of the 1961 report, it added two other disturbing pieces of information. It seems there had been another, unreported accident at Greenham, a 'crash landing' in 1963, and the recent MoD survey had found a hangar floor extensively resurfaced in a manner suggestive, at any rate to CND, of a nuclear clean-up.

At this, the MoD suddenly came out with its hands up – thanks largely, I suspect, to the no-nonsense instincts of the Armed Forces Minister Nicholas Soames. All the existing evidence was published, the relevant reports declassified. What is more, the various authorities finally accepted that public anxiety could not be allayed without a thorough re-examination of both the facts and their medical implications.

The Health Department immediately asked COMARE's medical experts to take another look. The MoD itself asked for an 'independent assessment' from the National Radiological Protection Board (NRPB, now a division of the Health Protection Agency), and even set up a helpline on which anxious Newbury residents could seek 'reassurance' from a health physicist.

Newbury's councillors, aghast that they might be deceived into buying back a contaminated airfield, turned for their reassurance to Southampton University and the Scottish Universities Research and Reactor Centre (SURRC). 'We're going independent', a man in the chief executive's office told me when I rang from the *Guardian*. 'We're cleared to spend up to a quarter of a million to knock this on the head once and for all.' He said the district council was beset with anxious residents worried about their children's health – or the effect on house prices. One woman wanted to know whether it was safe to retrieve her caravan from the airfield to go on holiday in Cornwall![59]

As the new investigations were completed, they did indeed offer considerable reassurance. Having taken measurements and soil samples from nearly 50 locations in and around the airfield – mainly in areas more or less undisturbed for the past 40 years – the NRPB found that radiation exposure from artificial sources such as fallout was 'no greater than anywhere else in the country'. Nor was the concrete excavated from the runway unusually radioactive.[60] The Southampton University–SURRC team concluded that the Newbury area had 'low environmental radioactivity compared with national and European averages'. To this extent, they too could find nothing to be frightened of, though they acknowledged that that they could not explain the 'perplexing ' incidence of leukaemia.[61]

COMARE's medical experts were the last to report,[62] paying close attention to suggestions of a nuclear accident they had known nothing about first time around, and dealing directly with public health worries. Like the others, they found only a low level of radioactivity around Greenham, which was

> due to natural sources together with a small contribution from man-made sources, including the worldwide fallout from global weapons testing, the fallout from the Chernobyl accident in 1986 and releases, including enriched uranium, from the nearby atomic weapons establishments at Aldermaston and Burghfield.

The updated COMARE investigation confirmed that there was a higher than average incidence of childhood leukaemia in West Berkshire and part of Newbury, but still found no reason to link these deadly illnesses with minimal local radiation levels. Even the hotspots measured by Cripps and Stimson in 1961 were in their judgement 'of no radiological significance'; the risk they posed to the public was 'trivial'.

So that was all right then; the new information had not changed the medics' judgement. But they went on to give the MoD the bureaucratic equivalent of a well-deserved kicking for not disclosing such vital evidence: 'We wish to make it clear that organisations whose predecessors have released radioactivity into the environment, whether those releases were authorised or accidental, have a responsibility to make that information available.' I say 'well-deserved' because the defence establishment has such a depressing record of withholding public information, especially in nuclear matters – a pervasive culture of secrecy, nurtured by self-importance and justified by misappropriating the genuine requirements of military security. The result, as here, can be a vast expenditure of time, expertise and taxpayers' money to investigate facts that could and should have been volunteered at the time.

As it turned out, however, the additional information still did not remotely answer the vital question of what was causing the Newbury cancers. Even the much simpler question of whether an atomic bomb was damaged in the 1958 fire was left tantalisingly unresolved.

The problem was that nobody could find any fundamental flaw in Cripps and Stimson's original measurements. In 1986 the AWRE itself took another look at the data and concluded there was no reason to doubt the earlier findings. So where had the contamination come from? COMARE clearly suspected Aldermaston, though it could offer no proof of this. Having studied the B-47 accident reports, it concluded that there was 'nothing to suggest that a nuclear weapon was involved'. Members of the committee were particularly impressed by the fact that firemen let the bomber burn itself out. They could not imagine this being allowed if there had been a bomb on board. Yet, as good scientists, they had to admit they had no absolute proof of this assumption. Reviewing the documentary evidence in the body of their report, they reminded readers that 'at no point in these documents is it categorically stated that a nuclear weapon was *not involved in the fire*'. Which makes one wish they had looked a little further, because there was yet another twist to this story.

No sooner had CND revealed the existence of the 1961 report, citing the B-47 fire in February 1958 as the only plausible cause of the airfield's uranium-235 contamination, than reports began to circulate of an earlier fire, in August 1957, also involving a nuclear bomber. CND suspected this first accident was more serious than the 1958 fire, even suggesting that an epidemic of Asian flu might have been used an as excuse to keep visitors away from the base while it was cleared up. The *Newbury Weekly News* then reproduced a letter from the late Frank Morgan (presumably the same Frank Morgan who wrote the covering letter to the Cripps–Stimson report, and one of Aldermaston's most senior scientists) which appeared both to confirm the earlier accident and to link it to the subsequent radioactive contamination.[63]

Writing at some time in 1959–61 (the letter is undated) to his distinguished Harwell colleague Sir William Penney, sometimes described as the 'father' of Britain's atomic bomb, Morgan began: 'You will no doubt recollect that I mentioned the high concentrations of U-235 found around Greenham Common, thought to arise from an accident there in August 1957 when a loaded aircraft caught fire.' He went on to explain that the 'excess material' was detectable to a distance of about eight miles and that in plotting it, allowance would have to be made for separate depositions around the AWRE.

At first glance (assuming the letter is genuine), it almost looks as if Morgan is writing about the same accident investigated by Cripps and Stimson, and just makes a careless mistake over the date. But the fact that he specifies the month as well as the year – August 1957 – rules this out. And whereas there was no evidence of a nuclear weapon being incinerated in the second fire, in February 1958, he says the earlier one occurred on 'a loaded aircraft'.

In pursuit of this intriguing lead, I contacted the Aldermaston department dealing with 'Freedom of Information' enquiries, asking whether they could find any correspondence or reports – including the Frank Morgan letter – relating to the mysterious 1957 accident. They consulted their corporate archive, but could find no trace either of the original letter or of any other relevant material. At Harwell, the UK Atomic Energy Authority also drew a blank. Apparently the only file that might have contained such correspondence with Sir William Penney has just five bits of paper in it, none of which is relevant. Meanwhile the request had been passed on to the MoD, where it seemed to disappear into the bureaucratic sand.

A formal response eventually arrived, simply repeating that nobody could find a copy of Dr Morgan's letter – the one item I already possessed, and therefore did not really need.

It is of course possible that the first fire was a minor one, quickly extinguished. The Pentagon appears to have no record of a nuclear 'Broken Arrow' at Greenham Common in 1957, any more than in 1958. Perhaps Cripps and Stimson knew of the incident but dismissed it as insignificant. Yet their boss evidently thought it serious enough to inform Sir William, and was sufficiently confident of his facts to state that the high concentrations of uranium-235 found around Greenham Common were 'thought to arise from an accident there in August 1957'. If all the relevant paperwork has been lost or destroyed, we shall probably never learn what happened. But it looks as if, once again, the MoD had forgotten to mention it to the people who needed to know.

Among those who desperately wanted some answers were Richard and Elizabeth Capewell, whose 16-year-old daughter Ann had died suddenly of leukaemia in 1993. They were living in south Newbury, not far from the western end of the Greenham runway. On hearing about the 1958 accident, and its possible implications, they began making their own local enquiries, plotting other cases of leukaemia on a map alongside their own (they both happen to be geographers). And they formed a small Newbury Leukaemia Study Group, hoping to prod councillors and health authorities into action.

Their research revealed a 'cluster' of 23 cases of leukaemia in south Newbury (excluding people over 60 years old) between 1971 and 1994. Among young people under 24, and especially among children under four, the incidence was substantially higher than the national average – findings broadly supported by the 1998 COMARE report, which acknowledged the Capewells' work. But, as with cancers elsewhere, it was one thing to show a statistical coincidence and quite another to establish a causal link sufficiently strong to prompt preventive action. Richard Capewell says he came up against two pervasive mindsets among the radiological experts. One focused on the medical consequences of massive radiation doses, such as the Hiroshima explosion, while the other (endorsed, naturally enough, by the anti-nuclear lobby) accepted that long-term exposure to low-level radiation was also dangerous and therefore worth investigating.

Newbury District Council clearly understood the strength of public concern and did what it could to support the leukaemia study group. Berkshire

Health Authority agreed to conduct an investigation, though somewhat grudgingly, it seems. Its experts accepted the information collected by the Capewells, but did not invite them – as they had perhaps naively expected – to take any part in preparing the subsequent report. The Newbury couple were not even invited formally to speak at its public presentation in April 1997. The assumption, presumably, was that parents who happened to have lost their daughter to leukaemia were neither objective nor competent enough to play any useful role in such complex epidemiological analysis.

In fact, the parents' published commentary on the health authority report suggests that they were well aware of the difficulty of establishing statistical 'significance'. The authority concluded that in general, cancer incidence rates in Newbury and West Berkshire were higher than national rates but in line with the surrounding region; that in the 0–4 age group, West Berkshire and Newbury cancer rates were higher than both national and regional rates; and that in one south Newbury ward there was a significant excess of leukaemias in the 0–24 age group.

While welcoming the BHA report, and its broad conclusions, the Capewells felt it was 'overloaded with caveats and one-sided statistical arguments' so as to play down the importance of the problem. They preferred, instead, to publish their own large-scale map, plotting a thick cluster of leukaemia cases running north-west from the end of the Greenham runway – that is, on the northern fringes of the contaminated 'lobe' identified by Cripps and Stimson many years earlier.

Whatever the source of Greenham's contamination, and its possible medical implications, the MoD land agents' immediate concern was whether the airfield they now wanted to sell was still radioactive. And in this they were reassured. In 1994 the Defence Radiological Protection Service, admittedly using somewhat rudimentary techniques, gave the base a clean bill of health apart from traces of caesium-137 (probably fallout from the Chernobyl explosion) found in one of the drains. The land disposal could go ahead.

Conflicting interests

The Ministry of Defence's first tentative proposals for the future of their airfield were not, at first glance, as crudely commercial as many local people had feared. Newbury's ancient commons were not going to become the site of a 'new town', or London's third airport, or some vast, haphazard industrial estate. The draft planning brief prepared by the Barton Willmore Planning Partnership for a meeting with Newbury's council in July 1993 began by confirming the MoD's previously stated intention that much of the central open space on which the vast runway was built should be retained as a public amenity. As soon as Chris Austin and the Commons Again watchdogs looked at the detail, however, their hackles began to rise.

The draft proposal's plans *did* include an airport – albeit only for light aircraft – making use of the control tower the protesting women had raided from their Violet Gate on the Burys Bank Road, and presumably adapting the existing northern taxiway as its runway. The western end of the airfield was set aside for sports facilities, including a football pitch and tennis courts. The main built-up area of the base behind the main gate was to be redeveloped for a mixture of commercial activity and housing, and a further 36 acres of land on that side of the runway was earmarked for additional housing. The former USAF command bunker nearby could perhaps become a military museum.

Such a scheme had the merit of catering for every conceivable interest, vested or otherwise. The end result, however, would have been to throttle what was left of the old heath in a more or less continuous ring of suburban development. Moreover, the residual open space might be cut in two by a road linking the airport to the commercial estate on the other side. All this may well have suited some Newbury people, but not those intent on major restoration.

Chris Austin accordingly pounced on the report's admission that Greenham commoners' rights – supposedly extingushed – had not yet been removed from the county register. 'If we can prove that commoners' rights still exist', he argued, 'the whole of Barton Willmore's plan is out of the window. You can't build on commons without the approval of the Secretary of State for the Environment, and the only things that he can approve are those that will improve the common for the local community. That certainly wouldn't include hundreds of houses.'[64]

The MoD had clearly failed to strike the right balance. But while it waited for public consultation to produce a better idea, its land agent immediately put several prime properties which lay outside the airfield up for sale – the listed Elizabethan-style Greenham Lodge (used as an officers' club by the USAF), its entrance lodge on the Burys Bank Road and the former American school at Crookham – so as to raise cash for maintenance and security elsewhere on the base. It also took immediate steps to find tenants for some of the military buildings, most remarkably the grass-clad, reinforced concrete silos (still subject to Russian inspection) in which the nuclear cruise missiles had been hidden. One of the things the MoD thought the empty silos might be used for was growing mushrooms – a gift to newspaper headline writers if ever there was one!

At this point in the Greenham story it would be nice to report a simple fairy-tale ending in which a born-again Ministry of Defence suddenly took the commoners' part, tore up its vesting deed, bulldozed the perimeter fence and escorted cattle back on to the heath as if nothing had happened since 1940. In reality the commons were so damaged by half a century of military occupation, overlain by miles of concrete, polluted by thousands of gallons of spilt aviation fuel, the recovery process was always going to be long, complex and expensive. And the remarkable concept eventually devised to manage their restoration reflected that: a private–public partnership operating simultaneously as both business enterprise and charity.

It sounds hopelessly complicated, like some politically correct 'initiative' cooked up by a Whitehall think-tank. Yet it worked, because in large measure it provided the main competing interests with what they wanted. The Ministry of Defence recovered enough money to show it was doing its duty by the taxpayer; the local economy gained a new business park; the profits from that helped fund the costly restoration of the commons so that Newbury District Council could afford to give them back to the local community and its commoners.

The idea came from Sir Peter Michael, a prominent local businessman. Having graduated in electrical engineering, he had built a highly successful career in the fast-expanding electronics industry while retaining a more parochial base in Newbury through his family hotels. His scheme was mooted in December 1993. Setting it up took another three and a half years of public debate, legal procedure and – initially – frustrating negotiation with Whitehall's bureaucracy. A ministerial decision finally broke the logjam.

In 1994 Newbury District Council formally 'adopted' a planning brief for the airfield. The following year it joined forces with a group of local businessmen to form the Greenham Common Community Trust, a non-profit-making charity whose sole declared objective was 'to ensure that the former Greenham Common air base is acquired, restored and developed in accordance with the Council's planning brief and managed for the benefit of future generations'. The Trust's management company accordingly put in a bid for the base, and on 25 March 1997 a deal was struck with the MoD at £7 million, most of which was borrowed from Barclays Bank. The Council promptly bought 750 acres of open airfield from the Trust for £1, leaving the main built-up area by the main gate – which was already attracting business tenants – to be commercially managed under the name of 'New Greenham Park'.

At one level the Park operates like any other business, for example obtaining EU funds to build a new Enterprise Centre providing premises for small local firms, particularly those just starting up. But its profits are then distributed through the Trust, both to help re-establish the commons and to support a growing list of other local causes – the Citizen's Advice Bureau, a school for deaf children, a community hospital in need of new X-ray equipment, a free musical instrument loan scheme for schoolchildren, a Newbury theatre renovation, and, within the Park itself, an arts centre in one of the former USAF buildings. A superb new purpose-built Mencap workshop enables people to surmount their learning difficulties by recycling furniture and domestic equipment for sale that would otherwise be dumped. In another setting, chief executive Stuart Tagg's well-rehearsed talk of turning private-sector energy and initiative to public benefit might be no more than political cliché. Here it really seems to represent the reality.

Without waiting for the scheme's elaborate managerial structure to be erected, the MoD had meanwhile made a start on an essential (and profitable) job it was familiar with from disposing of other RAF airfields: digging up the runway. The main runway stretched for more than 2 miles – reputedly the longest in Europe. Then there were taxiways on either side and clusters of circular pans on which big aircraft could turn, park and refuel. Together they contained more than a million tonnes of concrete and tarmac, and nothing much could be done about restoring the heath until it was removed. Given modern equipment – powerful hydraulic 'peckers', and those amazing machines that munch through chunks of concrete and spew it out as homogenous hardcore – the work itself was relatively simple. It just took a long time: 5 years, during which the airfield inevitably became a desert of heaped concrete and gravel.

In retrospect, it would have been easier if the other big clearance job, removing the labyrinthine aircraft fuelling system, had been tackled first. But the concrete raised some quick cash for the MoD, and later, when Newbury Council took over the contract, helped fund other restoration work. A few Greenham women were still around to watch great lorries taking the crushed material away, some of it to form the foundations of the Newbury bypass – the controversial object of protests almost as passionate as their own.

By 1995, two years had passed since the government said it no longer needed the airfield, yet the perimeter fence, potently symbolic for both Greenham women and commoners, was still barring public access. The latest explanation – or excuse – was that it must remain to keep people away from the dangerous concrete munchers. Commons Again was not impressed, and renewed its threat of legal action to assert what Chris Austin defiantly called the commoners' 'absolute right' to walk across this land. When an inner fence was erected to mark out parts of the base proposed for development, a group of Yellow Gate women challenged it in the County Court, hoping in the process to lure the MoD into the old debate about rights of commons – a trap government lawyers avoided by the Alice-in-Wonderland manoeuvre of admitting, 'for the purpose of this litigation only', that rights over Greenham did still exist.[65]

There was more legal confusion when somebody remembered the government's 'Crichel Down rules', dating from the 1950s, under which agricultural land compulsorily acquired by the government (typically for wartime purposes) has to be offered back to the former owners or their successors. Perhaps, after all, some local farmer was going to make a financial killing out of all this? Not really. In this instance the former owners were the old Newbury Borough Council, who bought Greenham Common at auction in 1939 and sold it on to the Air Ministry in 1960 (presumably under threat of compulsion), and the Tull family, who sold Crookham Common five years earlier. If this line had been pursued it might have provided a feast for the lawyers, but it was apparently blocked by another of the Crichel rules – that the government had no obligation to the former owners if the land had been 'materially changed in character' during its occupation. That was certainly true of the Newbury commons – except, of course, that they were now being altered back again. Here was a legal labyrinth in the Dickensian tradition of *Jarndyce* v. *Jarndyce*.

The cursed fence did not begin to fall until September 1997, when the district council decided to celebrate their acquisition in the by now time-honoured fashion: attacking the wire with a pair of bolt cutters. The man wielding them on this occasion, before an appreciative audience of council dignitaries, local residents and Greenham women, was the local Liberal Democrat MP David Rendel. It should have been straightforward enough. But Mr Rendel proved remarkably inept with the cutters. 'Oi, can I show you how?' called a female voice from the back, and one of the Greenham women stepped forward to help. The fence was down in a trice, and the crowd surged through the gap to enjoy their first officially sanctioned access in decades.

For a more formal celebration, Newbury had to wait another three years, by which time much of the rough clearance work was complete and it was finally considered safe to sweep away the rest of the barbed wire. On 8 April 2000 Jeremy Cottam, chairman of West Berkshire Council (successor to Newbury District Council), used yet another pair of bolt cutters to chop through the chains binding the gated entrance at Pyle Hill – still known to virtually everyone as 'Blue Gate', the name given it 17 years earlier by the women who set up camp there, and still splashed with distinctive paint.

David Rendel said, without exaggeration, that this was 'a truly historic day for the people of West Berkshire and indeed the people of the whole country'. Chris Austin was there, representing Commons Again, and Sarah Hipperson from the residual Yellow Gate encampment, soon to be abandoned. People wandered across the scarred heathland, gazing in awe at the massive nuclear silos still crouched gloomily behind their triple fencing, just in case the Russians should demand to check them out. As if collecting shells from a beach, kids took home bags of concrete chips, supposedly part of the millionth tonne recovered from the runway. Other children cut out a piece of chain-link fencing to be presented as a symbolic gesture to the forthcoming Nuclear Non-Proliferation Treaty review conference in New York. Mrs Mary Charles, interviewed by the *Newbury Weekly News*, collected soil from the flattened site of the cottage she came to live in half a century ago, just before her father left to fight in the Second World War. She said she intended to place it on her father's grave in Japan.[66]

Landscape surgery

Before the commons could once more be a tranquil haven for bell heather, birds or butterflies, they had temporarily to be turned into what looked like a vast industrial construction site. This preparatory work was in three stages: ripping up miles of concrete runway and taxiway, excavating a labyrinth of fuel tanks, and re-landscaping large tracts of gravelly Crookham Common that had been flattened to make a level base for the aircraft. It was not the obvious job for your typical conservationist, probably more used to cataloguing rare lichens than driving a bulldozer. But by a happy chance, the young man Newbury District Council found to take it on as project director felt quite at home with both.

Ed Cooper graduated in mechanical engineering before spending four years, as he puts it, 'milking cows in Dorset'. Then during the 1980s building boom he was off to London, to try the world of hard hats and donkey jackets he had trained for, working as a contracts engineer on vast sites at Canary Wharf and Broadgate. Not satisfied, he re-qualified in conservation management and landed a new job setting up countryside projects in the Pang and Kennet river valleys. So in 1997 he was nearby, as if waiting in the wings, to tackle the Greenham restoration – 'a massive opportunity to do something worthwhile on a large scale, and it matched all my skills'.

Removing the airfield's fuelling network proved to be a much bigger job than most people had imagined. Spread around the various aircraft parking bays were 21 fuelling points, fed from vast cylindrical tanks buried beneath the concrete, with an extraordinary combined capacity of 8 million gallons. (It was not just American cars, it seemed, that were extravagant with fuel. Some of the tanks were full of a nasty mixture of oil and water – about 1.5 million gallons of it. Ed managed to find a company that would separate the oil and take it away, but as the tanks were dug out a much worse problem was revealed. For years, fuel had been leaking from some of the rusting tanks and spreading to contaminate large areas of gravel. These had to be excavated and dispersed to allow bacterial action gradually to break down the oil. (Curiously, the MoD asked to retain the valve chamber connecting the tanks to the National Strategic Fuel Line at Crookham, near the women's Orange Gate, as if, even now, officials believed they might one day need their airfield back!)

As it happened, Ed was already intent on reconfiguring the north-east corner of the airfield, to replace the marshy gullies that used to drain the plateau with newly created ponds and hillocks that would partially replicate the original habitat. Not everyone was happy with this scheme. Some of the commoners, particularly Chris Austin, would have preferred to leave the flat landscape (some of which used to be farmland) more or less intact, so as to recover it quickly for grazing rather than wait many years for heather and grass to recolonise raw gravel. Residents of the Burys Bank Road even formed an 'action group' to protest at the disruption, and at the prospect of the nearby control tower being turned into a visitors' centre.

The counter-argument is represented by the shallow meres that are slowly beginning to acquire soft fringes of vegetation, and in the wading birds – redshank and ringed plover – that are attracted to nest on the bare gravel. Besides which, the million or so tonnes of gravel that was removed was sold to help fund landscaping and cleaning. Every stage of the commons' restoration involves striking some such balance between conflicting interests or objectives.

Nevertheless, Chris Austin is not alone in suggesting that the very word 'restoration' is questionable in describing some of the changes being made there. When I had the temerity to use it in a letter to Richard Adams, author of *Watership Down*, who remembers the heath from his boyhood, he replied scornfully that the 'so-called restoration' of Greenham Common is no restoration at all: 'The whole periphery of what used to be the common is now surrounded with housing and other development. The whole sense of a great, lonely expanse is gone forever.'

While respecting such nostalgia, I fear it risks missing a more fundamental point: that the common he remembers was not a natural environment, in the sense that mankind had no hand in creating it. On the contrary, as the process of recreating it clearly demonstrates, it was the artificial product of a particular kind of rural land management. Indeed the English countryside as a whole, that green patchwork we so readily admire when returning from some parched brown holiday resort in the sun, is much more the product of economic imperative than of aesthetic choice.

Ed Cooper was never going to be able to restore Greenham and Crookham commons precisely as they were before the Second World War, and
few would have thanked him for attempting to do so. The challenge was
to re-create a rare amenity still much appreciated by a modern, car-ridden
urban community like Newbury: an open, more or less uncultivated heath
to which there is full public access. Yet simply clearing away the detritus of
military occupation would not remotely have achieved that. The new heath,
just like the old, required positive human intervention. The difficulty was
deciding which aspects of the legal framework and land management that
produced our ancient commons were essential to this particular restoration
(or re-creation, or resurrection), and which could be discarded.

After one final legal challenge from the Yellow Gate women resulted in
an Appeal Court ruling that commoners' rights on Greenham really had
been extinguished, West Berkshire District Council decided it was essential
both to re-establish those rights and permanently to protect the public's
right of access. In December 2000 this was done, with the Trust's help, by
promoting the 'Greenham and Crookham Commons Bill' in Parliament.
A year later it became law. Here was the exact opposite of the eighteenth-
century Inclosure Acts – a measure dedicated to preserving common land
rather than seizing it as private property. The preamble solemnly defined
its purpose:

> To restore land at and in the vicinity of the Greenham and Crookham
> Commons as common land open to the public; to make provision for the
> conservation of the natural beauty of that land; to grant public access
> over that land in perpetuity and to make provision with respect to that
> public access; to restore and extend commoners' rights over that land;
> to constitute the Greenham and Crookham Common Commission for
> the management of that land; to confer powers on the West Berkshire
> District Council and on that Commission with respect to that land; and
> for connected and other purposes.

In other words, it addressed the two issues that had preoccupied first
the Greenham women and then Commons Again for so many years, and
settled them in favour of renewed commoners' rights and public access. The
one seemingly discordant note was the Act's explicit permission to erect a
new fence in place of the legally discredited, much-mutilated military one.
After all that desperate work with the bolt cutters, it must have seemed like
a betrayal. In fact the new stock fencing was so different, and so obviously
necessary, as to avert almost any criticism: a simple waist-high affair of

smooth wire stretched between wooden posts; enough to keep cattle from straying but not a serious barrier to humans who cannot bother to find the nearest gate. It was paid for by English Nature, the body which designates protected 'Sites of Special Scientific Interest' (SSSIs) on the new heath.

The Act also established a commission to supervise the commons' management, its members nominated by various local councils, the commoners, English Nature and the Trust. Among its specific duties are preserving this common land as 'a peaceful place of natural beauty', conserving sites of special scientific interest, promoting grazing, and encouraging public awareness of its ecological, cultural and historical significance. The Victorian founders of the Commons Preservation Society could hardly have wished for more.

Where rights of common survived, the Act extended them across the combined area known from then on in the singular as 'Greenham and Crookham Common'. Greenham commoners who had lost their rights could recover them, provided they paid back the £3,500 obtained in compensation from the MoD. Those rights not reclaimed within a year (either because the former owners preferred the money, or still possessed whatever rights they really wanted outside the old airfield boundary) would be sold, for example to local cattle breeders who intended to build up a herd on the new common.

Cattle were absolutely vital. If a lowland heath like this was not grazed, or continually cleared and mown as it was during its time as a military airfield, it would soon disappear beneath encroaching birch scrub, bracken and brambles. Gorse would probably survive, as it does elsewhere, but the expanse of open grassland and heather – the very reason we call it a heath – would be lost.

Cows were reintroduced to the common in 1999 – that is, 'suckler' cows, brown and white Herefords, which rear their own calves rather than providing human beings with milk. At the last count there were 60–70 animals, a number West Berkshire's Countryside Officer Simon Barnett would like to see doubled. Appropriately, the two largest herds belong to Chris Austin, now chairman of the Commons Association, and the Association's secretary Ken Neal.

Ken lives at Bunker Farm, on the edge of the common, down by the cruise missile silos which gave the farm its name. He describes himself as a building design consultant. His house, which he built himself, is one of the most spectacularly eco-friendly structures I have seen. The massive

After half a century of military occupation, cattle are once again grazing on Greenham and Crookham commons, helping to restore and maintain them as open heathland for the people of Newbury. On the horizon, derelict missile silos still stand as a permanent reminder of a nuclear past.

30-inch walls are made of cob – a mixture of clay and straw – smoothly plastered inside but quite raw outside. Timber framing came from the common woodland. He was going to grow straw for a thatched roof, but finally compromised by opting for modern tiles, which, I have to say, look somewhat incongruous atop the archaic mud walls.

His cows wander across the common in slow groups, searching this poor soil for the best of the coarse grass. They will also nibble the (relatively) soft tips of the evergreen gorse, but only when there is nothing else. On the north side of the common, where the Burys Bank Road crosses the fenced boundary, they hardly seem to notice passing cars – perhaps just a curious stare. Such insouciance occasionally leads to collisions.

These accidents are one of the reasons the Greenham herds are slowly being changed from Herefords to British Whites – which show up better in the dark! You might think dedicated conservationists would scorn such pragmatism, but I assure you it is one of four reasons quoted on the explanatory notice posted on a nearby gate. British Whites are an ancient breed, with a mouth more suited to the coarse vegetation found on the common. They are also a rare breed, intrinsically worth preserving, and they have no horns with which to threaten innocent hikers or birdwatchers. The vast white bull whose activity is gradually changing the herds' colour might seem threatening even without horns, but the notice insists: 'He is a very placid animal, far more interested in his cows than chasing about after people.'

The next step is to introduce Exmoor ponies, which already graze Snelsmore Common on the other side of Newbury. They have strong mouths and teeth capable of tearing up the invasive bracken roots and brambles Simon Barnett's team would otherwise have to tackle themselves. As for the unfenced Burys Bank Road, Simon is hoping life on Exmoor will have taught them how to cope without endangering either themselves or the passing motorists.

The Countryside Officer's long-term challenge is to weigh all the competing interests, human and otherwise, so as to find a balance which as near as possible sustains the heath without mechanical intervention or restrictive bye-laws. Many of the requirements of a modern common are recreational rather than economic, and reconciling them is not easy. Dogs, for instance, do not mix well with the ground-nesting birds local naturalists want to encourage, yet being able to walk a dog is one of the most obvious amenities the common provides. Where trees fringing the heath are no longer felled for local use, or coppiced in the traditional way – for example, to make besom brooms from young birch shoots – they still have to be controlled. It took several years to clear the suffocating birch scrub accumulated outside the old perimeter fence. A whole plantation of invading spruce trees was also cut down. It does not sound like conservation, but then it is not woodland that is being conserved, but open heathland.

The yellow-flowering gorse seems eager to re-establish itself on the former airfield. For this type of plant, the poor soil is not a problem. It was a characteristic feature of the old common, but it too will have to be monitored now that its natural predators – the commoners who collected and burnt it – are no longer interested. Nowadays it is the bird-watching enthusiasts who particularly welcome the spreading gorse, because it attracts sprightly little Dartford warblers.

Two other comparatively rare birds which draw 'twitchers' to Greenham are the woodlark and the nightjar, both of which need a subtly mixed habitat – something akin to a large woodland clearing. The nightjar has an alternative name, goatsucker, which refers to an extremely ancient superstition (recorded by Aristotle) that by sucking a nanny goat's udders, the bird would make the animal go dry and eventually turn her blind. Altogether an exotic creature, the kind of bird Breughel might have included in his mysterious symbolic landscapes as a change from magpies. It comes to Britain from Africa to breed, nesting on the ground. Its favourite food is moths and insects, gathered in a gaping mouth as it flits around after sunset, emitting a penetrating 'churr' as it does so. Few casual visitors to the common are likely either to see it or to hear it, but it features prominently on the council's publicity leaflets. At the last count there were seven or eight breeding pairs scattered round the edges of the heath. 'We could do with more', says Simon Barnett, describing in detail the sort of habitat he must produce to entice them: 'solitary pines, in an area cleared of birch, with some heather and a wooded fringe'.

If that sounds like a lot of trouble just to attract a few unusual birds, it is nothing to the complexity of the environment English Nature and the council are trying to develop for the smaller plants – heathers, orchids and grasses. The common already supports three different kinds of heather – ling (the commonest form), bell heather, with deep purple flowers, and crossed-leaved heath, growing in wetter areas. Among the orchids, the green-winged variety attracts a lot of interest because it does not normally appear on heathland.

For someone like myself, who can barely name a couple of dozen wild flowers, the intensity with which the new habitat is being scrutinised and recorded is extraordinary. This is a specialised scientific world where grass is not just any old grass, any more than the woodlark is just a 'little brown job'. For example, there is a particular bent grass on Greenham not found anywhere else in Berkshire, prompting speculation that seeds may have been transferred from East Anglia by American aircraft (echoing my conjecture, mentioned earlier, that the radioactive contamination discovered by the Aldermaston boffins in 1961 might also have been brought by visiting US planes). Intensive mowing of the common during its long years as a military airfield has also encouraged many tiny plants that would not normally survive on heathland.

It is not just the plant life that excites the scientists. Even beetles and snakes are loved by someone. Witness Ed Cooper's detailed explanation, in an essay he contributed to John Kippin's *Cold War Pastoral*, of why he insisted on bulldozing Crookham's bare gravel into uneven contours:

Small changes in hydrology, aspect, soil type, and fertility can provide niches for specialist plants and animals to survive. Burrowing insects such as the banded sand wasp, green tiger beetle and the minotaur beetle will use warm south-facing gravel banks and disturbed ground to nest, adders will bask in sheltered areas, cross leaved heather will thrive in slightly wetter areas and mosses and lichens will colonise open gravels.[67]

The adders, incidentally, have been given their own 'hibernaculum' made from old drainage pipes, so watch out!

With so much gravel exposed by removing the concrete runway and taxiways – about 250 acres – its treatment was fundamentally important. Rather than go for a quick fix by spreading topsoil, it was decided to let it regenerate 'naturally', but give it a helping hand. In late autumn each year, some of the existing heather is mown, and the cuttings spread on the bare stretches. Fresh shoots begin to appear a couple of years later.

It will be many more years before a permanent new balance is achieved and Newbury can finally see what sort of common has re-emerged from half a century of contentious military occupation. Once it does settle down, it is hoped to establish some sort of visitors' centre in the former control tower, which has been carefully preserved with this in mind. There will no doubt be a display showing where to find the rare orchids and the nesting birds (with a warning not to disturb them); maybe a café to replace the Ark Teahouse which used to stand a mile away to the west; and now those awkward women are safely out of the way, a reminder of their historic protest, which included breaking into this very tower one winter night to signal their presence to an astonished American sentry.

Chris Austin, who led the Commons Again campaign, is more or less content:

> Now there's an Act of Parliament, it would take another Act to undo the status quo, so I think basically we've got the common for ever. We've succeeded. It's now an open space, and every time I go out there and see people walking the dog, or jogging, or kids riding their bikes, I think – Yes, it's a job well done.

What's in a monument?

When the shutters are removed from the control tower's panoramic windows, Greenham's visitors will have fine views southwards, right across to Watership Down. The skyline immediately opposite contains the former hangars and workshops that have been absorbed into New Greenham Park. To the right, hunched low on land falling away towards the River Enborne, are two rows of vast grass-covered shelters. These are the nuclear cruise missile silos. They once housed enough destructive power to annihilate every major city in the western part of the former Soviet Union, from Leningrad to Odessa. A map reproduced in the official record of the 501st Tactical Missile Wing's mission, *The Last Crusade*, shows a 2,500-kilometre arc radiating from the UK so as just to include Moscow.

Of all the symbolic remnants of Greenham's military occupation, one might have expected that these grim nuclear bunkers would be among the first to be demolished as the common was restored. On the contrary, there is every reason to suppose they will be the last. For a start, they look almost indestructible, as if only an atomic bomb could remove them. The walls are 16 foot thick, composed of blast-absorbent layers of reinforced concrete and sand. Ed Cooper assures me, however, that if necessary his bulldozers could have brought them down. The initial reason for their survival was that under the 1987 INF Treaty they were subject to surprise inspection by the Russians, along with an associated workshop and hangar. Of course that treaty provision soon ceased to serve any direct purpose, because the actual weapons were publicly destroyed, but for some years after the end of the Cold War both signatories had an interest in maintaining their mutual inspection rights. So they were not abandoned until May 2001.

At that point the district council could have exercised its option to buy the silos for £1 (Greenham Common Trust snapped up the other two treaty-bound buildings for a similar sum) but declined to do so. Whoever bought them would have to pay for their maintenance and security (making sure, for instance, that inquisitive children did not come to any harm). Yet

The women's 'Green Gate' barring the way to the USAF's derelict cruise missile silos, the whole complex now scheduled as a national monument to the Cold War.

it was not at all clear what civilian purpose these strange semi-cylindrical buildings could serve – unless it was to grow mushrooms. Plans to set up another charity to run at least one of them as a Cold War museum came to nothing because the MoD, having fulfilled its obligations to Newbury, now put the Treasury's interests first by simply selling all the silos to the highest bidder.

Meanwhile English Heritage, of all people, had stepped in to schedule the silos as a monument! Which begs the fascinating question: to what are they a monument? American imperialism? Britain's 'special relationship' with the United States? NATO's 'victory' over the Warsaw Pact? The nuclear presence against which thousands of Greenham women hurled their protest? Or the protest itself?

On making inquiries, I found that English Heritage has its own lengthy and articulate answer. First, however, I had to shed a common misconception that all scheduled monuments are 'ancient' (though it seems to me a reasonable misunderstanding, given that the protective scheduling system was originally established by the Ancient Monuments Act of 1882). Evidently age no longer matters. Anything appropriately monumental can be designated, from a prehistoric burial mound to an abandoned twentieth-century coal mine.

This monument consists of what the Americans called the GAMA (GLCM Alert and Maintenance Area), a secure nuclear compound surrounded by a double fence, plus an outer 'patrol fence' topped by razor wire. Inside crouch the massive, hump-backed silos – six of them, unexpectedly camouflaged with turf so as to resemble some primitive Iron Age dwelling, yet designed to house state-of-the-art weapons of mass destruction. Each silo sheltered four missile launchers and two control vehicles, behind heavy steel blast doors that lowered like a drawbridge. A launcher contained four missiles, each far more destructive than the crude bombs dropped on Hiroshima and Nagasaki. In one of the six silos there was additional accommodation for a 'Quick Reaction Alert' crew, always at almost instant readiness to launch their missiles. Running through the site is Drayton's Gully, draining water from the common into the River Enborne, and alongside it are five nuclear bomb stores – or 'igloos' – built in the 1950s for Strategic Air Command's B-47s. They were refurbished by the missile warriors to serve as an armoury and fuse store.

Officially, the silos' massive construction was designed merely to protect the cruise missiles from conventional bombing, because during a nuclear alert the mobile launchers would disperse up to 200 miles from Greenham (Helen John's mysterious Sennybidge installation is within that range). In fact, according to Duncan Campbell,[68] the shelters were 'hardened' to the same degree as the US intercontinental missile silos, so as to survive a near-miss from a Soviet nuclear bomb. But of course it was not thought advisable to explain this to the people of Newbury. They might have got the wrong idea – about being sitting ducks.

The GAMA's entry in the Schedule of Monuments makes the point that latterly it was also protected against 'peace protestors who set up camp outside the perimeter fence in a series of camps which made the complex an internationally recognised focus of debate about the nuclear arms race'. A heavily patched section of the old perimeter fence containing the women's Green Gate therefore 'forms an integral part of the monument'. So their protest is commemorated here as well as at Yellow Gate.

Under the heading 'Assessment of Importance', the Schedule quickly corrects my lazy assumption that only sites like Sutton Hoo or Tintern Abbey can qualify as monuments. Even archaeology, it seems, is not necessarily archaic. 'The archaeological remains of the Cold War' the Greenham entry begins, 'are the physical manifestation of the global division between capitalism and communism that shaped the history of the late twentieth century.' The European cruise missile sites, it explains, 'testify to the resolve of the principal partners in NATO to maintain nuclear parity with the countries of the Warsaw Pact', while also representing examples of the Western post-war defence industry's leading-edge technological innovation. Moreover, the Greenham Common base was in commission for longer than any of the others, and is believed to be the only one in Britain to have housed operational missiles with nuclear warheads.

> The Greenham Common GAMA complex is internationally important as one of the key emblematic monuments of the Second Cold War, signifying an escalation of the nuclear arms race by the introduction of GLCM. Subsequent to the INF Treaty of 1987 most of the missiles and launchers were destroyed; GAMA remains as one of the few tangible relics of this technology. It remains a potent symbol of the positive power of arms control treaties to render advanced military technology obsolete. The site additionally includes a group of 1950s Igloo bomb stores which were reused in the 1980s but which also illustrate an earlier phase of Cold War nuclear deterrence.
>
> Beyond its significance as an exemplar of the infrastructure of GLCM technology, the site has a wider cultural significance in the late twentieth century as the focus of mass protest against the nuclear arms race.

It's all a long way from my outdated perception of English Heritage, and so much the better. But let me add one thought of my own. Nuclear weapons are not only uniquely destructive. They leave behind uniquely long-lasting contamination (the radioactive half-life of plutonium-239, the active component of most atomic bombs, is 24,400 years), which is the other big reason to fear their proliferation. And although Greenham's empty silos are indeed testimony to the success of the INF arms control negotiations, their looming presence is a reminder that while those particular weapons have been removed, the problems they posed have not been solved. Other weapons are still lurking out there in vastly dangerous numbers, waiting to achieve some new critical mass.

Most of the scars left on Greenham's and Crookham's ancient commons by half a century of military occupation are now being healed through a careful process of natural regeneration. The silos are different. They could squat there for hundreds, even thousands, of years. By the time their last traces disperse, the shingle ridge which formed the heath might itself be threatened by a resurgent River Kennet.

Herstory

> Human history becomes more and more a race between education and catastrophe.
>
> H.G. Wells, 1920

H.G. Wells shows a self-educated Edwardian's touching confidence in the progressive power of knowledge. At the beginning of this new century, having watched the Bush–Blair axis disastrously reassert the role of faith, intuition and superstition in political affairs, we may be inclined to doubt it. But if what he said was at all true in 1920, it is more so today, when we face, among other global problems, the complex dangers of nuclear proliferation.

The Greenham women's educational contribution was a simple one: to restore a human perspective. They sought to remind us (though to what effect is a matter of widely differing opinions) that NATO was gambling with our survival, using American nuclear cruise missiles as chips. They did not necessarily claim to understand the war game's arcane rules, merely that the stakes were far too high – potentially catastrophic.

Twenty-five years on, their concern has lost none of its relevance. At the last count,[69] there were still more than 16,000 operational nuclear warheads in existence: 7,000 of them American, 8,000 Russian, and the remainder distributed between China, France, India, Israel, Pakistan and the UK (which has 185). Most of these are long-range strategic weapons. Many are ready to launch at a few minutes' notice – a policy Robert McNamara, US Defence Secretary during the Cuban missile crisis, recently described as 'immoral, illegal, militarily unnecessary, and very, very dangerous in terms of the risk of accidental use'.[70] And although the numbers have been coming down year by year, the delicate legal and diplomatic structures erected to control them are being allowed to fall into disrepair.

In retrospect, the 1987 INF Treaty which removed the ground-launched cruise missiles from Greenham looks like a high-water mark for nuclear arms control, the first and only agreement to eliminate a whole class of weapons worldwide. Hopes of quickly following it with a comprehensive test ban that would stop the nuclear arms race in its tracks were not realised. Instead, there are now fears that more nations will feel the necessity to acquire such weapons, or, worse, that the revival of civil nuclear power programmes will enable terrorist groups to acquire some kind of 'dirty bomb'.

It was against this disturbing background that Blair's then Defence Secretary Dr John Reid called in 2005 for a national debate on whether Britain should replace its Trident nuclear missile submarines now the Cold War is over. When the women began their Greenham protest, the decision to 'rent' Trident from the United States had only just been taken – in July 1980. The main alternatives rejected at that time were CND's proposal for unilateral disarmament, endorsed up to a point by the Labour Opposition, and a submarine-launched version of the cruise missile the Americans were pressing NATO to deploy.

The odd thing is that, superficially, nothing much has changed. The obvious choice is still between another ballistic missile like Trident, a cruise missile, or no missile at all. The differences are nevertheless highly significant. The unilateralists' 'disarmament by example' is now a more plausible option for the UK than it was at the height of the Cold War, modern cruise missiles (already operated without nuclear warheads by the Royal Navy) are far more accurate than they were then (witness the attacks on Baghdad), and Washington's attitude to such an important technological transfer is in some ways less predictable.

One question that seems to me of continuing importance is how far the sort of uncompromising stand taken by the Greenham women, CND, or the 'peace movement' as a whole is likely to influence such a debate if there really is one. Does it matter whether academics engage in 'peace studies' or 'war studies'? Do mass demonstrations like the march against the Iraq war ever do more – at least in a British setting – than allow opponents of the political establishment to let off steam?

To provide a commentary that would address some of these points, I asked a number of people who might be expected to have relevant opinions – Greenham women themselves, politicians, academics, military figures and journalists – to answer an identical two-part question: 'What did the Greenham women's protest achieve, and what difference, if any, did it make to the outcome of the Cold War?'

The responses (given in full, in alphabetical order, in the next chapter) vary widely. Some argue that Greenham made absolutely no difference to the outcome of the Cold War, others that it played a significant part in promoting the INF Treaty which removed the cruise missiles, and thereby helped to bring the nuclear confrontation to an end. Those addressing the first half of my question – including some of the Greenham women – tend to be less interested in the protest's immediate influence on NATO policy than in the way it encouraged women to engage in a much wider political debate from which they had largely been excluded. Making a reality, in other words, of the painted slogan with which US Air Force personnel were often confronted – 'Greenham women are everywhere!'

For me, this emphasis on influence and inspiration, rather than cause and effect, is the correct one. It is admittedly true that the common de-nominator among the thousands who took part in the protest was their determination to rid Greenham Common of nuclear cruise missiles. The appearance of a permanent US base in Berkshire gave anti-nuclear campaigners like Ann Pettitt something tangible they could work with, a clear target, a destination for their march from Cardiff that was more than symbolic. Assessing what they actually achieved, however, is not that straightforward. In some respects their achievement was neither clear nor tangible. As one of the straw poll respondents put it, it is 'a bit like asking if it was the suffragettes who got women the vote'.

Besides which, just as the suffragettes campaign furthered women's in-terests other than the right to vote – men were forced to sit up and listen – so Greenham had a diffuse influence far beyond the nuclear issue. In fact both campaigns left such a deep imprint on our collective memory as to be important in themselves, regardless of their contemporary context or outcome – the sort of event requiring serious attention in any school textbook of twentieth-century history.

Karmen Cutler (Thomas), a key organiser of the original march, makes the point elegantly in her answer to my standard question:

> There are events in history which ignite feelings of passion and power, and which then inspire people to act. I believe Greenham was such an event. Whether the protest had any impact on the world's political stage is largely irrelevant. What is relevant is the impact it had on the women who became part of Greenham Common.

If you were looking for an analogy to explain this explosive burst of energy, the fundamental nuclear reaction that underlay the women's fears would coincidentally provide it. A fissile nuclear bomb material like uranium-235 will quietly emit neutrons to little effect – like the routine anti-nuclear demonstrations Helen John found so pointless – until it reaches a critical mass. Then it can suddenly explode. In terms of protest, Greenham created that critical mass, excited by what one of the women described as 'an infectious optimism'. The resulting outburst swept up thousands of women and metaphorically irradiated many thousands more. This energy was expended in some quite unexpected directions. For example, the relentless fashion in which the women drew attention, for their own purposes, to the continued existence of commoners' rights laid the legal foundations of the later campaign to recover the commons for the generally ungrateful residents of Newbury.

The peace camp was itself the result of a spontaneous impulse. When the marchers set out from Cardiff in August 1981 they did not intend to stay at Greenham, merely to demand a public debate. They fully expected to be back in their domestic routine by the end of the school holidays. Yet the camp became permanent. Women came for a week and stayed for years. Some, like Helen John, never went back to their former life. As the Irish proverb says: 'The seeking for one thing will find another.'

The women-only decision was also unexpected, completely changing the nature of the protest as well as vastly increasing its impact. It turned 'feminists into disarmers and disarmers into feminists', as one woman put it. The airfield's rainbow-coloured gates became an extraordinary, unprecedented and, for several years, successful experiment in anarchic feminist living. At times, a couple of the gates were also overtly lesbian, which for some women was itself a big attraction. Rebecca Johnson says she used to remind CND groups that were alarmed by this 'that Greenham wouldn't have existed much beyond the first couple of years if it hadn't been for the lesbians'. Her point being that heterosexual women with family responsibilities might support the camp from home by raising funds or visiting at weekends, but were less likely to make the drastic commitment of living there.

Some heterosexual women were understandably disconcerted, or frankly intimidated, by the lesbians. Others felt they gained a lot from the association, that here was another prejudice the camp's special atmosphere could help to break down. Women of different persuasions, different ages, different backgrounds, were working for a common anti-nuclear cause, and closed ranks against a common enemy, represented most crudely by the bailiffs and the vigilantes. In such circumstances normality was impossible to define. Eccentricities were ignored. As Lorna Richardson put it: 'Take away the dotty grandmothers, the teenage anarchists, the "burly lesbians", and there wouldn't have been all that many left.'

A certain degree of theatrical exaggeration was in any case appropriate. The airfield perimeter, with its barbed wire, arc lights and watchtowers, was in effect a political stage on which the argument between NATO's missile warriors and the anti-nuclear women was acted out. Songs, banners and witches' costumes were part of the scene. Occasionally, the production would transfer temporarily to a county courtroom. But all this was by no means the sum total of the protest, as the massive set-piece actions periodically demonstrated.

There were many thousands of women who heeded the call to 'Carry Greenham Home' to support groups throughout Britain. They led much more conventional lives but nevertheless found time to operate telephone trees, distribute leaflets, raise funds or even manufacture 'Getaways'. Hence the Greenham symbol of the spider's web. Without this great web, its longer threads stretching abroad as far as Moscow, Washington and Tokyo – a sort of political and social Internet before the actual electronic system was invented – the immediate spectacle around the base would have been nowhere near as sustainable or influential.

Against this wider background, the second part of my straw-poll question appears in better perspective. The fact is – though some of the women find this hard to accept – that identifying any direct linkage between the protest and the nuclear missiles' elimination, and hence with the outcome of the Cold War, is extremely difficult. The forces driving the arms race towards its conclusion – notably Gorbachev's realisation that military confrontation was economically unsustainable as well as appallingly dangerous – obviously swamped the effect of any one political demonstration, however spectacular.

Some Cruisewatch women who prevented missile convoys 'melting into the countryside' by publicising and disrupting their dispersal did feel that, in this way at least, they were striking a direct blow at NATO's military machine. This was not strictly true. The well-organised Cruisewatch campaign certainly caused the Americans a great deal of political embarrassment and inconvenience. It exposed the absurdity of training for nuclear Armageddon as if it were an extension of conventional warfare – a valuable lesson in itself. But these were political moves in a peacetime setting. In a real nuclear alert the Americans would have swept any protest aside to disperse as quickly and as widely as they could. Their operational concept was based on self-preservation. They knew that if it came to nuclear war, the airfield, along with the ancient town of Newbury, would have been wiped out.

Searching for simple cause and effect therefore does less than justice to the women's achievements. In this narrow sense one could argue that the women failed. The INF Treaty was the product of superpower diplomacy. Cancel the march from Wales, delete the Greenham protest from history, and the East–West nuclear poker game *might* have ended in a similar fashion. NATO had after all announced a 'twin-track' policy years before missiles arrived. Yet this is emphatically not the same as saying that persistent, widespread public alarm at NATO's precarious reliance on nuclear deterrence – vividly focused from 1981 by the Greenham actions – had no effect. On the contrary, it was from this background that positive diplomatic initiatives such as the twin-track, and the 'zero option' underlying the INF Treaty, somehow emerged. The fact that one cannot identify the myriad pathways along which pressure was exerted does not mean it had no effect. (If that were true as a general principle, economic forecasters in particular would long since have thrown in the towel.)

Our political leaders do not operate in a vacuum. They spend much of their time (some would say too much of their time) trying to assess public opinion so as to follow it or manipulate it. The Greenham women were exceptionally vigorous members of a wider movement, including CND and European Nuclear Disarmament (END), which alerted people to what was going on inside those Cold War bunkers. They dragged the fundamental issues out into plain daylight. Above all they changed public expectations, so that when a rare chance came to cut the knots into which the deterrence strategists had tied themselves, even the Iron Lady felt obliged to take it.

Although my arbitrary straw poll was not designed to find a consensus, a number of people – male and female – nevertheless agreed that Greenham's lasting achievement was to inspire/empower/politicise/energise/engage/galvanise women, almost regardless of the campaign on which they originally embarked. There is a lot of truth in that. But it is no reason to lose sight, almost condescendingly, of the nuclear issue that was at the heart of the women's protest. Whatever else it achieved, it should also be judged by its contribution to solving what is still among our most urgent problems: how to cope with the proliferating destructive power of nuclear weapons.

Back in 1980, when David Owen was still a Labour MP, albeit a thoroughly disillusioned one, he wrote a pamphlet called *Negotiate and Survive*. It was a calculated sequel to two earlier pamphlets: Tory Home Secretary

William Whitelaw's *Protect and Survive*, with its fatuous advice about white-washing windows against nuclear flash (in effect an official acknowledgement that Britain was defenceless against nuclear attack) and E.P. Thompson's *Protest and Survive*, calling for a Europe-wide anti-nuclear campaign. Owen summarised his response in a final sentence: 'In a nuclear age to protest is understandable, to protect is inevitable, but only if we negotiate will we survive.'

Twenty-five years on, our predicament has not changed that much, and nor has the answer. We survived the Cold War's nuclear confrontation as much by luck as by judgement. Its wildly irrational excesses have abated, but we now have the added anxiety that atomic weapons may soon be available to people with fewer inhibitions about using them. Governments still justify their nuclear weapons programmes by a doctrine of deterrence, with its deliberate uncertainties, though some begin to hanker for a more dangerous pre-emptive alternative. Negotiation in one form or another is still the only way we shall escape nuclear warfare's suicidal trap.

The Greenham women could not solve this intractable problem. They reminded us, in a fresh, clear, female voice, that it remains to be solved. And, along the way, they helped recover one of England's ancient commons.

THE QUESTION 'What did the Greenham women's protest achieve, and what difference, if any, did it make to the outcome of the Cold War?'

I chose this wording in the hope of prompting sharp answers both from those who believed strongly in the value of the women's campaign, as I did, and from those who dismissed it as hysterical nonsense. Besides which, it seems to me objectively important – now as much as then – to know whether such protests achieve results. Is anyone really listening, and, if so, how does a 'peace' movement's contribution measure up against that of other groups who also lay claim to being peacemakers or peacekeepers – the politicians, diplomats and soldiers.

The responses were every bit as provocative as I had hoped. Recorded here in full, they speak for themselves, but a few points of dispute and consensus are perhaps worth highlighting.

Denis Healey's typically blunt reply – 'I do not think the protest at Greenham Common had much effect on British politics, so it had no effect whatever on the Cold War as a whole' – seems to me to underestimate the political influence of public attitudes by comparison with the professional mechanics of arms control negotiations. It certainly contrasts with Michael Heseltine's dramatic contention that 'the continuing effectiveness of the strategy of the whole Western Alliance was at risk'[71] unless the anti-nuclear protest groups were defeated. And notice that NATO's supreme commander at the time, US General Bernie Rogers, admits to being anxious that 'the Ladies of GC', along with other European groups demonstrating against the missile deployments, might weaken their political leaders' resolve.

Jonathan Steele, who reported for the *Guardian* from Moscow, suggests that the Kremlin too was watching points, and may at times have been restrained by a desire not to look bad in the eyes of the Western peace movements. But then the former MoD mandarin Sir Michael Quinlan, the eminent theologian of deterrence strategy, speculates that if the women had any effect on Soviet policy, it would probably have been 'in the wrong direction' – encouraging a false belief in the Kremlin that it could manipulate Western public opinion to its own negotiating advantage. In his memoirs, Mikhail Gorbachev acknowledges this possibility, but adds that if the earlier Soviet leaders did think NATO would be impeded by the peace movement, they were 'more than naive'.[72]

At which point I can almost hear friends among the Greenham women exclaiming that so far these comments are coming from men. So how, in retrospect, do they rate their own achievements?

While generally accepting that the protest's direct influence was modest, the Greenham women show great pride in the way women across the world were inspired, politicised and ultimately empowered. They point to the ability of 'non-violence' to challenge the state's military strength, the way in which the 'idea of Greenham' changed other protest movements. In an especially vivid analogy, Ann Pettitt visualises women 'gatecrashing a private party at which the future of the world was being decided.'

Among the other respondents (of either sex), even those who give Greenham a low rating in terms of Cold War politics generally acknowledge that the protest made an important contribution to the wider feminist cause, though I realise there were those in the women's movement who believed all that energy would have been better spent elsewhere.

Professors Sir Lawrence Freedman and Paul Rogers, representing respectively King's College London's department of 'war studies' and Bradford University's 'peace studies' department, *do* offer distinctly different assessments. The London professor sees the protest as 'a symptom of a wider disquiet' about the conduct of nuclear deterrence, and its appeal as 'largely emotional'. His Bradford counterpart gives the women considerable credit, suggesting that but for their campaign, albeit as part of the wider anti-nuclear movement, the INF Treaty might not have been achieved – or at least not as early as it was.

THE ANSWERS

Chris Austin, Newbury resident, chairman of Commons Again:

> The Greenham women's protest achieved very little. However, locally it antagonised a lot of residents who had to put up with the nuisance of the encampments. Nationally, one of the women's DIY legal actions

produced a judgment saying that the minister's use of powers to compulsorily purchase the commoners' rights was lawful – something the commoners had deliberately avoided during the legal action they took. Internationally, the Cold War was won by President Reagan and Mrs Thatcher, who outspent the Russians on defence and by so doing began a process which has seen nearly all the nations of the Warsaw Pact and the Soviet Union join the democratic world.

Tony Benn, parliamentarian:

Their camp and campaign became known all over the world, and when I was in Hiroshima and Nagasaki in 1983 they were seen as beacons of hope. They were arrested and charged under the 1361 Justices of the Peace Act – although all they did was tie flowers to the barbed wire fence and sing – when inside there were enough nuclear weapons to destroy the human race.

Andrew Brookes, last operational RAF commander at Greenham Common, 1989–91:

The deployment of cruise missiles to Europe initiated the process that ultimately bankrupted the USSR. My level was more prosaic than that. I had a £750,000 annual budget for fence repairs, illustrating the costs of the peace women to the British taxpayer.

From my perspective, the women had no impact whatsoever on the withdrawal of the missiles from Greenham. Ironically, when the last missiles came to be flown out, some women tried to lie down on the runway to prevent the airlifter from taking off. Just being there had become their life.

Fiona Bruce, BBC journalist and (briefly) Greenham woman:

It's almost impossible to quantify exactly what the protest achieved. I think it failed in its grander ambitions – to hasten the end of the Cold War, to drive nuclear weapons out of Britain. But it certainly gave Britain's politicians a flavour of the extraordinarily tenacious opposition there was to nuclear weapons and probably made them considerably more cautious in their endorsement of them.

As a chapter in the history of feminism it was remarkable. With all its slight daffiness, dodgy knitting tied to the fences and tuneless chanting of Joan Baez songs, it showed that women can come together in a predominantly male arena as a force to be reckoned with.

Ed Cooper, project director for the restoration of Greenham and Crookham commons:

I think you have to be careful when generalising about the peace protest. In effect there were a number of different women's groups at Greenham and all behaved differently. Some groups managed completely to alienate the local population, whereas others gained some support. Overall, I believe the movement: raised public awareness of the threat of nuclear arms; increased public pressure on government to agree the INF Treaty; showed that committed protest could influence media coverage and hence raise awareness (a significant legacy for democracy); empowered other groups to feel that committed protest could achieve results (rightly or wrongly).

I believe the Cold War would have ended with or without the protest, for economic reasons, but it may have accelerated Western governments towards a solution.

Karmen Cutler (Thomas), joint organiser of the protest march from Cardiff to Greenham Common, August 1981:

There are events in history which ignite feelings of passion and power, and which then inspire people to act. I believe Greenham was such an event. Whether the protests had an impact on the world's political stage is largely irrelevant. What is relevant is the impact it had on the women who became part of Greenham Common.

Lynette Edwell, Newbury resident, supporter of Greenham women and Cruisewatch:

It got rid of the cruise missiles at Greenham. Otherwise the missiles would have stayed for as long as the USAF demanded. Our government would have had no say at all. In general, it empowered ordinary women, who had courage and conviction, suggesting original and imaginative ways of non-violent demonstration.

Michael Foot, journalist and author, leader of the Labour Party 1980–83:

Two contrasting events from those times stick in my old man's memory. One is a visit I made with my wife Jill Craigie to the women at Greenham Common – they were the people who were properly looking to the future, and could save us all. Jill had a special animosity towards nuclear weapons because of the injury they threatened to women, even in their production.

The contrast was the scene in the House of Commons when Michael Heseltine turned up to explain his conduct after a confrontation with some other women who were protesting (I think it was the nearest thing to real military strife he had ever seen). His report to the House was shocking. Nor did he worry about traducing a woman in the Government service who had done no more than fight for the same principles as the Greenham Common women.

Sir Lawrence Freedman, Professor of War Studies, Vice-Principal (Research), King's College London:

I don't think the Greenham women had influence on the outcome of the Cold War. They were a symptom of a wider disquiet about the West's reliance on nuclear deterrence for its security which was brought to a head by the intensification of the Cold War following the Soviet invasion of Afghanistan, the cruise missile and Trident decisions, and also some publicity about civil defence.

Whatever my differences at the time with the various expressions of disquiet, I always felt it was vital that the issues be addressed directly. There had been far too much complacency about the nuclear issue during the 1970s – really until the neutron bomb debate. There were good reasons to be anxious about the West's dependence on deterrence, even if the remedies were not as straightforward as often presented.

There were many symptoms of this disquiet – from the big protest marches in Europe to the Freeze movement in the US, and also the attempt of some security types, including myself, to try to suggest policies that would reduce the role of nuclear weapons in Western security. Greenham Common had the drama and the prominence, but its appeal was largely emotional, and so as the situation changed during the 1980s, particularly as Reagan and Gorbachev began to talk to each other, they had even less to contribute.

While many of the figures connected with CND and END had arguments that required attention and consideration, I can't say this was ever the case with any of the Greenham Common people. I don't mean this to sound condescending because I realise they had their own preferred ways of expressing themselves and relating to the issues, but they were just so off beam on the analysis that they were easily ignored.

The reason that policy-makers had to take notice of the concerns was because of the big protest movements, although they had lost all steam by the mid-1980s.

The Cold War ended because of the cumulative failures of the Soviet system which led Gorbachev to seek a variety of remedies, which included an easing of the Cold War. Contrary to the expectations of the protest movements, in their different ways Reagan and Thatcher responded to Gorbachev's initiatives. None of this happened within their analytical/political framework, so they were caught as much off guard as everyone else.

Roy Hattersley, member of the House of Lords, author and journalist:

I do not believe that the Greenham Common women had very much influence on the nuclear disarmament debate. They were an irritant to the Government and a wonderful example of the way some people are prepared to pay a personal price for the demands of conscience. But

the Cold War ended with glasnost in the Soviet Union, not because of
protests in Great Britain.

Denis Healey, member of the House of Lords, Defence Secretary 1964–70,
Deputy Leader of the Labour Party 1980–83:

I do not think the protest at Greenham Common had much effect on
British politics, so it had no effect whatever on the Cold War as a whole.

Peter Hennessy, Professor of Contemporary British History, Queen Mary
College, University of London:

I may be wrong, but I thought Greenham made absolutely no difference
to the ending of the Cold War.

Michael Heseltine, member of the House of Lords, Defence Secretary
1983–86:

The Greenham women were their own worst enemies, in that no matter
how much people sympathised with parts of their message, they found
no inclination to identify with the messengers.

Sarah Hipperson, Greenham woman:

Women developed, from a very simple method of non-violent resistance,
an effective strategy of dealing with the immense power of the state and
the military. At the root of its effectiveness lay an essential component
– commitment to a life that was entirely different from what had gone
before. Combining a simple lifestyle with revolutionary thinking, they
set down, in practical terms, a pattern of purpose and intent capable of
undermining aggressive power.

The conduct of the protest brought some light, and a change of mind,
into the nuclear war plans of the USA and the USSR, making them
abandon their policy of Mutual Assured Destruction (MAD) – hence
the words of the INF Treaty: 'Conscious that nuclear war would have
devastating consequences for all mankind...'. Cruise missiles were signed
away on 8 December 1987.

Jean Hutchinson, Greenham woman:

About our resistance and what it achieved, I would say we were
successful in removing Ground Launched Cruise Missiles from
Greenham Common. I was convinced of this when Mrs Thatcher – who
loved nuclear weapons – did not object to the signing of the INF Treaty
which banned these missiles. She had to go along with it because we
had invalidated the base.

Another answer, of equal importance, is that Ground Launched Cruise Missiles were vulnerable to our non-violent resistance. One of the main features of GLCMs was that they should 'fade away along the roads into the darkness', so the USSR wouldn't know where they were. Actions at Greenham Common and Salisbury Plain ensured that every convoy was plotted and watched, so the 'fading away' was never possible.

Helen John, Greenham woman:

The Greenham protest inspired women, very visibly, to oppose their own Government's policies – and this went right round the world. As for the Cold War, the protest played a part in preventing a particular weapons system functioning in this country – no doubt about that. But I always viewed the cruise missile as a red herring. The US was playing a massive poker game, to sucker the Soviet Union into again having to try to match an extraordinarily expensive weapons system.

Rebecca Johnson, Greenham woman, Executive Director, Acronym Institute for Disarmament Diplomacy:

Greenham was important because we had an impact on both sides of the Iron Curtain.

In the short term, it helped undermine military credibility in Europe through our persistent and successful obstruction of cruise missile deployment (while at the same time refusing to fit the heroic stereotype constructed for us by the Soviet media), by our links with dissident groups in Russia and Eastern Europe, and by inextricably connecting anti-authoritarianism and women's rights with our work against weapons and war.

By linking feminism, nonviolence and a concerted political challenge to military-focused concepts of security, Greenham had the longer-term impact of inspiring women around the world, imbuing generations of activists with a sense of direct political responsibility, power, and the possibility of creative change.

Bruce Kent, CND General Secretary 1980–85:

Perhaps the greatest achievement of the Greenham protest is one not mentioned often enough – the empowerment of women in many other parts of the world. I travelled to many countries in the eighties, some in the West, some in the Eastern bloc, and some non-aligned. Time and again at meetings held to discuss the nuclear arms race and ways of ending it, the first question would come from a woman. It would be about Greenham – How are they getting on? How many are there? How do the police treat them?

What effect did they have on the outcome of the Cold War? Some effect certainly if not a major one. The West was inevitably going to 'win' the Cold War since the Soviets, without anything like the same economic resources, ruined themselves trying to catch up or even get ahead. But when the USA decided to negotiate a zero option (no cruise, no Pershing II, no SS-20) their spokesmen always said that they took this option straight off our banners.

The voice of the Greenham women was a major part of the protest here, and contributed to the political pressure which made the zero option proposal a sensible one for the United States.

Rodney Legg, chairman Open Spaces Society:

That is a bit like asking if it was the suffragettes who got women the vote. There was much going on across a wider canvas. What Greenham did manage was to energise unrest inside the triangle of capitalism, communism and conflict. This encouraged those protestors on the other side of the Berlin Wall who took to the streets to bring down the Iron Curtain at the end of the decade.

Di McDonald, Greenham woman and Cruisewatch activist:

Greenham proved that long-term, peaceful, nonviolent protest was sustainable – we had the US forces, the civilian police, the MoD police, the judiciary and RAGE all against us, but we stayed there.

It uncovered a legal route to challenging the military. And it politicised women far beyond the confines of the camp – Greenham women spoke all over the world.

David Owen, member of the House of Lords, patron of the Greenham Common Trust:

The second part of the question (Greenham's effect on the outcome of the Cold War) is easy: it had absolutely no effect whatever.

As to the first question: it achieved something very important for women. Previously, women were identified with a variety of protest movements, but they'd never before been so dominant. Greenham Common was owned by women. During that period, in the early eighties, women engaged themselves on both sides of the argument. Greenham was a sort of injunction to get involved. Defence was not just a man's issue; it was also a woman's issue.

Essentially, what it did for women in politics – it made clear there were no areas where they couldn't go.

Evelyn Parker, Greenham supporter, Cruisewatch activist and member of Commons Again:

It changed attitudes. For example, Mrs Thatcher was quoted as saying that nuclear weapons were an evil, but a necessary evil – that made me realise that perceptions were changing.

Through Cruisewatch I think we proved quite conclusively that the missile dispersal system didn't work. The idea of dispersing along a limited system of roads to a destination that is supposed to be secret is actually quite silly.

Ann Pettitt, initiator of the protest march from Cardiff to Greenham Common, August 1981:

The purpose of Greenham was to gatecrash a bunch of nobodies into a private party at which the future of the world was being decided. In this, it was outstandingly successful: in between the kitchen tables of Wales and the negotiating tables of Geneva, Greenham women became one of the globally recognised symbols of the eighties.

Dan Plesch, founder British American Security Information Council (BASIC), former vice-chairman CND and Cruisewatch supporter:

The Greenham protests came to symbolise a much broader international mass movement. That movement had a decisive impact in preventing nuclear war, and helping ease the tensions so that the Cold War ended peacefully.

Greenham forced a badly needed and much resisted human reality check into the irrational logic of the arms race. More specifically, the protesters' main demand – 'No Cruise, No Pershing, No SS-20' – became the negotiating position of the US government, Ronald Reagan's zero option, and these weapons are to this day the only class of missiles possessed by the US and Russia that have been completely destroyed and banned.

Certainly, CND's demand of unilateral disarmament failed, but most at Greenham were not concerned with how the weapons were removed – just that they go – while some CND strategists argued that if we demanded unilateral disarmament we might get multilateral disarmament. Tragically though, with a handful of exceptions the movement dissipated and failed to follow up its success once the immediate threat had gone. Leaders used to mobilising on a diet of fear failed to celebrate a triumph when the INF Treaty was signed and use that celebration as the base to press on with the job.

Leslie and Wendy Pope, Greenham supporters, members of Commons Again and lifelong pacifists:

Firstly, the protest achieved a lot of publicity, which, along with the associated Cruisewatch campaign, kept the issue of nuclear weapons very much alive, so causing considerable irritation to government.

More permanently, it was a major factor in enabling many ordinary women – and men too – with strong convictions about nuclear weapons, and social issues, fearlessly to pit themselves against authority.

As a specific factor in power politics decision-making we think it was not significant.

Sir Michael Quinlan, Permanent Undersecretary, Ministry of Defence, 1988–92:

For what it is worth, my view is that the women made no substantive difference to policy or to the ending of the Cold War (and if they had had any effect in the latter regard, it would probably have been in the wrong direction, by encouraging the Soviet Union – as almost certainly happened over the 'neutron bomb' affair in 1977–78 – to imagine that they could sap the West's resolve and impede its actions by manipulating our public opinion).

Lorna Richardson, Greenham woman:

Greenham made an impact for several reasons. One was the practical day-to-day effect of having a peace camp outside a US base. Another was the network – composed of people who lived at Greenham but spent time elsewhere, and of people who spent most of their time at other places but then came to Greenham. And a third was the 'idea' of Greenham, and the effect that had on protest movements beyond those who actually came there.

US General Bernie Rogers, NATO Supreme Allied Commander Europe (SACEUR) 1979–87:

How well I remember the 'Ladies of GC'. I had some interesting discussions about the ladies, sometimes with Michael Heseltine, as well as about all the many demonstrations on the Continent which were against deploying the GLCMs and Pershing IIs. I think there were a number of us, who would be affected by the decision to deploy, who were concerned that all the demonstrations might cause nervous political leaders to become wobbly and not agree to the deployments, which were, in my opinion, absolutely necessary.

In the end, I do not believe the protests by the 'Ladies of Greenham Common' and the other widespread demonstrations on the Continent made any real difference to the outcome of the Cold War. What did make the difference was the steadfastness of most of the NATO political authorities to deploy those weapons on West European soil, where they represented, for the first time, a truly significant nuclear threat to the WP/USSR should the latter attack westward. (There was some conjecture that political authorities in some of the nations upon whose soil the deployments were to take place became so enraged by the demonstrators, such as the 'Ladies of GC', that they were determined the demonstrators would not be the ones who decided how their nations would be defended.)

Paul Rogers, Professor of Peace Studies, University of Bradford:

The Greenham Common protests had three main public effects – they had a major visual impact and added substantially to the growing nuclear disarmament movement, they greatly increased women's involvement in the movement and had an empowering role in the process, and they highlighted the particular dangers of highly accurate 'war-fighting' theatre nuclear systems.

In political and strategic terms, I don't think the INF Treaty would have happened (or certainly not as early as it did) without Greenham Common as part of the wider anti-nuclear movement. It is certainly the case that the INF Treaty was far and away the most transparent and verifiable treaty of its time.

Clare Short MP:

The Greenham women and other protestors stopped the development of a new generation of nuclear weapons in Europe and led Reagan and Gorbachev to disarmament agreements. It was a mighty achievement.

Jean Stead, formerly assistant editor, the *Guardian*:

The greatest lasting achievement was probably the assertion of modern feminism, ranking with the campaigns of the suffragettes, whose colours were adopted by many women. 'Carry Greenham home' was the slogan which encouraged women to become activists when they returned to their own areas.

Greenham added a substantial element to the ending of the Cold War. The unwelcome publicity which the women's action gave to the arrival of the cruise missiles, where they were to be targeted and the fact that each warhead was more than ten times the power of the Hiroshima bomb, was spread through the country and much of the Western world. People started to think about the dangers of possessing nuclear weapons. The women danced on the silos and the cruise missiles eventually went away, leaving them still occupying Greenham Common.

It is sad that the end of the Cold War was not followed by the same determination to rid the world of nuclear weapons which was started during the years of perestroika and glasnost after 1986.

Jonathan Steele, *Guardian* correspondent, regularly on assignment in Soviet Union and Eastern Europe during 1970s and 1980s, Moscow bureau chief 1988–94:

The Greenham women's peace camp was the single most effective initiative which British anti-nuclear protesters organised during the last decade of the Cold War. It commanded constant international and national attention and publicity. It inspired tens of thousands of other British people to volunteer for peace work and take part in demonstrations. Those who could not afford to devote as much time as the Greenham women nevertheless felt challenged to act in a lesser way wherever they could.

So the ripples which went out from Greenham travelled a long way. Greenham was the model, the touchstone, and the inspiration for thousands who never went there but admired the peace women's example.

The Greenham women, along with other peace protesters around Western Europe, put a third actor on to the Cold War stage, or at least created an engaged and alert audience sitting in the theatre. Whereas arms control negotiations used to take place in arcane private discussions between superpower leaders, with mind-boggling details on throw-weights and the numbers of multiple independently targetable delivery vehicles, the advent of the peace movement forced the core issues into the open.

Stuart Tagg, Chief Executive Greenham Common Trust:

You will need to ask someone wiser than me what impact the protest made on the outcome of the Cold War. It certainly made people think. For me, it raised the issue of where the duty of the citizen to act to prevent the government acting illegally starts and finishes. It also demonstrated the degree of sacrifice some people are prepared to make for a cause they are passionate about.

Polly Toynbee, *Guardian* columnist:

I never went to Greenham. My sister did, with her six-year-old son, but was sent away because he was a boy.

I think it had no effect at all on the Cold War, but had some galvanising effect on the women's movement in the Thatcher years.

Postscript

Where did they go from Greenham?

Helen John never went back to Wales. She has continued to campaign for the causes she embraced at Greenham – especially ridding Britain of its US military presence. Long since divorced, she now lives on her own in Otley, Yorkshire, conveniently placed to mount repeated protests against the US electronic eavesdropping facility at Menwith Hill and the prospect of Britain becoming a component in an American 'Star Wars' programme to take military control of space. During a recent general election, when she stood against the Prime Minister Tony Blair, she had to conduct part of her campaign from prison.

Eunice Stallard never really left her Welsh mining valley above Swansea. Now well into her eighties, she is still a member of the Labour Party, CND, Labour for Peace and the Peace Pledge Union. She attends chapel when she can get there. Much of her life these days revolves around that of her children, grandchildren and great-grandchildren.

Ann Pettitt, originator of the Greenham march, remains near Carmarthen, where the smallholding she worked with her partner Barry has evolved into a cottage industry producing high-class cabinet work and handmade tiles. Ann's latest campaign has nothing to do with nuclear weapons: it is to improve the maternal survival of women in the central African state of Chad.

Karmen Cutler (Thomas), who worked with Ann to organise the march, lives with her family at Brynaman, at the foot of the Black Mountain. She represents the trade union Unison, and is a volunteer warden at a local nature reserve.

Jean Hutchinson, one of the two Greenham women who successfully challenged the legality of the MoD's activities, has moved to the same former Welsh mining town as Karmen. With her husband John, a painter, she lives only a few hundred yards away. Jean rates it 'a real luxury' to have exchanged John Major's old constituency for one where the Welsh nationalist party Plaid Cymru is elected.

Georgina Smith, Jean's partner in the court battles with the MoD, now lives in Argyll, on the west coast of Scotland. Further south, near the Coulport Trident submarine depot on Loch Long, she has purchased land from the ministry, both to conserve it as woodland and as a convenient base from which to protest. She has not lost her enthusiasm for tastefully designed political banners and graffiti. Writing to me last year, she said her latest effort was still visible from the railway line between Helensburgh and Garelochhead.

Sarah Hipperson, another Greenham woman who relished taking on the MoD lawyers at their own game, has returned to a pretty house in Wanstead, Essex. She has recently published her own account of the many court cases in which she was involved: *Greenham, Non-violent Women v The Crown Prerogative*. She is still paying off the costs incurred in one of those cases.

Rebecca Johnson moved on from Greenham to organise campaigns for various peace and environmental organisations, and is now internationally known for her research on multilateral arms control and the United Nations. When not monitoring negotiations or putting pressure on bellicose governments, she can be found in Hackney, north-east London, from where she runs the Acronym Institute and publishes its journal, *Disarmament Diplomacy*.

Di McDonald continues to work full-time on peace and security issues for the Nuclear Information Service from a cluttered, comfortable Victorian house on the outskirts of Southampton. She is a member of the Greenham Women Everywhere network and the Aldermaston Women's Peace Camp. She says her adult children also continue to 'support disarmament and global equity based on the principle of nonviolence they learned at Greenham'.

The anonymous whistleblower who leaked MoD plans for the arrival of the cruise missiles in 1983 turned out to be 23-year-old Sarah Tisdall, a civil servant working in the office of the Foreign Secretary Geoffrey Howe. In a remarkable example of official vindictiveness, she was prosecuted and sentenced to six months' imprisonment. She now works in Bristol as a property manager for an organisation providing the voluntary sector – charities, co-operatives and other community groups – with affordable accommodation.

Chronology

1930	Crookham Common's owner grants right of public access
1938	Newbury Borough Council buys Greenham Common; deed later establishes public access
1941	Both commons requisitioned under wartime Emergency Powers
1943	US airborne division occupies airfield
1944	American airborne troops from Greenham Common join D-Day assault in Normandy
1947	Airfield de-requisitioned but not restored
1948–9	Berlin blockaded; NATO formed
1951	Commons re-requisitioned for USAF in spite of local protests
1952	Britain conducts first atomic bomb test
1955	Air Ministry purchases 400 acres of Crookham Common
1956	Air Ministry privately declares intention to extinguish commoners' rights
1957–8	Accidents involving US B-47 nuclear bombers at Greenham Common
1958	World War II Emergency Powers expire
	US Strategic Air Command puts Greenham B-47s on nuclear alert
1960	Air Ministry purchases 600 acres of Greenham Common
1961	Aldermaston scientists investigate airfield's nuclear contamination
1963	Partial test ban treaty reduces atmospheric nuclear tests
1964	US B-47s leave Greenham Common
1965	Commons Registration Act: Crookham and Greenham Commons Association formed
1966	Greenham becomes NATO standby base
1973	Commons and associated commoners' rights registered
1978	Plans to base US KC-135 tankers at Greenham abandoned after local protests
1979	NATO agrees 'twin track' to base nuclear cruise missiles in Europe and negotiate with USSR
1980	Greenham Common and Molesworth chosen as UK bases for NATO's US cruise missiles
1981	'Women for Life on Earth' march from Cardiff; Greenham protest begins in September
	Ronald Reagan becomes president of USA

1982   Falklands War
        First peace camp evictions – first arrests – in December 35,000
        women 'Embrace the Base'
1983   General Election: Margaret Thatcher re-elected
        First cruise missiles arrive in November – in December 50,000
        women demonstrate their protest
1984   First missiles operational; first dispersal from base in March; Cruise-
        watch formed
1985   Gorbachev assumes leadership of Soviet Union
        MoD introduces new trespass bye-laws in April; Jean Hutchinson
        and Georgina Smith convicted
1986   Chernobyl nuclear power station explodes in Ukraine
1987   Judge Josh Lait hears bye-laws appeal by JH and GS in Reading
        Crown Court
        Intermediate-range Nuclear Forces (INF) treaty signed
1988   Judge Lait rules in February that MoD bye-laws are invalid; women's
        convictions quashed
        In April MoD informs Parliament of intention to extinguish
        commoners' rights
        Soviet inspectors visit Greenham and Molesworth in July under
        terms of INF Treaty
        In September first cruise missiles leave Molesworth
1989   First cruise missiles leave Greenham in August
        Berlin Wall falls
1990   Commons Again formed in January
        Law Lords uphold Crown Court ruling that 1985 MoD bye-laws are
        invalid
1991   Gulf War
        Last cruise missiles leave Greenham in March
        Greenham (but not Crookham) commoners accept MoD compensa-
        tion for lost rights
        501st Tactical Missile Wing disbands in June
1992   Commons Again members arrested for cutting Greenham fence to
        assert rights of access
        Judge Lait rules in Crown Court in June that airfield perimeter fence
        is illegal
1993   MoD puts airfield up for sale in February
        In December Sir Peter Michael suggests partnership to recover com-
        mons and redevelop airfield
1994   Blue Gate peace camp closes in January
        Newbury District Council announces plans to recover and restore
        commons
1995   MoD begins breaking up runway in April
        Greenham Common Trust forms in July

1996   CND reveals nuclear contamination of airfield secretly investigated by Aldermaston in 1961

1997   Greenham Common Trust buys airbase; Newbury District Council acquires commons

Demolition of perimeter fence begins in September

1999   Grazing cattle return to commons

2000   Commons officially reopened in April

Last Greenham women leave Yellow Gate on anniversary of 1981 march from Cardiff

2001   Greenham and Crookham Commons Act re-establishes public access and commoners' rights

2003   Cruise missile silos scheduled as national monument

Notes

1. Chris Ashworth and Patrick Stephens, *Action Stations* 9: *Military Airfields of the Central South and South-East* (1990), gives airfield's detailed operational history
2. Margaret Gowing, *Independence and Deterrence: Britain and Atomic Energy 1945–1952* (Macmillan 1974), has a full, authoritative account
3. Duncan Campbell, *The Unsinkable Aircraft Carrier: American Military Power in Britain* (Michael Joseph, 1984).
4. Sasha Roseneil, *Common Women, Uncommon Practices* (Cassell, 2000), explores further antecedents.
5. Roy Hattersley, *The Edwardians* (Little, Brown, 2004).
6. J.B. Priestley, *The Edwardians* (Heinemann, 1970).
7. *Dictionary of National Biography* (Oxford University Press).
8. Rebecca Johnson in John Dewar, ed., *Nuclear Weapons, the Peace Movement and the Law* (Macmillan, 1986).
9. *New Statesman*, 17–24 December 1982.
10. Peregrine Worsthorne, *Sunday Telegraph*, 12 December 1982.
11. Richard Gott, *Guardian*, 15 December 1982, © Guardian Newspapers Ltd.
12. *Daily Express*, 13 December 82
13. Michael Heseltine, *Life in the Jungle* (Hodder & Stoughton, 2000).
14. Gillian Reeve and Joan Smith, *Offence of the Realm* (CND Publications, 1986), has Cathy Massiter's full account.
15. 'MI5's Official Secrets', documentary by 20/20 Vision for Channel 4.
16. Heseltine, *Life in the Jungle*.
17. Reeve and Smith, *Offence of the Realm*.
18. Stella Rimington, *Open Secret* (Hutchinson, 2001).
19. *Guardian* parliamentary report, 2 November 1983.
20. Paul Brown, *Guardian* 8 July 1983, © Guardian Newspapers Ltd.
21. Martin Wainwright, *Guardian*, 15 November 1983, © Guardian Newspapers Ltd.
22. David Fairhall, *Guardian* 19 September 1981, © Guardian Newspapers Ltd.
23. David Fairhall, *Guardian* 19 September 1981, © Guardian Newspapers Ltd.
24. *Guardian* Parliamentary report, 31 October 1983, © Guardian Newspapers Ltd.

25. Tony Higgott, *The Story of Newbury* (Countryside Books, 2001).
26. Ibid.
27. Gareth Parry, *Guardian* 2 June 1983, © Guardian Newspapers Ltd.
28. *Newbury Weekly News*, 24 November 1983.
29. Sarah Hipperson, *Greenham, Non-Violent Women v The Crown Prerogative* (Greenham Publications, 2005).
30. Heseltine, *Life in the Jungle*.
31. David Fairhall, *Russia Looks to the Sea* (Andre Deutsch, 1970).
32. Duncan Campbell, *The Unsinkable Aircraft Carrier: American Military Power in Britain* (Michael Joseph, 1984).
33. Reeve and Smith, *Offence of the Realm*.
34. *Jane's Defence Weekly*, 25 January 1986.
35. Alan Rusbridger, *Guardian*, 22 January 1986, © Guardian Newspapers Ltd.
36. Rebecca Johnson in Dewar, ed., *Nuclear Weapons, the Peace Movement and the Law*.
37. Jane Hickman in Dewar, ed., *Nuclear Weapons, The Peace Movement and the Law*
38. Jonathan Steele, *Guardian* 27 May 1983, © Guardian Newspapers Ltd.
39. Christopher Driver, *The Disarmers* (Hodder & Stoughton, 1964).
40. Hipperson, *Greenham, Non-Violent Women v The Crown Prerogative*.
41. David Fairhall, *Guardian*, 15 November 1986, © Guardian Newspapers Ltd.
42. Mikhail Gorbachev, *Memoirs* (Bantam Books, 1997).
43. David Fairhall, *Guardian*, 14 February 1996, © Guardian Newspapers Ltd.
44. Paul Clayden, *Our Common Land: The Law and History of Common Land and Village Greens* (Open Spaces Society 2003), has the full story.
45. Countryside Commission pamphlet, December 1979.
46. Kate Ashbrook, *Our Common Right: The Story of Common Land* (Open Spaces Society n.d.).
47. House of Commons Paper 397.
48. Richard Adams, *Watership Down* (Puffin Books, 1973).
49. 'Dstl's Hidden Treasures', *Sanctuary* (MoD conservation magazine) 33, 2004.
50. *Newbury Weekly News*, 6 February 1992.
51. David Fairhall, *Guardian* 31 May 1991, © Guardian Newspapers Ltd.
52. *Newbury Weekley News*, 22 Ocober 1992.
53. David Fairhall, *Guardian*, 27 November 1993, © Guardian Newspapers Ltd.
54. David Fairhall, *Guardian*, 28 January 1994, © Guardian Newspapers Ltd.
55. Hipperson, *Greenham, Non-Violent Women v The Crown Prerogative*.
56. F.H. Cripps and A. Stimson, *The Distribution of Uranium-235 and Plutonium-239 around the United States Air Force base, Greenham Common, Berkshire* (1961; declassified and released by the MoD 1996).
57. David Fairhall, *Guardian*, 30 July 1996, © Guardian Newspapers Ltd.

58. Duncan Campbell gives a full account of this accident in *The Unsinkable Aircraft Carrier*, p. 52.
59. David Fairhall, *Guardian*, 30 July 1996, © Guardian Newspapers Ltd.
60. F.A. Fry and B.T. Wilkins, National Radiological Protection Board (now a division of the Health Protection Agency) report NRPB-M752, December 1996.
61. L.W. Croudace, D.C.W. Sanderson, P.E. Warwick and J.D. Allyson, University of Southampton and Scottish Universities Research and Reactor Centre, report for Newbury District Council and Basingstoke & Deane Borough Council, February 1997.
62. Professor B.A. Bridges, Committee on Medical Aspects of Radiation in the Environment (COMARE) 5th Report, March 1998.
63. *Newbury Weekly News*, 15 August 1996.
64. David Fairhall, *Guardian*, 26 July 1993, © Guardian Newspapers Ltd.
65. Hipperson, *Greenham, Non-Violent Women v The Crown Prerogative*.
66. *Newbury Weekly News*, 13 April 2000.
67. Ed Cooper, *Cold War Pastoral* (Black Dog Publishing, 2001).
68. Campbell, *The Unsinkable Aircraft Carrier*.
69. International Institute of Strategic Studies, Military Balance 2004–2005.
70. Julian Borger, *Guardian*, 2 April 2005, © Guardian Newspapers Ltd.
71. Heseltine, *Life in the Jungle*.
72. Gorbachev, *Memoirs*.

Acknowledgements

Many people took time and trouble to help me with this project – not least my wife Pam, who also had to cope with the disruption it sometimes caused – and I want to thank them here.

Some gave long interviews – Chris Austin, Trevor Brown, Ed Cooper, Karmen Cutler (Thomas), Lynette Edwell, Michael Foot, Michael Heseltine, Sarah Hipperson, Jean Hutchinson, Helen John, Rebecca Johnson, Bruce Kent, Jim and Jackie Langdon, Di McDonald, Ken Neal, David Owen, Evelyn Parker, Ann Pettitt, Leslie and Wendy Pope, Lorna Richardson, Joan Ruddock, Eunice Stallard, Stuart Tagg – and then often found themselves dealing with my innumerable queries. I am grateful for their patient assistance, especially when this extended to active research on my behalf – as it did with Leslie and Wendy – or the extremely useful peace camp literature Di provided. Rebecca, the first woman to welcome this particular *Guardian* hack at the peace camp in the 1980s, has supported my project from the outset with essential facts, contacts and vivid personal accounts.

Many busy people (listed in the last chapter) took trouble to respond to the formal question as to what the women's protest achieved, a contribution I particularly appreciated. John Ledlie, Cathy Massiter and Gill Reeve helped in other ways to illuminate obscure corners of the story.

My thanks also to authors and publishers, such as the *Newbury Weekly News*, who gave permission to quote from their publications – above all to the *Guardian*, for which I worked at the time of the protest, and which provided so many valuable references. Richard Nelsson and Jackie Markham, librarians at the *Guardian* and the *NWN* respectively, kindly gave access to their files, as did Jane Burrell at the West Berkshire Museum in Newbury, whose permanent exhibition contains a highly informative section devoted to Greenham Common. The Women's Library in Whitechapel and the City of Westminster Archives Centre generously dealt with enquiries about suffragettes and suffragists.

I also want to acknowledge my indebtedness to studies of the women's movement, Greenham Common and the Cold War which helped provide the background against which to assemble my own account.

Jill Liddington's *The Long Road to Greenham* (Virago, 1989) was particularly valuable in putting the protest into a historical perspective. Sasha Roseneil's *Disarming Patriarchy* (Open University Press, 1995) and *Common Women, Uncommon Practices* (Cassell, 2000) helped reconcile a confusion of events, dates and conflicting attitudes, as well as offering a penetrating analysis.

Without Sarah Hipperson's detailed legal account, *Greenham, Non-violent Women v. The Crown Prerogative* (Greenham Publications, 2005), supported by the personal diaries assembled in Beth Junor's *Greenham Common Women's Peace Camp: A History of Non-violent Resistance* (Working Press, 1995), I would have been hard put to follow the long courtroom trail that led to the House of Lords judgment on commoners' rights. Jane Hickman and Rebecca Johnson's contributions to John Dewar, ed., *Nuclear Weapons, the Peace Movement and the Law* (Palgrave Macmillan, 1986) enabled me to understand something of the legal challenges the women faced in the US Federal Court and – day after day – in Newbury magistrates courts.

Duncan Campbell's *The Unsinkable Aircraft Carrier* (Michael Joseph, 1984) provided a unique, authoritative reference where historical details of the US military presence in Britain were concerned. Tony Higgott's *The History of Newbury* (Countryside Books, 2001) was another valuable source. Simon Barnett of West Berkshire Council's Countryside Department helped by sketching out plans for the commons' further restoration and by kindly allowing reproduction of a photograph of cattle once again grazing the heath.

Finally, let me record my gratitude to the Open Spaces Society, still not letting up after a century and a half"'s campaigning to preserve our common land. Kate Ashbrook and her colleagues were immensely helpful (as their predecessors were to the commoners of Greenham and Crookham), both directly and through publications such as Paul Clayden's *Our Common Land: The Law and History of Common Land and Village Greens* (5th edn, OSS, 2003) and Kate's own pamphlet *Our Common Right: The Story of Common Land.*

Index